Praise for *The Green*

'Here is all you ever wanted to kno[w] plethora of American presidents, particularly those who have calling since John Fitzgerald Kennedy's visit in 1963 . . . Kelleher has meticulously researched the "Irish connection" to the White House, and this book is a must for anyone who wishes to understand that relationship and those who made it possible.'

IRISH INDEPENDENT

'Kelleher is to be commended for the thoroughness of her research, and for having shaped all of it into a very readable, informative and entertaining package . . . this is without question the best book so far on the special link between Ireland and the White House.'

IRISH EXAMINER

'In this beautifully written book, Lynne Kelleher takes us on an exciting journey from the luxurious Kennedy compound in Cape Cod to the family's ancestral home in rural County Wexford, from the Watergate scandal to Richard Nixon's Irish setter named in honour of his County Kildare roots, from glamorous receptions in Obama's White House to pints of Guinness in County Offaly . . .'

BRIAN O'DONOVAN, RTÉ WASHINGTON CORRESPONDENT

'Captures the essence of a special relationship between a massive nation that is America and a little island on the periphery of Europe, a relationship that goes from the small farming fields of Ireland all the way to the most powerful office in the world, the White House.'

MARTY MORRISSEY, RTÉ

'Anybody with an interest in Irish-American politics and personalities will want to read *The Green and White House*.'

DICK SPRING

The
GREEN
and
WHITE
HOUSE

Ireland and the US Presidents

LYNNE KELLEHER

BLACK & WHITE PUBLISHING

First published in the UK in 2022
This edition first published in 2022 by
Black & White Publishing Ltd
Nautical House, 104 Commercial Street, Edinburgh, EH6 6NF

A division of Bonnier Books UK
4th Floor, Victoria House, Bloomsbury Square, London, WC1B 4DA
Owned by Bonnier Books
Sveavägen 56, Stockholm, Sweden

Where not otherwise acknowledged, quotes are taken either from reports
at the time or are from conversations held with Lynne Kelleher.

The publisher has made every reasonable effort to contact copyright holders
of quoted texts and of images in the picture section. Any errors are inadvertent and
anyone who for any reason has not been contacted is invited to write to the publisher
so that a full acknowledgement can be made in subsequent editions of this work.

A CIP catalogue record for this book is available from the British Library.

ISBN: 978 1 78530 424 8

1 3 5 7 9 10 8 6 4 2

Typeset by Iolaire, Newtonmore
Printed and bound in Great Britain by Clays Ltd, Elcograf S.p.A.

www.blackandwhitepublishing.com

For my dad, Tom.

CONTENTS

Foreword – Instruments of Policy –
          Seán Donlon, former US Ambassador   ix

Prologue – Cracking History Mysteries   I

  I. JFK   II

  2. PRESIDENT RICHARD NIXON   53

  3. PRESIDENT RONALD REAGAN   83

  4. PRESIDENT BILL CLINTON   113

  5. THE BUSH PRESIDENTS   151

  6. PRESIDENT BARACK OBAMA   171

  7. PRESIDENT JOE BIDEN   201

  8. THE SPECIAL RELATIONSHIP — WHERE IT ALL BEGAN   225

  9. FRONTIER PRESIDENTS IN THE MAKING OF AMERICA   237

  10. SHAMROCKS & SHENANIGANS & SILVER DOLLARS   269

Acknowledgements   308
Bibliography & Sources   314

INSTRUMENTS OF POLICY

Twenty-three of the forty-six US presidents have claimed, or have claimed for them, a connection with Ireland. This book examines the connections and in particular looks back on the state visits to Ireland by the presidents in the last sixty years. While the public focus has usually been on the glamour and emotional appeal of the connections there has frequently been a serious, behind-the-scenes political and diplomatic game at play. Successive generations of Irish politicians and diplomats have sought to take advantage of the president's Irish links, and successive presidents have been happy to demonstrate their interest in Ireland to US voters, especially to those with Irish backgrounds. The late historian Professor Ronan Fanning has accurately described these connections as very much 'instruments of policy'. This introduction gives a brief overview of what went on politically behind the scenes.

Even before independence, leaders of Irish nationalism sought US support for the achievement of their objectives. Charles Stewart Parnell visited Washington in 1880 and became the first Irish leader to address the House of Representatives. Pádraig Pearse personally lobbied Washington in 1914 and, as is now well documented, Éamon de Valera spent much time in the US in 1919–21 seeking to persuade political leaders there to support Irish independence. As luck would have it he got to know Roosevelt through seeking legal advice from him in 1919. When Roosevelt became president in 1933 de Valera had become president of the Executive Council in 1932, and although they never met personally, when both held high office they were in very frequent contact during Roosevelt's presidency from 1933 to 1944.

Initially, Irish nationalists sought support for and recognition for Irish independence. After the foundation of the state, the focus changed to seek support for the ending of partition. This was particularly the thrust of de Valera's approach throughout his political career. He believed that as the British had created partition, it was up to them to end it. He was convinced that the US could be persuaded of the injustice of partition, and given the special relationship with Ireland, they would prevail on the British to undo it. He never accepted that the special relationship that most mattered to the US was that with London and that no matter who was in the White House, London was unlikely to prevail over Dublin. This became starkly clear during the Kennedy administration in the early 1960s. Though there was no doubting President Kennedy's affection for Ireland and the importance he attached to his Irish roots, all efforts to have him press the British on partition during his historic visit to Ireland in 1963 were quietly rebuffed.

It fell to his brother, Senator Ted Kennedy, to take a public position in support of Irish interests from the 1970s until his death in 2009. By the early 1970s the Irish political and diplomatic approach in the US had modified. Led by Garret FitzGerald and John Hume, the focus shifted to accepting that the US had a special relationship with both Ireland and the UK and was therefore well placed to assist both governments and the Northern Irish political parties in coming to a solution. We were no longer asking the US to intervene in support of the Irish nationalist position. We wanted them to join with the Irish and British governments and the political parties in Northern Ireland in seeking a solution.

The breakthrough came in August 1977 when President Carter – improbably in many respects since he was not aware of an Irish connection and had never visited Ireland before or during his presidency – issued a statement calling for the establishment in Northern Ireland of a government which would command widespread acceptance and for a just solution which would involve the support of the Irish government. Carter's interest in human rights played a part, but the main factor was the influence of his Democrat colleagues in senior political positions in the US, Speaker Tip O'Neill, Senators Ted Kennedy and Pat Moynihan and Governor Hugh Carey of New York. They in turn were heavily influenced by Irish governments, by John Hume and by Irish diplomats.

Carter was succeeded as president by Ronald Reagan. He had visited Ireland a number of times before he reached the White House but his Irish roots were not definitively traced to Co. Tipperary until he became president in 1981. During his eight years in office he maintained an active interest in Irish affairs, and while it is well known that he had an excellent relationship with Prime Minister Thatcher, what is less well known is that on every occasion when they met, Ireland was on their agenda. Reagan played an important role in Thatcher's signing the Anglo-Irish Agreement in 1985, an agreement which for the first time gave the Irish government an internationally recognised role in the affairs of Northern Ireland. Reagan also initiated the creation of the International Fund for Ireland which aimed to give financial backing to the Agreement and which to date has involved the US, the EU and other countries contributing over £700 million to projects in Northern Ireland and in border areas.

Reagan, prompted by Speaker O'Neill, was also instrumental in establishing a St Patrick's Day event which has played a useful part in promoting Irish interests for the last forty years. As ambassador in Washington in 1981, I invited him to lunch at the embassy on St Patrick's Day. To everyone's surprise he accepted the invitation – it was the only embassy he visited during his eight years as president. At the lunch he was seated with Speaker O'Neill and there and then O'Neill invited him to attend a St Patrick's Day lunch on Capitol Hill, the seat of the US Congress, the following year. Reagan immediately accepted and that 1982 lunch began a tradition that has been followed by every president and every speaker since. Until then, presidents visited Capitol Hill only once a year, to deliver the State of the Union address.

The two Presidents Bush continued the now established practice of taking an active interest in Irish affairs. The senior Bush also had a keen interest in Irish golf courses and golfers. He frequently reminded me that the Walker Cup, a golf competition between the US and Britain and Ireland held every second year, had been established by his grandfather in 1922. When on one occasion there was a reference to the competition as one between the US and Britain, he wrote me a profuse letter apologising for the omission!

The role of US presidents in Irish affairs reached new heights with the election of Bill Clinton in 1993. He and his wife Hillary went on to involve themselves with skill and determination in brokering the 1998 Good Friday Agreement. The Clintons' Irish roots were somewhat remote but the president had long been interested in Irish political matters, an interest initially prompted when, as a student in Oxford in the late 1960s, he observed and was impressed by John Hume's approach to the Northern Ireland situation and by how much Hume was influenced by the US civil rights movement.

As president, Clinton visited Ireland on three occasions. He briefed himself fully on what was happening in relation to Northern Ireland and kept in close touch with the Taoiseach, Bertie Ahern, and the

British prime minister Tony Blair. He made two appointments which were to prove crucial in achieving the Good Friday Agreement. He appointed Jean Kennedy Smith, President Kennedy's youngest sister, as his ambassador in Dublin and Senator George Mitchell to chair peace negotiations in Belfast. Mitchell's task involved two long, hard years of cajoling and persuading the main political parties in Northern Ireland and the British and Irish governments to agree on a complex set of new structures for government in Belfast and new arrangements for accommodating the relationships between Dublin, Belfast and London. President Clinton's personal involvement was central to the achievement of the Agreement.

The involvement of US presidents in developments relating to Northern Ireland is now so well established that it is almost taken for granted. The presidents after Clinton all maintained the interest. Both Obama and Trump have visited Ireland while in office and they have continued to mark St Patrick's Day by the greening of the White House. Both also appointed special envoys for Northern Ireland to ensure that they were fully in touch with the situation there and could, as needed, influence proceedings.

In 2021, Joe Biden became president. If Kennedy was the most emotionally connected and Clinton the most politically connected, Biden is, of all the presidents, the best connected to Ireland both emotionally and politically. He has long been aware of his Irish roots, and on arrival in the White House he was exceptionally well informed on political matters in Ireland, north and south. Since he was first elected to the US Senate in 1973, he has taken an active interest in Irish matters and was one of the first members of the Friends of Ireland in the US Congress set up in 1981. As vice president, he visited Ireland in 2016. The British are very well aware of his interest and detailed knowledge, and there is no doubt that it will be an important factor as the post-Brexit situation develops.

Ireland is fortunate to have had and to continue to have US presidents who have become instruments of Irish policy. Our history and geography have connected us to Britain in ways which do not always work to our advantage. Without the White House – a building incidentally designed by an Irishman and modelled on Leinster House in Dublin – the achievement of Irish policies would have been enormously more difficult.

SEÁN DONLON
Irish Ambassador to the US (in the Carter and Reagan Administrations)
Secretary General, Department of Foreign Affairs (1981–87)

CRACKING HISTORY MYSTERIES

I'm always curious how far back you have to go in anybody's family tree until you hit immigrants . . . it's surprising by any measure how many of our presidents have had Irish ancestry.

T HE TOMBSTONES HAD LAIN side by side in an obscure Ohio cemetery for more than one hundred and fifty years. One of the tablets, edged by grass and smoothed to a mottled, blue tinge by the passage of time, was almost split in two. The letters, painstakingly carved by a stonemason, had survived the elements, although one or two words had been chipped away by more than a century of hard winters. It read:

> TO THE MEMORY OF WILLIAM KEARNEY . . . BORN IN MONE . . . ,
> KINGS COUNTY, IREL . . . , JUNE 24TH, 18 . . . AND DEPARTED THIS
> LIFE OCTOBER 1ST, 1855, AGED 22 YRS.

The neighbouring stone, where the young man's father was buried, filled in the blanks. The carved-out letters read:

> TO THE MEMORY OF JOSEPH KEARNEY SEN, BORN IN
> MONEYGALL, KING'S COUNTY, IRELAND.

King's County, now known as County Offaly, is located almost slap bang in the centre of Ireland, around 3,500 miles away from the Midwestern state of Ohio as the crow flies. These stone-cut words held the key to the puzzle of Senator Barack Obama's lineage. World-famous genealogist Megan Smolenyak, of *Who Do You Think You Are?* fame, had been on the trail of the African American's pedigree for months, and here was her *eureka!* moment chiselled into a flat stone slab in a Protestant cemetery in the rural heart of Fayette County, in southern Ohio. The ancestors, who crossed the Atlantic and eventually died in their new home, left a clear marker pointing backwards across the ocean for their descendant, who would go on to become president of the United States.

Megan Smolenyak's genealogical interest was piqued by Barack Obama early in the presidential election. 'I just found him interesting,' she said. 'One of the things I'm always curious about is how far back you have to go in anybody's family tree, until you hit immigrants.' The first hint to his Irish ancestors popped up in a record relating to his great-great-great-grandfather contained in the 1870 American census. It listed a Fulmoth or Falmoth Kearney – the name written in ink over a century earlier was hard to decipher – as the father of Obama's great-great-grandmother, Mary Ann Kearney. The column next to his name stated he was born in Ireland.

'I'm half Irish American myself, my mom's side is one hundred per cent Irish, so as soon as I saw that it sparked my attention; I went chasing that,' said the genealogist, who was working for ancestry. com at the time. 'So I figured out Obama was one thirty-second Irish.'

Five days before St Patrick's Day in 2007, a light-hearted press release was issued by the genealogical website titled: 'Ancestry.com Uncovers Irish Roots of Barack "O'Bama"' – resulting in a deluge of calls from Irish news outlets inquiring about the location of these ancestors. It was also news to Barack Obama and his mother, Stanley Ann Dunham, who were quite unaware of the connection until the renowned family historian went trawling back through the centuries.

This was a quintessential case of long-lost relatives. Since arriving on the boat over a century and a half earlier, the knowledge of their origins in the Irish Midlands had faded away in the intervening generations of forward-looking immigrants forging a new life at America's frontier.

During her digging, Megan Smolenyak would find the distinctive name of Barack Obama's nearest Irish relative spelled as Fulmoth, Fulmouth, Falmouth, Fulmuth and Falmuth in different written records, but most importantly it stood out amid all the multiple John Murphys and Paddy O'Briens crossing the ocean to the United States. In addition to his atypical name, it was discovered that the onward destination of Obama's shoemaker ancestor had been fortuitously logged on his arrival records as Ohio when he stepped off the *Marmion* ship in New York on 20 March 1850.

Further checks into the family records stretching from Ohio to Indiana, along with the discovery of two weather-worn Kearney headstones emblazoned with King's County referenced in a family tree website set up by Roger Kearney from the American branch of the family led to the pieces of the epic genetic jigsaw puzzle starting to slot into place. For that era, it was not unusual for tombstones of Irish immigrants to spell out where they were from in Ireland, at least the county, sometimes the town. 'I got very lucky; two of the family tombstones mentioned Moneygall,' Smolenyak said, explaining how she now had to link Fulmoth to the William and Joseph Kearney in the Ohio graves. 'It was a matter of doing the research to substantiate Fulmoth's connection to these others to give myself permission to claim Moneygall.'

After establishing the connection, she set about contacting the thirteen churches in the vicinity of the village in Co. Offaly, and eventually – with the help of Canon Stephen Neill, the rector of Templeharry Church outside Moneygall – records were found matching the names on the flat gravestones in Ohio. Meticulously kept baptism and marriage records dating back for close to two centuries confirmed that the Kearney family in Moneygall were in fact related to the first African American president of the United States of America.

While births, deaths, and marriages were logged in Catholic and Protestant churches, the survival of the records kept by Catholic churches in the eighteenth and the nineteenth centuries was more precarious. Ireland also lost millions of records in a string of mishaps with the census returns for 1881 and 1891 pulped during the First World War, most likely owing to a paper shortage, while a fire at the Public Record Office at the beginning of the Civil War in 1922 saw four decades of records from 1821 to 1851 go up in smoke, apart from a few boxes which were saved from the blaze.

'It was really unfortunate because the Irish census was one of the best that existed – a bunch of what would have been outstanding records got destroyed,' said Megan Smolenyak. 'Civil registration didn't kick in until 1864. Immigration records in America don't get good until 1906, in terms of the details. Prior to that, it mostly was just name, age, country, with those rare exceptions like Obama's family.'

Interestingly, Megan Smolenyak has also used her detective skills to delve into the family tree of 'Born in the USA' rock legend Bruce Springsteen. In recent years, she's discovered that his family were from Kildare, the same county which produced President Nixon. In fact, in the *Renegades in the USA* podcast presented by Barack Obama and Bruce Springsteen, the pair swap notes on the surprise of their shared Irish heritage, in a conversation on a feeling of difference in their childhoods.

'My grandparents were basically Scots Irish – and the Irish were outsiders for a long time,' shared the former president. 'Yeah,' the 'Born to Run' singer agreed, adding, 'My grandparents were old-school Irish people; they were very, very provincial, quite backward, quite country people . . . we all lived in one house, my parents, my grandparents on my dad's side, and me. I was brought up by the Irish side of my family and they were just as eccentric as American Irish could be.'

Scrawled entries on shipping records, census entries along with birth, death, and marriage certificates, and even a piece of gifted furniture, are among the clues linking twenty-three US presidents with Ireland. As Megan Smolenyak observes: 'It's surprising, by any measure, how many of our presidents have had Irish ancestry.' Since records have gone online in recent years, it has become easier for a string of renowned genealogists to join the ancestral dots which link around half of the forty-six American presidents back to Ireland. Genealogical pointers to the blood ties of these presidents are scattered across the United States.

The connection is as close as parents or a grandparent or as distant and as far back as five, six or seven generations in the case of presidents such as Bush and Ford. It can be as clear-cut as an irrefutable biological bond or as tenuous as a scrawled census entry or the political gift of a gaming table inlaid with five hundred pieces of Irish wood given as a mark of ethnicity.

Across four centuries, millions of Irish sailed across the Atlantic to North America. This is reflected in the family lines of the White House commanders-in-chief. Antrim is the birthplace of the ancestors of at least half a dozen presidents, while Down can lay claim to around three commanders-in-chief, with Donegal and Armagh also among the known birthplaces of presidential ancestors. The presidents descended from Ulster-Scots emigrants were in office mainly in the eighteenth and nineteenth centuries and the first half of the twentieth. In the second half of that century and into the twenty-first, the descendants of Irish immigrants from the south of Ireland, from counties like Kildare, Limerick, Wexford, Mayo and Tipperary, are sworn into office.

In the post-revolutionary days of the nineteenth century, the presidents with Irish blood ties were Andrew Jackson, James K. Polk, James Buchanan, Abraham Lincoln, Andrew Johnson, Ulysses S. Grant, Chester A. Arthur, Grover Cleveland, Benjamin Harrison and William McKinley. In the twentieth century, the more familiar-sounding Irish American presidents included Theodore Roosevelt, Woodrow Wilson, John F. Kennedy, Lyndon B. Johnson, Richard M. Nixon, Gerald R. Ford, James Carter, Ronald Reagan, George H.W. Bush, and William J. Clinton. With the twenty-first century came George W. Bush. Barack Obama and, now, President Joe Biden.

In recent years, President Obama's Irish ancestry only emerged in the form of a great-great-great-grandfather during the presidential race, but President Joe Biden's family had never completely severed their ties with their Irish relatives after they first crossed the Atlantic during the famine. The details would emerge once again when one of America's leading history detectives started digging into his family tree.

'Every once in a while, I do some research just out of respect and admiration. My dad is from Wilkes-Barre, Pennsylvania, which is right next door to Scranton where he is from, so I've known of Joe Biden for a long time, and I know he's very proud of his Irish heritage,' said Megan Smolenyak. Raised in a family steeped in Irish Catholic traditions, she was familiar with this world.

'Being proud of Irish presidents was part of that. I'm of the era where everyone had a photo of Kennedy in their house. Currently, we have probably the president who is the proudest of his Irish heritage ever in the Oval Office.' Along with the Blewitts on his mother's side of the family, she unearthed long-lost Galway relatives on his father's side, while Irish genealogists tracked down the maternal lines of the Kearneys and the Finnegans on the Cooley peninsula in Louth.

The *Who Do You Think You Are?* expert spends much of her time poring over records and visiting old churches and graveyards to unearth clues from the past, but very occasionally she gets to see tangible results from her explorations back through the generations. If she hadn't found the tombstones marking the resting place to his Kearney ancestor in Ohio, it could have taken years longer to find Obama's relatives. Mingling among the 100,000 Irish people waving stars and stripes in College Green in Dublin in 2011 as President Obama introduced himself as 'Barack Obama . . . of the Moneygall Obamas,' she felt deep pride. During that week in Ireland in 2011, Megan's sister, who had accompanied her on the trip, would proudly announce she was the ancestry authority who had linked Obama to Ireland. 'They wanted to shake my hand. It was just really lovely.'

Standing mere feet away from Obama as he spoke to the crowd on that day in May, she was pointed out to the president, who came down the line to shake her hand:

> In the speech, he says, 'I want to thank the genealogist,' and a voice goes, 'She's right here!' and someone started pointing at me. I was right at the front and when he came down to do the rope line, he and Michelle came over to me. It was the first chance I got to meet them. It was so celebratory; it was a wonderful time to be there. I had been to Ireland a number of times over the years, but that occasion was extremely memorable.

The significance of her painstaking research also hit home that day.

> It's just a kick as a genealogist because you don't really expect your work to have any obvious outcome other than perhaps correcting a piece of history. But when you see something like that happen or when you see the Obama Plaza... the chance to see a noticeable outcome is very rare. When I was researching him, he was running for president and I was curious and so to be there in that celebratory moment was really cool. Obviously, there was so much that happened between those tombstones and that moment in Dublin. So many parties involved. But it's great to get the ball rolling with something that people have forgotten: some little, tiny hidden connection.

The churning forces of religious turmoil, famine and colonialism, along with the pull of adventure, wide-open spaces and voting rights, lured millions across the Atlantic. *The Green and White House* examines diaries, speeches, and handwritten letters which give glimpses into the thoughts of twenty-three presidents on their ancestral island thousands of miles away when they were in Oval Office. The enduring bond of the blood tie was regularly acknowledged privately and in diplomatic missives between Ireland, England and the United States through the American Revolution, the Irish Famine, the American Civil War, two World Wars and the founding of the Irish Republic.

There remains something of an enigma around why this familial tie is claimed and celebrated even when the relationship is as distant as an eighth cousin, but still these presidential family trees spawned a succession of homecoming visits of US leaders to star-struck rural outposts around Ireland.

Of course, the romance between Ireland and the White House began in earnest when President John F. Kennedy touched down on the tarmac in Dublin Airport to a 21-gun salute on 27 June 1963.

In 1961, Irish Ambassador to the US, Thomas Kiernan, presents
the traditional bowl of shamrocks to President John F. Kennedy.

CHAPTER ONE

JFK

---

*Ireland is not the land of my birth but it is the land
to which I hold the greatest affection . . . And I certainly
will come back in the springtime.*

I N HIS FINAL VACATION in his oceanside home in Hyannis Port,
JFK spent many evenings repeatedly playing the black and white
footage of his euphoric trip to Ireland for his extended family. His
house at Irving Avenue, which became the summer White House
while he was president, was two doors down from his parents'
sprawling clapboard beachside home. These properties, along with
the homes of his brother, Bobby, and his sister, Eunice, made up the
legendary Kennedy Compound, a piece of paradise on the southern
shore of Cape Cod where his family had holidayed for generations.

When he arrived with his wife, Jackie, and their children, Caroline
and John, that July, JFK was still on a high from his four-day homecoming visit to Ireland weeks earlier. Photographs of those last
halcyon days in the salty air of the Massachusetts shoreline capture
the president sailing his yacht, *The Sequoia*, driving a gaggle of kids
around on a golf cart and swimming in the Atlantic. But his fixation
in his downtime in the balmy evenings was reliving the homecoming
tour he would refer to as the four best days of his life. Family friend

and former CEO of the JFK Trust in New Ross in Ireland Sean Reidy remembers Jean Kennedy Smith telling him affectionately of her brother endlessly playing the footage of his jam-packed tour of Ireland's cities.

> They would all gather in Hyannis in the summer, and she talked about the first night they were there. [JFK] said, 'You all have to come over and watch the video of my Irish visit...' Then she said he would play it time after time, they were plagued with watching his Irish visit with him. It had such an impact on him that he wanted to share it with everyone all summer long.

The US president's love affair with Ireland began sixteen years earlier, when he took on the role of family genealogist in 1947, tracking down his father's side of his family to a farmyard full of chickens and pigs. Their paternal line is undoubtedly the most visceral for America's fabled family. In his home in Dunganstown in New Ross in Wexford, Patrick Grennan, a third cousin once removed to JFK, walks around his yard indicating the spot where the American president had tea with his grandmother, Mrs Mary Ryan, pointing out the tattered leather Morris Minor seat where the president perched next to his matronly relative at the fire, the moving letter a widowed Jackie Kennedy wrote from a residence nearby requesting to visit with her small children. Treasure troves of memories of two brief visits by a president in his prime linger down through the decades all around the Wexford courtyard.

For years after that historic visit in 1963, sightseers would travel down the winding road to the farmyard, peering in over the gate. The ever-hospitable Mrs Ryan would invite them in for tea, especially if they sported a collar or a veil. Lifesize pictures and exhibits in a newly built museum building off the farmhouse now tell the tale of the origins of the political dynasty who were dealt triumph and tragedy in almost equal measure since their ancestors first set foot in Massachusetts around the time of the Irish famine. Their trajectory from tenant farmers to coopers to shopkeepers and bankers and on to Congress, Senate and the White House is an extraordinary hop, skip and a jump up through American society.

When the gangly, youthful congressman arrived in Dunganstown fresh from being elected to the House of Representatives in 1947, he had left the company of the cream of British society in Lismore Castle in the neighbouring county of Waterford. It was August and the thirty-year-old was spending the month visiting his sister, Kathleen 'Kick' Kennedy, who was married to the Duke of Devonshire, along with a party that included future British prime minister Anthony Eden, Irish writer Sean Leslie, and Kick's friend Mrs Pamela Churchill, the daughter-in-law of Winston Churchill. Armed with a letter from his father's sister, his aunt Loretta, giving him directions, he swung into the farmyard of Jim Kennedy. 'He found my grand uncle Jim Kennedy's place and met Jim's family . . . then Jim said, "You really need to go up to my sister's house up the road because she's in the home place." What the kids remembered is they got a spin in the big station wagon he had,' explains Mr Grennan.

Although his father, the former British ambassador Joe Kennedy, had come over to Ireland to receive an honorary doctorate from Éamon de Valera in Dublin in July 1938, he had not searched out his homestead during his time in London. Joseph Kennedy, a millionaire many times over by the time he reached his thirties, famously disliked the term Irish American, preferring to be known as American; and he had eschewed sending his children to Catholic schools like most wealthy Americans with an Irish background.

But his father, PJ, did make a trip back to Ireland in 1907 to see where his immigrant parents had spent their childhood. A newly unearthed letter dated 24 December 1907, among the boxes of files in the JFK Library, gives a fascinating glimpse into his grandfather's impressions of a turn-of-the-century Ireland. Addressed to James Kennedy, Ballydogan, New Ross, Ire, it begins with 'Dear Cousin Jim...' He opens the long letter referring to the matter of the estate of his mother's relatives in Wexford after the death in Ireland of his first cousin, Martin Roach, the eldest son of his maternal aunt, Catherine. It indicates he was heavily involved in the family's affairs on both sides of the Atlantic:

> I suppose the matter of the Roach farm has been settled by this time, although I have not talked with Jim Roach about it for some time ... When I came home, he had about made up his mind to go home to Ireland, but after I had explained the condition of the farm, it did not seem to me that it would be worth his while to spend the money that it would be necessary for him to spend in order to settle the estate.

PJ, just a few months short of his fiftieth birthday, expresses regret at not having more time in Ireland 'especially among the country people' and was already talking of another long trip. On his return to Boston, he was dismayed to find his pictures had been destroyed by a 'bottle of cordial we had brought with us from Rome ... I was very much disappointed in not being able to show my family the birthplace of both my father and mother.' But he treasures a memento he received in Wexford of his father who died when he was a baby:

> It was with a great deal of pleasure that I showed to my children and I showed my sisters and the friends gathered around when I arrived home the copy book my father used when he went to school ... the fact that I had never seen my father to remember him — so one of the pleasures of my whole trip was the fact of bringing that copy book home.

PJ tells of his role in a political campaign for the Democratic Party for none other than his son's future father-in-law, John 'Honey Fitz' Fitzgerald, the father of Rose Fitzgerald: 'You remember my speaking of Mayor Fitzgerald . . . He and the party went down in defeat after a very exciting campaign.' The following decade, the wedding between their children would take place.

Later in the letter, he makes several observations about his ancestral country, comparing it favourably with England, France and Italy, which were part of his grand tour of Europe, a mark of status for monied Americans of that time. 'It has often been said here in America . . . in going through Ireland one is bothered by beggars . . . I never had one living person ask me for one copper, excepting one little boy at the station in Dublin, but that was not true of London, Paris or Rome.'

He also delighted in riding on Irish horse-drawn jaunting cars: 'When I first looked at one, I felt I was taking my life in my hands . . . but after having ridden in one once, I took great delight in riding at every opportunity I got.' He added: 'The horses I saw in Ireland were the best I have seen anywhere,' in stark contrast to Paris where they had the 'poorest horses that I ever saw in my life'. He also talked economics, Irish farming, the Land League and the fall-off in immigration to the US. Clearly in close contact with his large extended family, he talks of seeing Jim's cousin, Bridgie, and signs off asking his Irish cousin to remember him to 'Father Hayden, Hannah Mulloy, Pat Kennedy and his family, your brothers Patrick and John and your sisters Catherine and Johanna and all inquiring friends'. The elucidating letter is signed off, 'Your cousin, Patrick Kennedy'.

Wexford historian Celestine Murphy says the correspondence is significant. 'It confirms that the Kennedys in the US never lost the connection with the Kennedys at Dunganstown.'

While PJ was closely connected to the families of both his parents,

Patrick Grennan believes his son, Joe Kennedy, was so occupied with forging his business empire, he never got around to returning to his grandfather's birthplace. But his Dunganstown relative described his Harvard-educated, history-mad son, JFK, as a 'bolter from the norm'. 'He was with the Who's Who of society in England in 1947, but JFK was a bit different and wanted to look up his roots,' said his Wexford cousin.

In a letter penned to Professor Jim Burns, who was writing a biography of JFK, on 25 August 1959, JFK explained his feelings on driving over to Jim Kennedy's farmyard accompanied by Pamela Churchill, who he referred to as 'an English lady'. He wrote:

> We drove in and sure enough, the Kennedy family was living in the house, which had been described to us in my aunt's letter. There was a husband and wife and seven or eight children – all very bright and energetic. We were greeted with friendliness especially as they've never seen a station wagon before, but they had no idea which of the Kennedys I was. The farmer did say that Patrick Kennedy from Boston, who of course was my grandfather, had come to visit the home some thirty-five years before when the farmer was a boy . . .

The letter goes on to say:

> I spent about an hour there surrounded by chickens, pigs etc and left in a flow of nostalgia and sentiment. This was not punctuated by the English lady turning to me as we drove away and saying, 'Just like a Tobacco Road.' She had not understood at all the magic of the afternoon. We returned to Lismore Castle.
>
> Best regards,
> John F. Kennedy.

The famous novel she referred to in her derogatory remark angered the young congressman as it depicted a family of poor white sharecroppers in the Great Depression. 'What my grandmother remembers of him visiting in 1947 is that he looked very feeble, and she thought he needed a bit of food, in that Irish granny way. I've read that he was actually anointed two weeks later,' said Mr Grennan today of the 1947 visit. The president, who endured acute physical pain with his back for most of his adult life after he was shipwrecked in the Second World War, would become so gravely ill on board the *Queen Mary* that September while returning to the United States from visiting his sister that he was given the last rites while still at sea. But he survived the scare and went on to serve three terms in the House of Representatives before being elected to the US Senate in 1952 and being voted as the first Irish Catholic president of the United States on 8 November 1960.

From ghettos to the White House

John F. Kennedy's eight great-grandparents, from Limerick, Cork, Clare, Wexford and Cavan, were all born on tenant farms deep in rural Ireland, arriving in Boston after surviving gruelling journeys across the Atlantic to escape the famine and grasp the economic opportunity offered in a fresh new world free from colonial rule. Initially residing in overflowing Boston tenements, they had no choice but to overcome the harsh, widespread discrimination against Irish-Catholic immigrants at that time. His great-grandparents worked as peddlers, coopers and labourers but quickly moved up the social strata to become tavern owners and shopkeepers.

Patrick Grennan believes that President Kennedy's great-grand-father Patrick Kennedy left his 31-acre holding in Wexford to join his wife-to-be Bridget Murphy in America. 'He is going for love, I think, to marry Bridget, to start a new life.' Patrick, who marries Bridget in

Boston on 26 September 1849, initially works as a cooper making wooden barrels before he opens up a grocery store. 'He probably has a serious work ethic, they are opening a grocery store nearly straight away, he's still working in the cooperage and they're starting a family,' said his Irish Kennedy cousin.

Genealogists such as R. Andrew Pierce, the leading expert on the Kennedy family tree, have tried to pinpoint the exact dates of their departure, but it is almost impossible to determine when someone with a name as common as Bridget Murphy exited Ireland. Along with the name, there were scant records of departures from Ireland around the time of the famine, along with the added factor that many fleeing emigrants first went from New Ross to Liverpool before crossing the Atlantic as it tended to be a cheaper fare.

What is certain is that the Wexford couple married and had five children before the former farmer died of consumption, or what we now call TB, nine years after his wedding in Holy Cross Cathedral in the American city. 'He's been used to country air,' muses Mr Grennan, who still farms the land in the Kennedy homestead.

> He goes on an arduous ship journey and the next thing he's working in a cooperage in squalor, and I'd say his lungs weren't able for that. He's used to a healthy life in rural Ireland. He dies and leaves Bridget with four kids, things should have gone downhill, but Bridget now has the support of her cousins and a whole family network around her.

New research unearthed by Wexford historian Celestine Murphy uncovered evidence that Bridget Murphy is the forgotten heroine behind the Kennedy political dynasty. It is uncertain exactly when she left her one-roomed stone cottage in a patchwork of green fields in the townland of Cloonagh of Wexford, eight miles outside New

Ross. But sometime in the late 1840s, the young woman walked down the path of the grove leaving behind everything she knew, her parents, her older brother, James, and younger sister, Johanna, never to set eyes on Ireland again. 'The big question I'm always asked is if the Murphys and the Kennedys knew each other but you couldn't say for certain.'

Most likely, she set sail sometime around 1848. Landing into a heaving, tenement ghetto in the streets near Boston port would have been an assault on the senses of the twenty-something woman, used to rain-drenched greenery and the stillness of the countryside. Despite the beauty of the surroundings, it is almost certain she had endured hunger and hardship as her father desperately tried to eke out a living on their seventeen-acre tenant plot of barely farmable land on a vast estate run by British landlords.

After her marriage on 26 September 1949, Bridget has five children, her son PJ, his three sisters, and a baby brother, John, who dies at twenty-one months from cholera. The killer disease which first spread across the world from its original reservoir in the Ganges delta in India was epidemic in the American city in the middle of the nineteenth century.

A largely unsympathetic and condemnatory report on Asiatic cholera by Boston city's health committee gives a rare insight into the pitiful conditions endured by desperately poor famine immigrants crammed into ghettos in the Irish neighbourhoods in North End and Fort Hill. The 1849 report details the 'very wretched, dirty and unhealthy condition' of tenement houses with rooms from 'garret to cellar' crammed with families, sometimes with two or more families to a room. Residences were 'polluted with all manner of bad odours' with conditions allowing 'no cleanliness, privacy or proper ventilation, and little comfort'. One scathing passage reads:

It is sufficient to say, that this whole district is a perfect hive of human beings, without comforts and mostly without common necessaries; in many cases, huddled together like brutes, without regard to sex, or age, or sense of decency; grown men and women sleeping together in the same apartment, And sometimes wife and husband, brothers and sisters, in the same bed. Under such circumstances, self-respect, forethought, all high and noble virtues soon die out, and sullen indifference and despair, or disorder, intemperance and utter degradation reign supreme.

During an inspection visit, it was found some had neither drains nor toilets; there is a description of an open sewer running down one staircase in one dire tenement. Families in the worst conditions were crowded into cellars with the only light or air coming from the passage that led into them. The physician said it was a wonder life existed for a day in these underground dwellings; there were 586 such cellars in use at the end of 1849. The author of the report deduced that there could be no surprise that a statistical table carried out by a Mr Shattuck found the 'average age of Irish life in Boston does not exceed 14 years . . .'

In the grim, unsanitary conditions of tenement life in Boston, it's not surprising that Bridget Kennedy's son died of cholera, which causes acute diarrhoea, in September 1855 and her husband Patrick died of consumption on 22 November 1858. Two years later in the 1860 census, Bridget is living with her three daughters: eight-year-old Mary, seven-year-old Joanna, six-year-old Margaret and two-year-old Patrick Joseph, later known as PJ. Eight other families are living in the house. Her possessions were valued at just fifteen dollars. PJ, who would go on to be a grandfather of a future president, was just ten months old when his father died. But in the dockland ghetto, new information unearthed by Celestine Murphy now shows the 31-year-old widow had the support of her large extended family of sisters, Catherine, Ann and Margaret, and their spouses and their children who had all journeyed across the Atlantic. In the 1860 census, she is also sharing her room with her sister, Margaret, and her eighteen-year-old niece Mary Roche, Catherine's daughter.

'Bridget has acquired a great deal of agency and she goes from strength to strength. I'm often lost in admiration for her,' notes Celestine Murphy. 'She sent PJ to a good school, and presumably she had to pay. PJ become a state senator, that's all down to her.' Bridget ends up establishing what was called a 'notions' and stationery shop which sold everything from a 'needle to anchor'.

'She was a seamstress, her daughters were all schooled and the next thing in the censuses they're all seamstresses, coat makers, dress makers. From census to census her fortunes improve hugely. She was resourceful, unbelievably courageous, she didn't marry again, she went out and made a life for herself and her children. That's heroic in the 1860s,' said the Wexford historian.

Eventually Bridget acquires a house, and her son ends up running a saloon on the docks and becomes a state senator for Massachusetts. 'She has three businesses working by the time her kids are in their early twenties. Her son is the frontman, but she is the boss by all accounts. PJ Kennedy is a saloon keeper, he is a very good barman, he's lending money, getting lads work, then gets involved in politics. His bank starts loaning money to dock workers,' said Patrick Grennan.

The young man, who began his working life as a dockhand after leaving school at fourteen, had soon acquired three bars and a whiskey import firm. He was elected to serve in the Massachusetts House of Representatives in 1884 and five years later to the Massachusetts Senate. By the end of the century, he had forged a friendship with John 'Honey Fitz' Fitzgerald, who was also elected to the state senate in 1892 and would go on to become the first Irish Catholic mayor of Boston. In June 1903, a letter – about red tape over shop licences for a constituent called Mrs Carrnotta – from PJ Kennedy to the 'Hon John F. Fitzgerald' starts with 'Friend John . . .'

Over a decade later in 1914, with the marriage of their children, Rose Fitzgerald and Patrick Kennedy, America's most mythical political dynasty was born. Bridget Murphy lived long enough to see the birth of JFK's father, her grandson Joseph, who was three months old when she died, who would go on to become a multi-millionaire tycoon and serve as the US ambassador to Britain in the late 1930s.

Meanwhile, Joseph's second-eldest child, John Fitzgerald Kennedy, would go on to do just about as well as any man could do in the United States of America when he surpassed the achievements of his grandparents in the local senate and the congress, and his father's ambassadorial role, by being voted the 35th president of the United States by the slimmest of margins ahead of the Republican candidate, Richard Nixon.

During his campaign, the 43-year-old Harvard-educated senator faced criticism over his youth and lack of experience, but his gentlemanly glamour wooed the public. His elegance and eloquence as an orator and his self-deprecating style also endeared him to voters. But, while his Irishness has often been thought to have helped him clinch his narrow win, his Catholicism was certainly a hindrance during the campaign as there was a prevailing attitude that the Pope would cast undue influence in the White House. But a landmark speech in front of the Greater Houston Ministerial Association in Texas in September 1960 helped to defuse the situation.

But because I am a Catholic, and no Catholic has ever been elected President, the real issues in this campaign have been obscured – perhaps deliberately, in some quarters less responsible than this . . . I believe in an America where the separation of church and state is absolute – where no Catholic prelate would tell the President (should he be Catholic) how to act, and no Protestant minister would tell his parishioners for whom to vote – where no church or church school is granted any public funds or political preference – and where no man is denied public office merely because his religion differs from the President who might appoint him or the people who might elect him.

All the Kennedy siblings were pressed into canvassing for their brother, often encountering a fascination with their big family on the doorsteps. And so, Kennedy won the presidency in one of the closest elections in American history – by a surplus of 118,000 votes out of 69 million.

The happiest four days of a president's life

JFK's trip to Ireland came over two years into his term and, by all accounts, it was not a popular choice among his stable of advisors. 'I remember one historian saying it was totally off the Richter scale that a US president would spend four days in Ireland,' observed Sean Reidy, formerly of the JFK Trust. The four-day stop-off in Ireland during his European trip, which also took in powerful nations like Germany, England, Italy – and the Vatican – was seen as an indulgence, but the president insisted, and he got his way. 'This is the image that went back to America,' said his Irish cousin in the Kennedy homestead, pointing at the picture of JFK sitting next to his granny in their sitting room. 'It's not him making a speech in Dáil Eireann, he's sitting at his ancestor's fireplace. He's now the leader of this nation of emigrants and he's back to Europe and showing he's proud of his peasant roots. It's this gesture that he wants to go back to America to help his own nation feel comfortable with who they are.'

On his arrival at Dublin Airport on 26 June, straight from

visiting the Berlin Wall in Germany, the American leader was greeted by Ireland's elder statesman, eighty-year-old Éamon de Valera, before his motorcade weaved through the streets of the capital where people hung off lampposts and out of windows to get a glimpse of the glamorous leader. As he was cheered by the multitudes, office workers threw out confetti-like pieces of paper from the windows in a ticker-tape parade, an old custom for honouring returning war heroes and heads of state. A raincoat-clad president persisted with the open-top motorcade alongside a hat-wearing de Valera as the clouds opened with showers of summer rain as he went through the gates of Dublin's Phoenix Park to Áras an Uachtaráin, the presidential seat.

The following day, the US president arrived to the Dunganstown homestead he had first visited in 1947, but this time he came in a Marine One helicopter. US Embassy and security officials spent around a month preparing for his return to meet the rural relatives who had captivated him sixteen years earlier. His cousin, Josie, who passed away in 1979 from a brain tumour, spoke of her memories of the president back in 1966 for an oral history interview for the JFK Library: 'We were all very excited, but we regarded his coming as a cousin coming home . . . We liked to meet him that way and receive him that way.'

He didn't disappoint when he arrived first at the Ryan home with his sisters Jean and Eunice for a farmyard tea party, which descended into cheerful chaos. The president drank cups of tea and ate salmon sandwiches, jokingly asking if the fish had been illegally poached, before handing around slices of cake to a gaggle of policemen, local dignitaries, neighbours and spruced-up schoolchildren. When he entered the house, he pointedly spoke to neighbours helping out in the background, shaking hands with some two or three times.

Proposing a toast, he said: 'We'll drink a cup of tea to all the

Kennedys who have gone away and to all that have remained at home.'

Patrick Grennan says his granny, Mary Ryan, was not fazed by the attention. 'She was taking things in her stride. Sure, anyone could visit, she had brothers and sisters who went to America, and everyone came back and stayed here. JFK came in and sat at the fireplace.' Later, in another part of the house, he points to a battered car seat. 'There is the actual seat the President sat on. It's an old Morris Minor car seat. We told people that's where he sat, and they would pull bits out of it,' he says, explaining why the worse-for-wear seat is now tucked away.

There was one gesture from the president that day that showed he had the measure of Mrs Ryan, according to her grandson. 'At the end of the visit, most of the cake and sandwiches were left uneaten. So, JFK stepped back, and invited the newspapermen and cameramen to eat the food. He saw the effort that had been made for his visit.' Before he left, he helped local schoolchildren to plant trees, ruffling their heads affectionately as he went along the line before walking away to fly off in Marine One with a last beaming smile.

At the much more formal affair at his next stop on the Wexford docks, he laid a wreath at a statue of John Barry, the Irishman dubbed the father of the American navy. He singled out the Irish Republic as a beacon of hope for nations caught up in their own struggles:

> It seems to me that in these dangerous days when the struggle for freedom is worldwide against an armed doctrine, that Ireland and its experience has one special significance, and that is that the people's fight, which John Boyle O'Reilly said outlived a thousand years, that it was possible for a people over hundreds of years of foreign domination and religious persecution – it was possible for that people to maintain their national identity and their strong faith. And therefore

those who may feel that in these difficult times, who may believe that freedom may be on the run, or that some nations may be permanently subjugated and eventually wiped out, would do well to remember Ireland.

He also spoke of his pride that his own country 'welcomed so many sons and daughters of so many countries, Irish and Scandinavian, Germans, Italian, and all the rest, and gave them a fair chance and a fair opportunity'. He added: 'In Ireland, I think you see something of what is so great about the United States; and I must say that in the United States, through millions of your sons and daughters and cousins – twenty-five million, in fact – you see something of what is great about Ireland.'

At the next stop in New Ross on 27 June, he caused amusement when he spoke about the serendipity of emigration, the *Sliding Doors* moment which had ripple effects through generation after generation. 'When my great-grandfather left here [in 1848] to become a cooper in East Boston, he carried nothing with him except two things: a strong religious faith and a strong desire for liberty. I am glad to say that all of his great-grandchildren have valued that inheritance.' He added – to laughter – in his distinctive trans-Atlantic tones: 'If he hadn't left I would be working over at the Albatross company . . . or perhaps for John V. Kelly [a shop]. In any case we're happy to be back here.'

The next day began with a helicopter flight to Cork, where in the midst of throngs of well-wishers outside City Hall, he showed his humanity when he observed one Garda using a little force on an over-enthusiastic spectator, gently saying: 'Don't do that, that man is a good friend of mine.'

That afternoon, the first serving US president to visit Ireland visited Arbour Hill where he laid a wreath at the grave of the executed leaders of the 1916 Rising. After the 36th cadet class provided a guard of honour, the president remarked to their superior officer, Lieutenant Frank Colclough, that it was the best honour guard he had seen. After leaving, he went to Leinster House, becoming the first foreign leader to address the Houses of the Oireachtas before rounding off the day at St Patrick's Hall in Dublin Castle, where he received two honorary degrees and the freedom of the city.

In Galway, on his final day, he famously told the crowd in Eyre Square in his clipped tones: 'If the day was clear enough and if you went down to the Bay and you looked west and your sight was good enough, you would see Boston, Massachusetts – And if you did, you would see down working on the docks there some Dohertys and Flahertys and Ryans and cousins of yours who have gone to Boston and made good.' So heartfelt and demonstrative was his reception by the people of Ireland that President Kennedy remarked before departing Galway, 'You send us home covered with gifts, which we can barely carry, but most of all you send us home with the warmest memories of you and your country.'

Over the course of three days, he received the freedom of five Irish cities, but the president's Bostonian charm and impish humour reduced the most ceremonious of occasions into laughter-filled events, while his empathetic eloquence on famine and immigration infused hope and energy into an ancient nation stepping out as a young republic on the global stage.

Force of nature: who was the 'F' in JFK?

The international media interest in the Fitzgerald side of the family was first piqued when John F. Kennedy was sworn in as the 35th president of the United States on Friday 20 January 1961, in Washington, with his hand resting on a bible held by a clerk of the Supreme Court. The brown leatherbound bible with a gold-leaf cross had traversed the Atlantic with Thomas Fitzgerald from the town of Bruff in Co. Limerick more than a hundred years earlier. Inside, the cover contained five handwritten pages of the Fitzgerald family records. There are notes for the engagement of Rose E. Fitzgerald and Joseph P. Kennedy, their marriage in October 1914, and a list of births for their nine children, including a record of the birth of John Fitzgerald Kennedy on 29 May 1917, alongside various other extended family members.

The 'F' in JFK may be the lesser-known consonant in the iconic acronym, but the maternal grandfather signified in the middle initial is certainly not a character to fade into historical obscurity. In fact, the first two letters of the famous abbreviation are taken from the president's larger-than-life grandpa, John 'Honey Fitz' Fitzgerald. While the first of the Kennedy boys, Joe, was called after his father, the future president was called after his mother's father, a former mayor of Boston. 'Grandpa Fitz took up all the oxygen in the room,' remembers his grandson, Tom Fitzgerald Jnr, fondly.

The eldest son of Irish immigrants, Thomas Fitzgerald and Rose Anna Cox, the politician was a five-foot-seven force of nature, known by Boston citizens simply as John F. long before his grandson would become the first Catholic to become president of the United States. In a family collection of anecdotes called *Grandpa Stories*, his grandson Thomas A Fitzgerald Jr. recalls his astonishment at the parting of traffic in Boston to make way for his grandfather while they were en route to a Red Sox baseball game at Fenway Park in a cab when he was eight years old.

> As we got closer to the ballpark, the traffic grew very heavy, and we got tied up. But that didn't stop Grandpa. Suddenly he had the window rolled down and shouted to the nearest policeman, 'John F., John F., John F.' And the traffic would vanish as if he were Moses

parting the Red Sea. This continued until we were safe in our seats inside the park.

The fast-talking Bostonian – 'They said he could speak 210 words a minute,' said his grandson – who was mayor of the city as well as one of the first Catholics elected as a congressman, appeared to have carte blanche to stroll into the Red Sox locker room or to carve his way through the traffic in a city where everyone knew his name.

The colourful politician took up residence in a suite at the Bellevue Hotel in downtown Boston, right next to the State House, later in his life. JFK also resided at the hotel for most of 1946 after returning from the Second World War, a time when he would engage in long chats with his grandpa. Even before then, when he and his older brother, Joe, were at Harvard, they would regularly call at the Boston hotel to lunch with Honey Fitz.

'Rose Kennedy worked hard maintaining that connection with the Fitzgerald side of the family,' recalled her nephew, Tom Fitzgerald. In the family book of stories, Ted Kennedy remembers how visits to the hotel on Saturdays became a lifeline to him while he was boarding in Fessenden School in Massachusetts. 'In so many ways Grandpa was a second parent for me,' the senator recalled in *Grandpa Stories*:

He was someone who would listen to my adolescent chatter, my hopes and dreams. We would often eat lunch or dinner in the hotel dining room, but I never got much to eat. Grandpa was always introducing me to someone sitting nearby or taking me into the kitchen so the staff could meet me as well. Grandpa simply knew everyone, and if he didn't, he acted as if he knew them anyway.

Grandpa loved the city and took great pride in the things he had done for the citizens of Boston when he was mayor – things like the zoo, the Christmas tree on the Common, the Park Street bandstand, things that everyone could enjoy. He was very conscious of the welfare of everyone. With so many grandchildren, I suppose one might wonder, did he have a favourite? He did – the one he was with at that moment.

In the same family tome, Eunice Kennedy Shriver – the future founder of the Special Olympics – describes her mother dispatching her down to the oceanfront with her grandpa while he sat soaking in health-giving seaweed during visits to their summer house in Hyannis Port. While her grandfather was usually a magnet for people, Eunice has a distinct memory of listening to him hold forth about women's rights as he steeped in the saltwater shallows during one of their snatched one-to-one conversations in the sea.

'Grandpa pointed out to me that most of the news in a newspaper covered the activities of men. Grandpa said papers should talk about the good works women were doing in all walks of life. Here again, Grandpa was ahead of his time,' she recalled in the stories curated by Tom Fitzgerald.

The rise of the man from a Boston tenement to City Hall was almost as unfathomable as his biblical ability to part gridlocked traffic in the heart of his native city by sheer force of his personality. The short, blue-eyed politician was born in overcrowded conditions in Boston's North End, which was heavily populated with Irish emigrants. 'He came out of a neighbourhood, a tenement ghetto in Boston, that was very Irish. He did talk about his early days of growing up in a housing arrangement that had eight families and just one bathroom,' said his grandson, Tom, who was one of JFK's first cousins.

His ancestor, Thomas Fitzgerald, had left Ireland reluctantly around the time of the Irish famine, according to his namesake great-grandson. 'It's suggested that he wanted to try to make it as a farmer in Bruff, and, finally, he saw it wasn't going to work and that's when he decided to come to Boston and work with his brother Jim.' Initially, he hoped to work in the city and earn enough money to purchase a farm in the Midwest, but he changed his mind and instead started, with his sibling, a grocery store-cum-saloon where Irish people would gather in the evenings. 'It had two floors above it where the family could live and the big thing was, they had their own bathroom,' said Tom Fitzgerald. This was the start of the stratospheric climb out of the poverty of the famine and into the highest echelons of American society and political power.

Honey Fitz's eldest sister Ellen Fitzgerald had also succumbed to the rampant cholera in Boston when she died in 1870 at the age of just six months. Nine years later, 45-year-old Rosanna and Thomas, who had ten sons, lost their only other daughter, Mary, to debility (which translates as a state of weakness), at just five days old, on 9 January 1879. But just over two months later, the still-grieving mother died in a tragic circumstance of what was called on her death certificate an 'apoplexy', which was in fact a sudden violent attack in her home at 469 Hanover Street. It is believed it was caused by the shock of being mistakenly told her husband and sons had died in a train crash by someone who'd ridden down to their neighbourhood in the North End. 'She thought she had lost her husband and her sons, and she collapsed and died of a heart attack. It was one of those terrible times,' said her great-grandson, of an accident that had not involved the family at all.

In the aftermath of her death, Thomas sent his son, John, to a Boston Latin school and on to Harvard Medical College, but before he could complete his medical degree, he was summoned home to the North End to care for his younger brothers after his father suddenly died in 1885.

'There was going to be a push to disband the children and put them in foster homes, so Honey Fitz quit and joined in with the political crowd in the North End and got a paying job, which allowed the brothers to stay together,' said his grandson, who believes his grandfather's tough tenement upbringing shaped him for a life of public service. 'It's important to understand what becomes important when you come out of those circumstances. I think he was so consumed with this spirit of public service that he didn't spend a lot of time talking about the past, about his father or his mother.' Just sixteen when his mother suddenly passed away, he was still only twenty-two when his entire family was orphaned and he became the sole guardian of his brothers.

Honey Fitz became a consummate politician, winning a seat on the state senate before going on to win a seat as a congressman in the US House of Representatives in 1894. After three terms in Congress, Fitzgerald was voted mayor of Boston in 1906. He had finished his first term of office when he visited Bruff with his two daughters, Rose and Agnes, and his wife Josephine, during a tour of Europe at the start of the twentieth century. A picture still exists of him standing on the pedestal steps of the Treaty Stone monument in Limerick with a hat-wearing Agnes Fitzgerald on 5 August 1908.

Around this time, Rose had already become acquainted with Joseph P. Kennedy at Old Orchard Beach in Maine where their families vacationed together. On 7 October 1914, they were married in a modest ceremony in a small chapel at the residence of Cardinal O'Connell, who officiated. In 1938, when Honey Fitz returned to Ireland after first visiting his daughter Rose in London, where her husband was serving as US ambassador to Britain, a local hackney cab driver in Bruff, Denis Conway, would later recall bringing the sandy-haired politician on the four-mile trip to Lough Gur. Halfway out down the road, he told him he was the mayor of Boston, on his way to visit his father's birthplace.

Mary Ann Fitzgerald was the mother of Honey Fitz's wife and President Kennedy's maternal grandmother, Mary Josephine Hannon. She was also from Bruff, while her father, Michael Hannon, was from Lough Gur, which means that JFK had three great-grandparents from two neighbouring parishes in the same small corner of east Limerick. In fact, Thomas Fitzgerald and Mary Ann Fitzgerald were first cousins, which in turn made Honey Fitz and his wife Mary Josephine Hannon second cousins, who required special dispensation to marry in 1889 in Boston.

When Thomas Fitzgerald first moved to Boston in 1852, he went to work on his uncle Edmund's farm. Edmund was the father of Mary Ann Fitzgerald, the mother of Mary Josephine Hannon. Research by Boston genealogist R. Andrew Pierce suggests that she came over to New York aboard the *Josephine* from Liverpool with her father and other family members in 1850 before moving to Boston. In his petition for naturalisation, Thomas Fitzgerald says he arrived in Boston in 1850 while Edmund listed his occupation as a peddler and their address was 5 Ann Street in the city. Records uncovered by Mr Pierce in a tithe applotment book show him with a holding of four and a half acres in Bruff parish before he left Ireland.

Rose Kennedy, JFK's mother, reminisced about growing up in Concord, Massachusetts as a small child in the late 1890s with her Limerick-born maternal grandparents, the Hannons:

> As a little girl I lived on a farm . . . outside of Boston. Those were the days when we slept in feather beds and read to the lights of kerosene lamps and got our milk in a five-gallon tin can. But I was happy and contented, helping my grandmother in the garden and riding home proudly with my grandfather on a load of hay after the men had piled it high . . . in the old farm wagon drawn by the farm horse. I heard about the hardships, too, in those days . . . when the rains did not fall

and vegetables were parched ... and the other grey days when there were too many peas and beans in the market at one time and the prices would fall and the apples would lie rotting on the ground because it was not worthwhile to pick them.

When her grandfather Michael Hannon first arrived from Bruff, Limerick, he worked on the railroads like many Irish immigrants and was later listed as working as a labourer to support his wife Mary and their six children in the 1880 census. The crumbling ruin of the house where Mary's mother, Mary Lenihan, was born has only recently been unearthed in Bruff through further examination of land records by local historian Declan Hehir. Although her husband left for America around the time of the famine, JFK's great-great-grandmother died in her hometown shortly after the birth of her baby daughter, Mary Ann. The ivy-clad stone cottage, which now has brambles and trees growing up through the old kitchen, is just outside the village. This traditional farmhouse was the residence of young Mary Lenihan, before she moved a few hundred yards down the road after marrying her neighbour in 1828. Mr Hehir pieced together the origins of the derelict cottage by checking through nineteenth-century land registries of tithe applotments. The sites of the Fitzgerald family homesteads are marked out on a trail in the town, but the buildings in all other cases are long since gone.

Fitzgeralds make *Life* magazine

In the backroom of a country pub at a sleepy crossroads in Limerick, Pat Moloney takes out a cardboard box and unpacks his memories of JFK's visit to Ireland in 1963. Weeks before the four-day homecoming trip, two photojournalists from *Life* magazine had pulled up at his grandmother's house in Kilballyowen outside the town of Bruff in a big yellow sedan. The publican was ten years old at the time, and his third cousin was about to make his euphoric state visit to Ireland, the first US president to do so. In the magazine printed on 5 July 1963, the youngster, smart in a buttoned-up checked shirt and a brown knitted jumper, stares solemnly at the cameras from beside his grand-uncle, Ned Fitzgerald, and his grandmother, Ellen Fitzgerald Hallahan, who has wisps of silver hair escaping from her bun. The elderly siblings were first cousins of JFK's grandfather, John F. 'Honey Fitz' Fitzgerald.

The unvarnished image taken in their kitchen was printed over a headline, *Kennedy's Irish Kin – A Sturdy People Share A President's Heritage*. For his part, Pat, who would go on to travel the world, was wide-eyed at these American journalists arriving on his doorstep. He remembers excitedly bundling into their hire car to drive off around Lough Gur, a hauntingly beautiful lakeside townland, and neighbouring Bruff, where three of President Kennedy's great-grandparents were born. The lake, which curves around the hill of Knockadoon, is walking with history. Driving around the winding roads past stone walls and sloping meadows and patches of forest, they motored by an ancient stone circle and the ruin of a seventeenth-century castle. 'They had this big car and all these cameras, and a briefcase full of chocolate. They took loads of photographs, every time they took a photo, I got a bar of chocolate,' said Pat with a smile. 'I remember they had me up on a tree and looking out a window of an old shack house. I got about twenty big bars of chocolate, at that time you would never have them because you couldn't afford them.'

Although it was the 1960s, the images captured with the backdrop of a brooding landscape depicted an Ireland untouched by time, little changed from the previous century when many of the Fitzgerald family departed for the east coast of America. In the pages of *Life*, Ned Fitzgerald was shown sitting on a wooden stool hand-milking one of his two cows into a metal bucket with the caption: 'Thomas

Fitzgerald, the President's maternal great-grandfather, may have been born in a now-ruined house in a bog near here.'

Caught unawares when her brother jauntily arrived up to her home with the American visitors in June 1963, Ellen Fitzgerald Hallahan was dismayed over the stark family portrait which ended up on the magazine's pages in millions of American households, their desire for rural realism at odds with her understandable wish to look her Sunday best. When a car arrived at their house, on the day President Kennedy famously addressed a huge crowd fifteen miles away in Limerick city's racecourse on the last day of his visit, she declined to go in, still smarting over being pictured in her apron with untidy hair. 'They sent out a car to her and to Ned to go in and meet him, I would have tagged along if she went but she didn't want to go in,' remembered Pat. Her brother, on the other hand, was 'delighted' to be chauffeured into Limerick city to meet his famous cousin.

At the Green Park Race Course that afternoon, the president with movie-star charisma drew huge cheers when he said: 'I asked your distinguished Ambassador to the United States, Ambassador Kiernan – he has sort of an elfish look about him, but he is very, very good – I said, "What is this county noted for?" and he said, "It is noted for its beautiful women and its fast horses." And I said, "Well, you say that about every county." And he said, "No, this is true about this county,"' before breaking into a huge grin at the roar of approval. Then he turned at the podium saying: 'I want to express my pleasure at seeing the Fitzgeralds. I wonder if they could stand up? One of them looks just like Grandpa, and that is a compliment.' And he smiled, to more cheers.

Pat Moloney was always told that JFK was pointing to his uncle Ned that day, a second cousin once removed. 'President Kennedy when he was speaking in Limerick turned and said, "Doesn't he even look like Honey Fitz?"' said Pat. Looking at his printed family trees,

Pat says now, 'Ned knew all the time, but he didn't have the proof I have now. Ned was very proud of the whole thing.'

Their photoshoot under moody skies wasn't their first experience with a big-selling American publication looking to unearth the relatives left behind in the old country. A journalist from *Look* magazine had pulled up at their household over two years earlier, shortly after President Kennedy was inaugurated. At the time, it was one of the highest circulation magazines in the US, reaching millions every week. To coincide with St Patrick's Day in 1961, the magazine, with 1960s movie icon Ingrid Bergman on the cover, ran a four-page spread on the bloodlines of the most Irish of all US presidents with the headline, 'If There's a Dollar In It, I'm related.' This was reportedly quipped by one of the patrons in the public house of Gus O'Kennedy in New Ross.

Back in Bruff, Ned Fitzgerald had been pictured for the same feature almost blending into the craggy landscape as he stood, chest out, dressed in his brown overcoat and wide-brimmed hat, standing among rocks in a boggy field. A white-horned goat added to the rugged look of the picture captioned: 'Fitzgerald Bog and the Old Homesite In Limerick.' Ned was pointing at the rubble of an old ruin where he believed Thomas Fitzgerald – President Kennedy's maternal great-grandfather – had been born.

In the aftermath of the JFK visit, Pat remembers his grandmother getting a letter from the former Archbishop of Cashel, Dr Thomas Morris, a patron of the GAA. 'He used to throw in the sliotar at the All-Ireland finals. She got a letter from him asking her, would she write to the Kennedys and recommend that they give a donation for the doing up of Holy Cross Abbey.' When another letter came from the *New York Times*, from a journalist called Wilbur Jennings, an eleven-year-old Pat took it upon himself to send a reply as his grandmother was not interested in any more interactions with the American press. They corresponded for years afterwards. 'He would send me all the cuttings of the famous people he would be interviewing. He lived in Bridgeport, Connecticut, and years later I drove up when I was over in America, as I remembered the address. He had since died but his daughter remembered I had sent him over an Irish tablecloth.'

Another fourth cousin, Michael Fitzgerald, who is still living in Bruff, was aware from a young age of their famous relative. 'I always remember in the sitting room at home you would have the picture of the Sacred Heart and you have the picture of Robert and John Fitzgerald Kennedy both beside each other. My father's grandfather, James Fitzgerald, was a first cousin of Honey Fitz's father, Thomas Fitzgerald, who left Bruff in 1852.' His grandfather spent time in Boston in the 1920s, where Michael believed he would have encountered the Boston mayor. He noted there was often talk about a family resemblance between the Bruff Fitzgeralds and the Boston Fitzgeralds. 'My own grandfather was supposed to be this spit of Honey Fitz.'

Although the lesser-known side of the family, the Kennedys did keep in touch with the Fitzgerald relatives over the years. Pat Moloney remembers corresponding with Ted Kennedy, who was said to have an Irish roadside signpost for Lough Gur to match the one for Dunganstown in his Senate office. He was due to visit Lough Gur in the 1990s, but a family member fell ill, and he sent his apologies.

However, his older sisters, Jean Kennedy Smith and Patricia Lawford, spent several days touring around Bruff and Lough Gur in October 1994, going through old records and visiting the sites of family homesteads. The down-to-earth siblings stayed in a local guesthouse, mixed easily with locals and happily tucked into a pub dinner in the company of Irish comedian Jon Kenny, who lived nearby.

Ms Kennedy Smith, who was the US ambassador at the time, spoke of her emotion at returning to the birthplace of her great-grandfather, Michael Hannon. 'It's very moving to visit the place where your great-grandfather was born. I have already been to Wexford with my late brother, President John Kennedy.' She remembered her grandfather Honey Fitz as 'always central to our family'. 'He was particularly close to Bobby,' she added as she opened a theatre in his name in Lough Gur. During her stay, she was full of anecdotes about her grandpa, explaining that he acquired the name Honey Fitz as a result of his singing the song 'Sweet Adeline' at the end of all his political rallies with her mother, Rose, often accompanying him on the piano. 'He adored my mother – in fact she often campaigned with him,' she remembered.

Her sister, Pat Lawford, who had been married to the famous British actor Peter Lawford, described the visit as a stirring experience. She recalled how, as an old man, her grandfather had described his visits to Lough Gur and Bruff as one of the highlights of his life, calling the area 'indescribably lovely'. She said at the time, 'Our mother would never forgive us had we not paid a visit to Lough Gur to see where it all began.' Rose Fitzgerald died a few months later in January 1995 at the grand age of 104, safe in the knowledge her ancestors had been acknowledged. Her *New York Times* obituary described her as a 'child of the Boston Irish' in its opening sentence.

Ambassador Smith would return the hospitality she received in Limerick later in 1995 when she invited a delegation up to her Phoenix Park residence for a Thanksgiving celebration, where a fledgling young traditional music group called The Corrs performed.

When JFK returned from the Second World War, he lived at the Bellevue Hotel for months alongside his much-loved grandfather.

Upon being elected to Congress in 1946, Honey Fitz sent his young grandson a Western Union telegram saying:

CONGRESSMAN JOHN F KENNEDY, HEARTIEST CONGRATULATIONS BOSTON PAPERS CARRY YOUR PICTURE ON FRONT PAGE WE ARE ALL VERY PROUD OF YOU JOHN F FITZGERALD.

Although the Boston politician died in 1950 at the fine age of eighty-seven, his grandson paid homage by naming the 93-foot presidential yacht *Honey Fitz* after his grandpa. During the presidency, he regularly sailed down the Potomac River in DC to Cape Cod.

Tom Fitzgerald, JFK's younger first cousin, remembers the Secret Service arriving at his Boston home just before the president's inauguration. 'My dad was burning trash in a barrel out in the back of the house in Dorchester, when he said, all of a sudden three men came out of the trees, and said they were the FBI,' he laughed. 'They were coming to pick up the Bible that JFK wanted.' Growing up, he would pore over the pages of notes which kept their family history. 'I used to be fascinated, looking at the births and deaths pages, and trying to figure out whose handwriting it was. And I knew it was Thomas Fitzgerald and then Grandpa Fitz's and then my father's handwriting was very recognisable and then I ended up in charge of the Bible.' Although Honey Fitz had died over a decade before JFK's inauguration, his presence must have been felt by his grandson in the leather under his palm as he was sworn into office.

Tom Fitzgerald was still in high school when his much older cousin became a senator, but he would see him occasionally in the summer when he would visit his aunt Rose with his father in Hyannis. 'Sometimes we would walk along the beach with Joe Kennedy and my dad and JFK was there in a couple of those walks.' He does have vivid memories of attending the reception in the White House after the inauguration. 'It was a grand affair. Like a lot of things in life, you were so lost in the moment. It was busy, it was exciting, it was hard to imagine what was happening, that you were a fringe part of it.' He remembers being struck by the young navy lieutenant, with a briefcase handcuffed to his wrist, next to the president that night. 'It had the nuclear codes and I thought he's never going to be alone again. As president, you are not alone.'

Michael Collins and the Cork connection – ancestors of twentieth-century icons born half a mile apart

There are also three lesser-known great-grandparents in the family tree. JFK's great-grandmother, Margaret M. Field, has a surprising link to one of Ireland's most iconic revolutionary figures. The farm, where she was born in 1835, was in the townland of Coorleigh North, around four miles outside Clonakilty in Cork, and less than half a mile from the house where Republican leader Michael Collins was born in the neighbouring townland of Woodfield. Michael Collins' father was seventy-five when he was born, the youngest of eight children. It had been a very late marriage for the bachelor farmer, who was sixty years old when he married the freedom fighter's 23-year-old mother, Mary Ann O'Brien. Michael Collins Snr was around twenty years old when President Kennedy's great-grandmother arrived into the world so it's almost certain he would have met his young neighbour and been on familiar terms with her parents.

Local historian Tim Crowley was fascinated to discover the families of two of the most significant political icons of the twentieth century lived in such close proximity. 'An old lady pointed out the Field site to me about twenty-five years ago and it's there on the map. They were just over the ditch. We heard Margaret Field emigrated during the famine; she would have only been around twelve.' He believes there is even a possibility there could be a distant blood tie between JFK and Michael Collins, through the Sheehy lines of their families. 'Johnny Collins, Michael's brother, is recorded as saying that the first Collins to come into Woodfield, several generations before Michael Collins, actually married into a Sheehy farm. So, at the very least they were neighbours and there is a possibility that Kennedy and Collins are distant cousins,' he said referring to the fact that JFK's grandmother – Margaret Field's mother – was called Mary Sheehy. Maybe Jean Kennedy Smith was cognisant of this chance connection in her cameo role in the 1996 film, *Michael Collins*, in a scene with the fleeing revolutionary hero.

When he gives tours at the Michael Collins Centre outside Clonakilty in west Cork, the historian puts pictures of the two leaders side by side for visitors.

> If I said to you, they were brothers you would take my word for it, there is a bit of a resemblance. They were both charismatic leaders of the twentieth century, they both died from shots to the head under controversial circumstances, Collins on the 22nd of August, Kennedy on the 22nd of November. They were both traveling in open motor cars leading up to the time of their deaths. There's a lot of quirky little coincidences. If they were related it would be an amazing bit of history.

In another interesting twist, Éamon de Valera, Ireland's other legendary Republican figure, grew up in the village of Bruree, around six miles away from Bruff. The Irish statesman was born in Manhattan in New York on 14 October 1882, but was sent home as a toddler by his mother, Kate Moll, a native of the Limerick village, to be reared in a labourer's cottage by his grandmother, Elizabeth.

Meanwhile, the Clare husband of Margaret Field, James Hickey, is among the more enigmatic of President Kennedy's great-grandparents. About twenty years ago, on foot of a request from Kennedy genealogical expert, R. Andrew Pierce, it was established that President Kennedy's great-grandfather James Hickey was born in the parish of Kilnasoolagh in Clare in 1835, near the grounds of Dromoland Castle, to Michael Hickey and Kate Hassett, and that he emigrated to Boston in 1852. James Hickey is thought to have married Margaret Field in 1857. His father, Michael, was renting a house on five acres from Lord Inchiquin near Dromoland Castle around the time of his birth.

It was also discovered by Mr Pierce that James Hickey would have worked at the castle as a servant along with his siblings. In the 1860 census, he is listed as an engineer living in the tenth ward of Boston with his wife and two infant children, one of them Mary Augusta Hickey, who would grow up to marry Patrick Joseph Kennedy and become President Kennedy's grandmother, dying just a few days short of JFK's sixth birthday. By 1870 he is listed as a steam engineer; by 1880 he is a machinist, and his grown-up sons are working in shoe stores.

The springtime promise JFK would never get to keep

On the packed last day on his homecoming tour to Ireland, JFK light-heartedly told crowds in Limerick, it was 'not the land of my birth but it is the land to which I hold the greatest affection'. He added: 'And I certainly will come back in the springtime.'

A month before he was assassinated, his first cousin, Tom Fitzgerald, remembers the president stopping off at his Boston family home to pay a visit to their grandma Fitz, who was living with his father, Tom Snr. By that time she was unable to speak, but she was the only grandparent who lived to see him sworn into office. 'In photographs of that visit that JFK made, you could see the delight in her eyes, in her face.'

She also lived to see the president felled by an assassin's bullet just weeks later. On 22 November 1963, shortly after noon, President Kennedy was shot in the head as his open-top car drove slowly past cheering crowds along Dealey Plaza in downtown Dallas. The murder of the president next to his terrified young wife sent shock-waves around the world. Announcers delivered the news in one newsflash after another in sombre tones.

Mary Ryan and her daughter Josephine were sitting at their Wexford home listening to the radio when it was interrupted with the announcement. In the following weeks, thousands of letters of sympathy were delivered to their farmhouse. Within a few hours of the shooting, Lee Harvey Oswald was charged with the murder, but on 24 November, another man, Jack Ruby, shot and killed Oswald, thus silencing the only person who could have shed light on the killing. In the wake of his death, JFK's widow sent a request to Mrs Ryan to attend the state funeral, but it was decided her daughter, Mary Ann, a young midwife working in the Rotunda Maternity Hospital in Dublin, would represent the family at the service. Mr Grennan states:

My aunt Mary Ann went out to Shannon Airport and got on a plane out to New York with European dignitaries attending the president's funeral. A military plane brought her to Washington from New York. She sat beside Martin Luther King at the funeral. She travelled in the funeral cortège with JFK's sister Patricia and her husband Peter Lawford. When he sat at our fireplace, the president had asked if he could bring his wife and children back the next year. He must have spoken of his wishes to Jackie for her to have thought to invite Granny to the funeral.

Jacqueline Kennedy had also sent word asking if the Irish cadets who had so impressed the American leader with their drill movements during his Irish visit would fly over to Washington five months later to form a guard of honour at his graveside. One of the rifles used in the Arbour Hill and at JFK's funeral now stands in a glass case at the museum in his Wexford homestead.

After the funeral, Mary Ann was taken aside by Jackie Kennedy, who handed her JFK's rosary beads and his presidential identification tags. 'The rosary beads were given to my aunt by Jackie the night JFK was buried and his commander-in-chief dog tag,' said her nephew Patrick. 'She took her aside and said, "Would you give this to your mum, Mrs Ryan?"' It was an extraordinary gesture by a grief-stricken widow at a funeral which was attended by hundreds of foreign dignitaries.

After the funeral, Mary Ann also had a surreal interaction with Irish president Éamon de Valera at Massachusetts Avenue in Washington. 'She had no place to stay so she was brought to the Irish Embassy and had dinner with de Valera,' explained her nephew, 'and she told him she had lots of first cousins she could visit while she was over there, but she had to go home to go back to work in the Rotunda Hospital. He said, "You stay here, I'll go back and talk to the matron," so de Valera came back to Ireland and cleared the way for her to stay in America and visit her cousins in St Louis and New York.' He added that one of his granny's proudest moments came at the opening of the John F. Kennedy Arboretum near the homestead in 1968 on 29 May, the president's birthday. When President de Valera officially opened the garden dedicated to the US president 'she got to link arms with de Valera and walk up to the ribbon'.

The rosary beads stayed in the attic of the Kennedy homestead for decades, but in more recent years they have been put on display in the museum. The significance of the gesture was brought home to

Patrick Grennan during a recent visit by Robert Kennedy's son, Douglas, to the museum, as he stood in front of the glass case containing his uncle's prayer beads. 'You'd rarely see anyone in Ireland with rosary beads now, but Douglas was standing there, and he pulled out his rosary beads from his pocket. He told me he would see photographs of his dad, Robert, with his hands in his pockets and Douglas knew he would be counting the rosary beads.'

Years later, the former CEO of the JFK Trust in New Ross and a family friend of the Kennedys, Sean Reidy, remembers bringing a Norwegian emigration expert out to visit the homestead in Dunganstown, where they met Mary Ann. As the visitor had studied immigration, he remembers asking Mary Ann if she would mind showing him the items she was given at JFK's funeral, which at that time were kept in a press upstairs.

> I can remember the man crying because he was so moved. Here was someone who took out a little box, a dog tag of an American president and the rosary beads he carried on him the day he was assassinated, one of the most iconic figures in world history, and here she was taking out a box in her living room and putting it on the table. The enormity of it really struck him, because he was someone who studied immigration.

Tragically, of course, JFK was unable to keep the promise he made in Limerick on the last day of his fabled trip to return to Ireland the following spring, but his family have kept coming in his name in the ensuing decades. The most poignant visit to the Kennedy homestead was undoubtedly the arrival of Jackie Kennedy with her children, Caroline and John Jnr in June 1967, fulfilling the pledge her husband had made to bring back his family to see Mrs Ryan, as at that earlier time Jackie was pregnant and therefore unable to make the trip.

Four years on and his widow was now one of the most recognisable people on the planet, but seeking a haven of normality for her children away from the constant glare of cameras. She sent a note to Mrs Ryan from where she was staying in Woodstown House in the neighbouring county of Waterford.

Dear Mrs Ryan,

At last we really are in Ireland, and the children and I are looking forward so much to coming over to see you and meeting all of our cousins. I wondered if this coming Wednesday might be convenient for you? I would have asked to come much sooner – but there have been so many newspaper men and television cameras around, I didn't want them all to follow us and spoil a happy family meeting – The children have been looking forward to Dunganstown for such a long time – They both have pictures of your house in their room at home – and I thought for little children, all the impressions of seeing the place their family came from, might be ruined if we were surrounded by photographers, so I hope you will forgive me for waiting until now to write to you. Please know how very much we're all looking forward to seeing you. If that day is inconvenient for you – I am sure any other that you choose will be fine for us.

Sincerely,

Jacqueline Kennedy.

When the children and Jackie Kennedy arrived on the farm, the youngsters were smitten by two kittens with six-year-old John pleading with his mother to bring one home, but quarantine laws wouldn't permit their passage back to the US. The following day they were sent back down to the farm by their mother, arriving in bare feet with a security officer, and spent the day roaming the fields and playing with a sow and her young piglets.

It was around 1980 when Ted Kennedy visited the homestead which had charmed his brother. 'We got a spin on the helicopter,' remembers Patrick Grennan. A few years later in 1984, he went with their aunt Mary Ann to his office in the US Senate where he vividly remembers being taken on the train in the bowels of the US Capitol that ferries lawmakers from Senate chambers over and back to their office buildings. On another American trip by Mary Ann to see Jackie Kennedy, Patrick recalled how she brought home a drawing and a piece of artwork that young Caroline and John Jnr had made at school.

JFK had once said he wanted to become an ambassador to Ireland after completing two terms in the White House. It was not to be. But his sister, Jean Kennedy Smith, was appointed to the role by President Bill Clinton in 1993, following in the diplomatic footsteps of her father, Joe. The US ambassador and her brother, Senator Ted Kennedy, are among the key architects of the Good Friday Agreement, which brought peace to the island their great-grandparents fled in the middle of the nineteenth century.

Today, the Kennedy connection has put New Ross on the global tourism map, not unlike Graceland in Memphis or Paisley Park in Minneapolis. Sean Reidy, CEO of the JFK Trust from 1991 to 2014, first connected with Ted Kennedy on Capitol Hill in 1993 in a meeting that ran an hour over time, and his sister Jean later that day, as he told of his dream of building the life-size Dunbrody Famine Ship, which now stands on the quayside in the Wexford seaside town. In raising funds to build the replica of the tall ship which carried JFK's ancestors, the currency of the Kennedy name magically opened doors. 'If you had the Kennedy link, it made an awful difference in Irish government circles,' commented Mr Reidy.

When the JFK Trust was set up in the late 1980s, New Ross was one of Ireland's unemployment blackspots, but the footfall to various memorials to the Kennedy family has transformed the town, as Mr Reidy recalls:

It was to commemorate the legacy of JFK in projects that would enrich the lives of the people in the ancestral hometown of New Ross. There is nowhere in Ireland where Irish-American heritage is celebrated in such a significant way. There is a ship, a visitor centre, a statue, you have the arboretum, the homestead, the emigrant flame, the Irish-American Hall of Fame and the Rose Fitzgerald Kennedy Bridge. We probably bring in about 100,000 people a year to New Ross. It's worth millions every year.

In 2013, thirty members of the Kennedy clan piled into coaches and cars to make their way down to Wexford to mark the fiftieth anniversary of the president's visit to Ireland. Before arriving on the east coast, Caroline Kennedy, the most private member of her famous clan, journeyed to the pretty Limerick village of Bruff with her husband, Edwin Schlossberg, and her children, Jack, Rose and Tatiana, on 24 June. She strode up the main street with hundreds of villagers in her wake before taking to the podium, where she exuded the Kennedy charm. 'Grandma always had it that the Fitzgeralds were the better half of the family and the ones with the brains. And everybody knew Grandma was the best politician of all,' she said to beaming faces, showing off her own political genes.

Although some Fitzgeralds departed and others stayed behind, there is a lingering pride in the family members who reached the highest offices in the United States. 'To think they ended up getting one of the highest offices in the world. We're really proud of how quickly Honey Fitz became mayor of Boston in one generation. Of course, it doesn't stop with JFK, there was Robert and Ted. It is a political dynasty that goes on to this day,' said Michael Fitzgerald, JFK's fourth cousin.

When Caroline Kennedy came with her children to Bruff in 2013, they were the fifth generation to return since three emigrants left to carve out a new life across the Atlantic. Michael Fitzgerald had a sense of them walking in their ancestors' footsteps:

> They walked from the Protestant church up through the town right up to the Thomas Fitzgerald centre at the top of the town. I think what they felt was that one of their relations, going way back, came from this town and probably walked that road in the 1840s, 1850s, before he went to America. I think that means a lot to all of us, to go back where it all began, and see where your people came from. No matter how long they live they'll always be Irish, and I think that's why they'll always keep coming home.

The Kennedy mystique was still tangible in New Ross later that week in celebrations of the fiftieth anniversary of JFK's visit when a few dozen of the clan watched an 'eternal flame' from JFK's grave in Washington light the emigrant monument on the New Ross quayside where his great-grandparents had boarded a ship to America. But the event nearly didn't happen because of concerns by his sister, Jean Kennedy Smith, over the sanctity of his memory. When it was suggested that the flame might first travel around parishes and appear on RTÉ's *Late Late Show* before reaching New Ross, his sister strongly objected. After some frantic diplomacy by the former CEO of the JFK Trust in New Ross, Sean Reidy, and the Irish government over a number of days, it was agreed that the flame could be taken from the grave for the first time, but only under state escort. 'She wanted this flame to be treated with state honours the whole way. She guarded his legacy very carefully,' recalled Sean Reidy.

The Irish army, and later the Irish navy, did guard the flame on every inch of its journey from Washington to Dublin and then down by the Irish Sea along the east coast to New Ross, where Jean Kennedy Smith, Caroline Kennedy and the Irish Taoiseach Enda

Kenny took three torches and lit the emigrant monument on the quayside. The Irish air corps did a fly-by in salute as the flame was lit on the Wexford coast where so many emigrants left their country never to return. It was on that quayside, in an electric speech, that the glamorous US president would change the perception of emigration for millions around the globe as he told his audience, 'I'm glad to be here. It took 115 years to make the trip and 6,000 miles and three generations.'

Fifty years later, the last thing Jean Kennedy did before she left the Wexford town for the final time was pull up in her car on the quayside and walk over to the emigration flame where she spent five minutes in deep contemplation on the edge of the Atlantic. In June 2020, she was the last of her nine siblings to die at the age of ninety-two. But on that trip to Ireland in 2015, she took her leave of New Ross and stepped back into the car and drove off, safe in the knowledge that her brother's memory would continue to burn brightly.

Irish Ambassador William Patrick Fay pins a cluster of shamrocks on President Nixon's lapel on 17 March 1969.

CHAPTER TWO

PRESIDENT RICHARD NIXON

---

*I can assure you that the Irish have the best grips of anybody
in the world. This is the first time anybody has shaken hands
with me and broken a cufflink in the process. But they were
friendly handshakes and I enjoyed it very, very much.*

S IT, KING. SIT!' COMMANDED PRESIDENT NIXON. But the red
setter he had named after his ancestral home in Ireland was not
in a cooperative mood for the photo call in the Rose Garden with
seventeen-year-old Kildare student Marian Scully on the morning
of 19 September 1972. After several spirited attempts to get King
Timahoe to pose for the press cameras, there was laugher as the
president's national security advisor, Henry Kissinger, offered to
see if he would follow the command in German while the president
suggested his valet, Manolo Sanchez, speak to the dog in Spanish.
The gun dog eventually followed orders, sitting obediently between
President Nixon and the teenager in the yellow dress amid the
popping flashbulbs, and the photo shoot wrapped up successfully. 'I
knew we'd get it,' commented the president in triumph. 'We got
some historic footage,' remarked his press secretary Ziegler. The
light-hearted exchange with Nixon, the teenager and the Irish setter
named after her hometown in Kildare was captured in the White

House tapes which would later play a pivotal role in the Watergate scandal.

Minutes earlier, Nixon had wrapped up high-level talks with future president George H.W. Bush, who was the then US ambassador to the United Nations, and Mr Kissinger, on the hijacking of a Swedish airliner, letter bombs and US relations with the Soviet Union. Kissinger was still in the Oval Office when the White House appointment's secretary, Stephen Bull, entered and briefed the president on his next engagement with the young Irish woman, explaining to the commander-in-chief that his helicopter had landed in a field on her family's farm in Co. Kildare during his visit to Ireland two years earlier. 'Mr President, Marian,' announced one of his aides as she walked into the Oval Office as President Nixon and Mr Kissinger gathered up papers.

'Well, how do you do? Nice to see you, have you had a good time over here? Where have you been all this time?' President Nixon asked the teenager, who replied she had been staying in Connecticut since June. 'In Connecticut? Well, there are a lot of Irish out there . . .'

Nearly half a century on from her summer working as an au pair in the US, the young woman, who now goes by her married name of Marian Moore, and is back living in Kildare, vividly remembers the surreal audience with the US leader. 'President Nixon was asking how I enjoyed my holidays and Henry Kissinger wanted to know how this happened and I told him [President Nixon] had landed in my dad's field in Ireland.' When the teenager was planning a working summer in the US two years after Nixon's state visit to Ireland in 1970, her father, Kildare farmer Jack Scully – who was very proud his Timahoe field became a landing strip for Marine One – insisted that she drop the embassy a line informing them of her upcoming trip to America.

That July in Connecticut the letter had been long forgotten when she got a phone call from her father, who had been visited by a puzzled sergeant in Kildare to say the FBI were looking for her address in America. Her letter had resulted in a reciprocal invite to the White House two years after her family has hosted the president on their farm. After getting instructions to keep her impending trip to Washington confidential, she was chauffeured from her flat in Connecticut to La Guardia Airport where she was put on a plane under a diplomatic pass, before being taken off the jet by Irish embassy staff ahead of all the other passengers and driven direct to the White House.

It was nearly four years into the Nixon administration and the Californian president had ordered that all his meetings and phone conversations would be recorded to preserve an accurate record of his presidency on the advice of his predecessor, President Lyndon B. Johnson. The extensive White House taping system would later prove to be Nixon's downfall in the Watergate scandal which led to the president's resignation in August 1974.

Two years before his departure, this equipment was listening in on a much more innocuous encounter with a young Irish girl who was granted a private audience which would be the envy of the leaders of many small nations. A few minutes into her meeting, the recording reveals the president being asked by an aide to step outside the French doors of the Oval Office to pose for the 'press picture'. As they walked out the French doors, he asked Marian: 'We might get the big setter out there, you heard of him?'

During the photo session, the White House pet was initially oblivious to the entreaties for him to be seated. 'There seemed to be a lot of cameras flashing. I know the Miss Worlds were there at some time that morning. No dog is going to sit with all that. To me King Timahoe was grand. He did sit eventually when we were nearly finished so they got the photograph,' remembered Marian.

The president then brought her back into the Oval Office to give her gifts with the presidential seal for her family, brooches for her sister and her mother. On the White House tapes, he can be heard saying, 'Let's get something for your dad too, these are cufflinks that have the [presidential] seal.'

She remembers him talking of memories of his Irish visit. 'He said it was lovely to see where his ancestors were buried and it was nice to make the connection because Pat, his wife, is from Mayo and she knew more about her connection than [he] did about his,' recalled Marian. As she was leaving the White House, tapes capture him saying, 'Except for ancestors migrated I might be there myself, it's where we all came from . . .'

As the teenager touched down in La Guardia Airport that evening, she saw her photo call with President Nixon and King Timahoe flashing up on primetime news in the US terminal. 'It was kind of nice to be chauffeured around in a big black sedan, it was fifteen minutes of fame that I suppose that everybody should have in their lifetime.'

Americans she had met over the summer months were agog. 'Myself and my friend had got jobs as au pairs. I had met people through my friend, it was a party summer. They were all ringing asking, "Is that Marian?" They couldn't believe it. I had parties out of it.'

Direct line from cemetery to White House – and the Quaker custodian who spoke truth to power

It was over two years earlier, in April 1970, when Marian's father got the first inkling that President Nixon would follow in JFK's footsteps with a trip to Ireland. Nixon's great-great-great-great-grandfather Thomas Milhous, born in 1699, went from the tiny eastern parish of Timahoe in Ireland to Chester County, Pennsylvania in 1729. A surviving certificate, used to introduce

Milhous to the Society of Friends in Pennsylvania, explains that Thomas and his wife, Sarah Miller, and their three young children, along with her parents and a sixteen-year-old servant girl called Ann Cunningham wished to settle in America. The document signed by twenty-six Quaker men in Dublin stated they were 'sober and orderly in conversation, as becomes our Holy Profession'. On arrival, Milhous bought two hundred acres and a home in Chester County in Pennsylvania.

An official paper on the ancestry of President Nixon detailing research carried out in 1972 mentioned another distant relative called James Nixon, who also may have come from Ireland. A third descendant, another great-great-great-great-grandfather, James Moore, migrated from Ballymoney, Co. Antrim in Ireland to Lancaster County, Pennsylvania before 1759. In his marriage certificate in Pennsylvania, he is listed as, 'James Moore, son of James Moore, deceased, of Ballymoney, in the Kingdom of Ireland.' Another great-great-great-great-grandfather, Alexander Brown, was born in Ireland around 1773 before emigrating to Hampshire County, West Virginia. Meanwhile an ancestor called Issac Brown from Ireland, who emigrated to Ohio, is a closer relative as a great-great-great-grandfather, but there is no conclusive location for where he came from in Ireland.

As the US Embassy scoured the country for any living relatives of Mr Nixon in the run-up to the visit, they were initially flummoxed by the identification of two parishes of Timahoe – one in Co. Laois and one in Co. Kildare. Officials of the Laois town were quite insistent that their village, which had just won the Tidy Towns competition, a dahlia-dazzling contest for the country's most spruced-up parishes, was in fact the birthplace of Nixon's forefathers. Meanwhile, newspapers articles went back and forth on the Timahoe tug-of-war over the sought-after position of presidential birthplace.

People were swayed by the round tower in Laois's Timahoe, which was possibly more picturesque than its Kildare counterpart, but then the Kildare Timahoe did have a Quaker community. The US Embassy decided to dispatch US ambassador John Moore for a spot of in-person reconnaissance. On a bright spring afternoon, locals watched in amusement as an embassy car tried to manoeuvre up their narrow country lane leading to the disused Quaker cemetery with the diplomat barely managing to squeeze out between the door and a very overgrown ditch.

Local farmer Jack Scully, who has since passed away, would later recall seeing a pair of well-polished shoes appear while he was repairing a fence.

> This rather large black sedan pulled up at the gates and a very tall, well-dressed man introduced himself as Mr Moore, the American ambassador at the time. He said it was confidential, of course, but there was talk of Mr Nixon coming to Ireland and he wanted to visit his ancestors' original place and they had traced them down the Quaker graveyard in the top field.

Mr Scully brought the ambassador clambering across ditches to the cemetery to personally verify the Milhous grave. His daughter remembers the Quaker graveyard, which was well overgrown with broken headstones and a rusted little gate. 'He was able to tell him he was looking for Milhous or Nixon, or maybe just Milhous. So, they went around the headstones and they found it. He was a very normal man; there was no problem, although my dad was worried about his very polished shoes.

Local historian Seamus Cullen claims it was all a moot point as President Nixon was well aware of where his ancestors lived in Ireland. 'Nixon knew more than they knew. The Milhous relatives were disgusted with this two Timahoes situation because they knew exactly where their family came from,' said Seamus, who was at the graveyard the day Nixon flew in. The story goes that, in 1952, Nixon's maternal aunt, Rose, and her husband travelled to Timahoe to look up their relatives while on a world tour. On the drive back to Dublin with a member of the Society of Friends, who had acted as their tour guide, they began talking about the upcoming American presidential election. As they got talking about a General Eisenhower, who was the Republican candidate, they then dropped into the conversation that they felt their nephew – who was a Californian senator – had a good chance of being selected as Eisenhower's running mate in the election. 'So, little did the people in Laois know that Nixon's family had already been to Ireland, to Kildare and to Timahoe,' said Mr Cullen. The arrival of Nixon's Irish red setter, King Timahoe, in the White House in 1969, a year or so before he set foot in Ireland, would certainly indicate he was aware of his connection to the Kildare village.

Once Timahoe's graveyard had been newly landscaped, telephone poles were erected and a phone was installed to ensure there was a direct line to the White House. 'The amazing thing at the time was the big, long telephone line and at the end of it a white telephone with a big light on it. Nobody was to touch it, it was sitting on a box and there was a guard standing at it,' remembered Marian. 'You could lift the phone and you were directly through to the White House in a matter of seconds from the hill of Timahoe. The phone was gone in seconds when he pulled away.' She remembers the embassy staff casing out the farm for a helicopter landing spot.

It was all very exciting. The day dawned and there was a fierce Garda presence, and the roads were all cleared. The security was around for weeks before, looking under stones and behind hedges, because there were anti-Vietnam demonstrations all over the world at the time.

There was a couple in Dublin, and there was Troubles in the north, so they were afraid it might all spill down to Timahoe.

Jack Scully would tell people afterwards he was amazed to see the Irish and American flags flying on two very tall poles at the gap at the top of his field that day. 'The thought that the president of America was in my field was hard to believe,' he said.

That day, Seamus Cullen arrived at the graveyard with his sister and mother. To the twenty-something – who was sporting a typically long-haired 1970s look – he felt like he was on the set of *Hawaii Five-O* with President Nixon as the show's star character, Detective Steve McGarrett, as he and his wife flew in on the Marine One helicopter.

It would remind you of going to a rock concert: the excitement, the blocked cars waiting to go into a car park and then suddenly over a hedge this helicopter appears. All glass, and you could virtually put your hand out and touch it, it was so close. I was there, my sister went into the crowd and shook Nixon's hand, I saw Nixon looking at me, but we knew the story, Nixon didn't particularly like hippies, and I was like a hippie, it was the period of the 1970s with the long hair.

He described the film-star glamour of the president with his winter tan and lightweight navy suit, worlds away from the heavy wool suits sold in Irish department stores like Cleary's in those years of the early 1970s. 'He was very smiley and when he began to speak, he was the Nixon you'd see on TV. He seemed to be very, very friendly,' Seamus remembered, 'and he came across as a man who was enjoying himself. There were eyes looking at him in excitement. It was the American president coming to our village.'

For the locals it was a chance to get red tape magically melted away. Public services were abruptly diverted to Timahoe, which received a makeover in the weeks before the visit. Hedges were neatly cut all the way up the boreen to the cemetery. Mr Cullen recalled one local man, on a waiting list for a phone for close to twenty years, finding himself with a brand-new telephone two weeks before Nixon's visit.

With its entourage of busloads of US newspaper journalists and TV crews, the arrival of an American president soon put a tiny village like Timahoe on the global map, but it was causing sleepless nights for one 72-year-old lady in the area. For a few short minutes in the remote cemetery, the world's cameras would be trained on Olive Goodbody, the curator of the historical library of the Society of Friends in Timahoe. Highly active in her local area, the energetic Quaker mother and grandmother was also a Cub Scout leader, volunteer at a Dublin children's home, custodian of Quaker records and dedicated pacifist in line with her religious beliefs. As the Vietnam War had raged on the other side of the world, Mrs Goodbody had agonised over the US Embassy's plan to welcome President Nixon publicly into the graveyard of the Timahoe branch of the Society of Friends. At the crux of her dilemma was the Quakers' peace testimony, which is a clear testimony against war or violence of any kind.

'To have somebody who is actually a member of the Society of Friends involved as he was in Vietnam was certainly controversial and left a bad taste in many Quakers' mouths,' said Olive's grandson Rob Goodbody. He believes most Irish Quakers would have preferred if Nixon had made the visit as a private individual and not as a commander-in-chief of hundreds of thousands of soldiers engaged in combat in a highly divisive war. Still, Mrs Goodbody received no judgement from Quakers over her decision to present the records to

Nixon at the public ceremony in her role as a genealogist rather than a representative of the Society of Friends.

After handing the president replicas of the will and the inventory of his great-great-great-great-great-grandfather, John Milhous, the registers of births and the certificate given by Timahoe Friends to Friends in Pennsylvania in order to offer our ancestor a welcome in Pennsylvania, the last lines of her speech gently called on the president to examine his conscience. In the news reels, the voice of the lady in the tweed coat and cap shakes as she delivers her short speech:

> These documents are usually started by the words, 'Loving Friends', and it is in that form I perhaps may address you now. We hope that the courage, the faith, and the integrity of your ancestors will help you through the sorrow, the trials, the anxieties, and the sadness which come to every man in your great office, Mr President.

Her grandson has his own supposition as to why there was a distinct tremor in her voice. 'You could read that as somebody not used to public speaking in this incredibly public scenario with radio there, TV cameras there and the press there. But I think it's just the importance of what she is saying. It's heartfelt.' Her words are conveying her hope that Nixon finds his way out of the war that he inherited with the office of president and into some resolution for it in accordance with his Quaker principles. 'She spoke truth to power in a subtle way,' said her grandson.

Three of Nixon's Milhous ancestors were buried in the graveyard, according to Seamus Cullen, but the unveiling of a headstone that day by the president to his relatives was also a source of unease to Irish Quakers. On that day, the historian remembers a Quaker from Dublin making a casual anti-war protest before leaving.

The stone says: 'In memory of Irish Quakers of Timahoe dedicated October 5th, 1970, by Richard Milhous Nixon, President of the United States of America whose maternal ancestors are resting here.' It's a simple headstone, but Irish Quakers knew that Nixon's Milhous ancestors would have objected to the erecting of monuments: it was not the Quaker way of doing things when they were buried in the 1800s. It wasn't until the 1850s that headstones appeared in Quaker graveyards in Ireland – there wouldn't have been a single headstone during his ancestors' time in Timahoe – although Nixon might have been unaware of this, as plain headstones were widespread in the twentieth century.

Seamus Cullen believes Nixon was genuinely moved when he saw the freshly tidied burial spot of his relatives. 'Nixon was waving and shaking hands and then he saw this outline and the expression was like that of any American who would have ancestors in Ireland, when they would go to a cemetery. There is an expression of excitement but very serious; I saw that for a few seconds in his eyes. The man was moved.' He believes the name of Timahoe would have been handed down through the generations of Milhous relatives as the last place they lived in the old world. Although he also adds: 'The motive was electioneering. There was a cartoon saying the first 1972 primary was Timahoe.'

In his speech that day, the president said he was very proud the plaque had not been there to indicate where his ancestors lived just before the American Revolution. In addressing the crowd, he alluded to the fact that Irish Quakers who lived in Timahoe and in County Kildare were always treated equally by Irish Catholics, who were in the great majority. He also caused a stir among the throngs of reporters when he started talking about pacifism after Mrs Goodbody's speech.

Nixon addressed the Quaker 'passion for peace', which was talked about by his cousin, the writer Jessamyn West, who had accompanied the Nixons on their trip to Ireland:

> My mother was a pacifist. My grandmother was a pacifist. Jessamyn's mother was, her grandmother, her grandfather, going back as far as we know. And I know that if they were here today that they would reflect the views that I am now going to express. Their greatest desire for anyone in their family, who held any office, would be whether he could make a contribution to peace. I can assure you, the greatest purpose and the greatest goal I have, and the greatest purpose and the greatest goal the American people have, is to play a role to bring peace, not only to America but to all the world. If we have that, we can build on from that, and, if we make that contribution, then I can truly say that I have lived up to what I think my ancestors, who worshipped in this place so many centuries ago, would have wanted one of theirs to be, if he ever got to the high office that I now hold.

That day, Nixon went on to do a whistle-stop motorcade tour of Kildare. While passing Naas Racecourse, there was an impromptu stop at the Curragh to chat to two female riders out exercising their horses. The heavy security presence – and a possibly heavy-handed approach by the FBI agents – reportedly ruffled feathers in the local Gardaí, but locals tell how the Irish force had their own way of making their point to the American agents. The trip to Timahoe from Kildare was a mere twelve miles, but it crossed over three canal bridges built in the 1780s with sharp, almost 45-degree angles. The Gardaí took the lead in their small cars with the agents in much larger American vehicles tailgating along the winding country roads. As they reached the first bridge, the Gardaí hit the accelerator giving the unsuspecting agents a jaw-shuddering jolt as they vaulted the humpback bridge.

The misplaced machine gun, the situation room in the Limerick stud farm and the church donation

The day before had been taken up with the more personal part of Nixon's trip to the country estate of his long-time Irish friend, millionaire businessman John A. Mulcahy, outside the sleepy Limerick village of Hospital. Crowds of locals waved stars and stripes as his black Lincoln Continental eased through the main street flanked by two sharp-suited Secret Service men. They formed part of a phalanx of agents on the presidential detail as the motorcade stretching to almost one hundred vehicles, carrying US newsmen and officials, rolled into the hamlet. In the previous few days, teams of American agents in dark sunglasses had raised eyebrows in the village deep in rural Ireland with their forensic inspection of manholes which had been welded closed.

But now, President Richard Milhous Nixon and First Lady Pat Nixon proudly stood waving through the sunroof of the limousine as the earpiece-wearing agents ran along each side. The date was 3 October 1970; just hours after Air Force One had touched down in Shannon Airport, bringing the Republican president and his entourage to Ireland for a state visit. The vision of the Californian president and his wife, the latter sporting a designer lilac suit and a blonde bouffant, was an incongruous sight in this agriculture outpost, around twenty miles outside Limerick city.

It seemed like nearly every one of the village's six hundred or so residents had come out for their once-in-a-lifetime look at a US president, along with hundreds more intrigued bystanders from neighbouring parishes in this fertile patch of Ireland famous for its horse-racing studs. They didn't know it yet, but a few of these spectators would shortly find themselves helping to narrowly avoid an international incident as they jovially returned a loaded weapon to a stricken Secret Service agent.

The year 1970 was when sixteen-year-old Irish singer Dana, clad in a white Celtic-emblem minidress, had won the Eurovision Song Contest with her pure-voiced 'All Kinds of Everything', while Dublin broadcaster Gay Byrne was in the first decade of his legendary run in the world's second longest-running chat show. And that very week, 'Band of Gold', by US singer Freda Payne had just hit the top of the Irish charts, reflecting the permeation of all things American to its neighbour on the other side of the Atlantic.

But music of the time also gave urgent voice to political discontent. When the California senator was sworn in as the 37th president of the United States nearly two years earlier in January 1969, there were more than half a million young American troops fighting against communist North Vietnamese troops in the deeply unpopular Vietnam War. Then, in November that year as many as half a million US citizens staged what is believed to be one of the biggest ever anti-war protests in Washington, culminating in the crowd singing John Lennon's 'Give Peace a Chance'.

Coming as he was from an American electorate disgruntled with the war, the 57-year-old US president looked thrilled by the reception from the Irish spectators who had waited until late in the evening to catch their glimpse of the world's most powerful leader.

Local historian Michael O'Sullivan, who was acting as a steward that night, remembers spectators spilling off footpaths as his car slowed down at the top of the town. Nixon spontaneously hopped out to greet the crowds to the alarm of the agents and long-coated Gardaí trying to hold them at bay. As the crowed surged to shake his hand, he was pinned up at the side of the car, but Mr O'Sullivan and his fellow steward, Michael English, came to the rescue by pushing their backsides out to the crowd and using their hands to vault the president up onto the roof of the limo.

He was delighted with himself; he stayed there and shook hands with half the town. There was an almighty rush to try and get to him. He would have stayed there for the night with the crowd, if he was left. Of course, there was pandemonium among the Secret Service men, because they thought he was, and he probably was, very vulnerable, if anybody wanted to have a pot at him. I always say I saved Nixon and changed world history.

Many of the crowd were quite unaware of just how exposed Nixon was to become in the following seconds. As one Secret Service agent was jostled by the crowds, his loaded weapon fell out of his holster onto the roadside. In a country used to a largely unarmed police force, this was a novelty which prompted a very Irish reaction.

'People were passing it around from one person to another and eventually handed it to one of the guards,' said Kevin Mulcahy, whose family were hosting the president at their lavish Limerick estate. 'They were looking at it, smiling, saying look at this. It was an Uzi submachine gun. I'd say your man came in for quite a sounding-off for losing his weapon.'

From his vantage point as a steward, Michael O'Sullivan saw the local man waving it aloft with a look-what-I'm-after-finding air. 'Luckily one of the guards grabbed him and took it down because the Secret Service were edgy anyway. You wouldn't know what would have happened; it could have been a very serious incident.'

In a reception with the American press corps in Dromoland Castle in County Clare in the following days, Nixon commented he had lost a cufflink during the marathon hand-pressing affair. 'I can assure you that the Irish have the best grips of anybody in the world,' remarked the president. 'This is the first time anybody has shaken hands with me and broken a cufflink in the process. But they were friendly handshakes and I enjoyed it very, very much.'

The upshot of the unscheduled stop was that President Nixon never halted at a podium set up for VIPs and speeches further up the town as he was due for dinner at Kilfrush House, a few miles outside the village, owned by his Irish friend and Republican donor, John A. Mulcahy.

The millionaire tycoon had left Dungarvan in Ireland for America in 1923 after spending several months in jail as a seventeen-year-old for fighting on the anti-treaty side during the Irish Civil War. Being a member of the IRA was a capital offence, but it is thought Mulcahy escaped death thanks to his young age, and instead he boarded a ship in Cobh destined for New York after his release the following year.

After putting himself through accountancy college, he first got a job in the United States Rubber Company with Mr Prescott Bush, who would go on to be father and grandfather to two US presidents. Coming back in the 1950s, he was the true embodiment of the American dream. With a fortune wrought from steel, he purchased some of Ireland's most storied properties including Ashford Castle, Waterville's Golf Club in Kerry and the splendid Limerick estate called Kilfrush House. As Air Force One touched down in Ireland nearly fifty years after his release from his jail cell in the Curragh, Mulcahy must have been reflecting on his journey from teenage prisoner-of-war to host of the US president in his native country.

Nixon was coming in from Heathrow, fresh from his meeting with the Queen and Edward Heath at Chequers, the English prime minister's country residence. As the Boeing 747 flew in, the philanthropist and businessman was flanked on the tarmac by his Irish brothers and the Taoiseach Jack Lynch and his wife, Maureen. 'It was quite a thrill for my dad to introduce his brothers to President Nixon,' remembers his son Kevin Mulcahy.

And there on the tarmac of the Co. Clare airport, Jack Lynch offered the traditional 'hundred thousand welcomes' to the land of 'your forefathers'. Light-hearted about his claim to Irishness, which was much further in the distant past than his wife's Mayo grand-father, Nixon told the gathered crowd, 'I have never had the opportunity of driving through the Irish countryside, of going back to where they say my great-great-great-great-great-great-grandparents came from.' He went on:

> I know for sure, however, that in Mrs Nixon's case the proof is much clearer. As a matter of fact, I can't find anybody in Ireland that will claim me, but I am sure that as far as Mrs Nixon is concerned that her grandfather, of course, came from Ireland, and if her credentials were open to any question, I can tell you that when I married her, her name was Patricia Ryan, and she celebrated her birthday on St Patrick's Day. So that must prove something.

The president jovially continued his charm offensive, telling them that he was looking forward to a rare day off from his packed whistle-stop tour of Europe. As he told the crowd:

> I can't think of any country in the world I would rather have a day off in than Ireland. I would say to you finally that in my travels over the world that have taken me to over sixty-five countries, I have had many very great and warm experiences. I can tell you that none is one that I look forward to more than this one – I look forward to it because I do probably claim, as do almost all successful American politicians, an Irish background.

Indeed, the Irish-American vote was widely considered to have helped clinch President Kennedy's victory when he narrowly defeated Richard Nixon in the 1960 election. Nixon, who had served as vice president for President Dwight Eisenhower from 1952 to 1960, later succeeding Lyndon B. Johnson in 1969, must have had his eye on the votes of the Irish diaspora in the upcoming 1972 election as he set off to tour the byroads of the Irish countryside. The motorcade made a brief stop in Limerick city, where Nixon was presented with a hawthorn stick by Mayor Liddy. He told the mayor: 'Having heard of Limerick all my life, and recalling in the eighteenth century when the famous Irish Brigade was fighting all over the world, the song was "Will You Come up to Limerick?" and here I am. I am glad to be here, and I am glad I came.'

He may have been thousands of miles from the US, but Nixon hadn't totally left his Vietnam War woes behind. While he was welcomed in Hospital, about a thousand demonstrators had marched through the centre of Dublin hours earlier to the US embassy in Ballsbridge to protest his visit to Ireland. This rally was organised by what national papers termed 'Maoists'. The group carried a coffin inscribed 'Mourn for the dead children of Vietnam' and chanted 'Victory to the Viet Cong' as they marched along for two miles. They also sang 'We Shall Overcome', a song synonymous with the African American civil rights movement, which was adopted by many of the civil rights protesters in Northern Ireland. Then, outside the embassy, protestors burned an effigy of President Nixon.

That day, as dusk fell, in the rural countryside dappled with dairy farms and racehorse studs, the vehicle bearing the presidential eagle seal swept down the long tree-lined driveway of a manicured 286-acre Limerick estate. This area is Ireland's answer to Kentucky, famous for its limestone soil which is reputed to be the secret ingredient in the breeding of the country's line of elite racing winners. Ahead of Nixon's visit, the Kilfrush estate – the private residence of one of his closest Irish-American confidantes – with its old stone fountains and a white-painted mansion, was renovated to include a guest wing with three huge bedroom suites and a leisure complex with swimming pool, gym, hot tub and sauna. The ivy-clad Georgian property was still getting its last few coats of paint and carpets fitted in the final frantic hours before the president's arrival.

Sitting heads of state would stay in an ambassador's residence or a state building or even a hotel, but it was somewhat of a diplomatic departure for a US president to reside in a private home, even one as lavish as a sprawling country estate built in 1835. But, in doing so, he was fulfilling a promise to John A. Mulcahy, a long-time friend and major Republican donor. In a letter to Mr Mulcahy on 5 August 1968, in the run-up to the presidential election later that year, he writes:

> Dear Jack, I have not forgotten your invitation for me to come to Ireland a short time after the convention. The plans are still somewhat nebulous though, through that period of time and I'm somewhat in doubt I'll be able to come because I'm sure I will be busy with my staff on campaign planning. Should I find it possible to spend a few days with you I will certainly get in touch with you. In any event I hope to see you soon again in New York.

He signed off all his correspondence as 'Dick', indicating their familiarity. 'The original thought was prior to the election that he would come to Ireland,' said Kevin Mulcahy. 'But, as he states, it obviously wasn't possible with so much going on with the election. There was an open invitation for when it was convenient for the president to come and visit Ireland.' It finally became a possibility in October 1970, when Ireland was pencilled into a European tour which also included Italy, Yugoslavia, Spain and Great Britain.

The Secret Service might have been nailing down manhole covers in the local village, but Kilfrush House was almost turned inside out by agents in the run-up to the visit. 'That meant going through this house with literally a fine-tooth comb and looking in every cupboard and on top of this and behind that,' remembers the son of the late Mr Mulcahy. The White House also vetted all eleven of the staff working there at the time. 'Immediately outside the president's bedroom there was a Secret Service agent positioned, halfway up the stairwell there was another agent and, at the bottom of the stairwell, another agent, and every fifteen minutes they rotated positions. Security was extremely tight,' he recalled.

Officials also set up their own switchboard in the basement of Kilfrush House, so the president could get straight through to the White House switchboard. This installation was vital in the 1970s to keep a US president in constant contact with the White House during foreign tours – requiring a complexity of technology and organisation that it's difficult to imagine in our 21st-century age of broadband and instant communications. Kevin Mulcahy, who was helping his father host the American presidential party, distinctly remembers the constant presence of an Air Force general, who carried a black box. He believes now that it had the capacity to launch nuclear missiles, but they were told at the time that it contained a telex machine.

On Sunday morning, the congregation of the local church in Hospital were joined by almost the entire presidential party, flanked by a heavy security detail for what would prove to be a rewarding visit. Missing was President Nixon, a Quaker by faith. John A. Mulcahy would habitually attend the second Mass on a Sunday when he was staying in his Limerick estate. On this occasion, under the watchful eye of FBI agents, Williams Rogers, Secretary of State; Harry Bob Haldeman, White House Chief of Staff; Henry Kissinger and White House Press Secretary, Ron Ziegler, all filed into church pews alongside him. On seeing the US arrivals, the church organist, John Enright, and a singer called Jim Canty decided to play the Battle Hymn of the Republic during the ceremony in the newly done-up church. As he belted out the final strains of 'his truth is marching on . . .' the Limerick singer was unaware of the effect it was having on an emotional Mr Mulcahy in the congregation.

Afterwards, the Waterford tycoon went into the sacristy to thank the parish priest, Canon O'Grady, for the rousing rendition of the patriotic American anthem in honour of his US delegation. Knowing that the church had just been redecorated, Mr Mulcahy asked O'Grady, 'Is there a debt still outstanding in this church?' On being informed that there was a bill of something in the region of £14,000, quite a substantial sum in 1970, he took out his cheque book then and there and wrote a cheque for the entire amount. 'I used to always joke with Jim Canty afterwards that in 1970 he was the highest paid entertainer in Ireland!' commented Michael O'Sullivan.

But such a gesture was not so out of character for the millionaire businessman, who became intent on spreading his wealth across most of the Irish provinces. For the man who had to take a boat from Cobh and leave everything he knew behind at just eighteen years of age, he wanted to play his role in firing up his native country's economy. When he returned in the 1950s, he bought a string of properties and, through his ties with Nixon and American businessmen, is said to have been instrumental in persuading companies such as Pfizer to locate in Ireland.

During that Sunday, things took an even more surreal turn in this manicured estate in the heart of rural Ireland, as the newly decorated drawing room was turned into a situation room hosting intense talks on the Vietnam War with Nixon and Henry Kissinger, who had flown in from talks on the Paris Peace Accords. Just under 18,000 US troops were killed between 1969 and 1979 in the controversial war, many of them young men who were drafted. By October 1970, with anti-war sentiment escalating in America with regular peace demonstrations, the public were demanding the withdrawal of troops and the release of US prisoners of war.

Nixon's national security advisor Henry Kissinger had been in secret peace talks with North Vietnamese representative Le Duc Tho in Paris for months, while also attending the public negotiations in the city known as the Paris Peace Accords. The timing of these high-level negotiations also meant Nixon had been able to fit in the trip to Ireland around the talks to start withdrawing troops completely from the war-torn Indochina region. 'Essentially the Secretary of State William Rogers, Henry Kissinger, the president and two other gentlemen, who I don't know, really cocooned themselves for the day in discussions and kind of went outside a couple of times for some photo opportunities,' recalled Kevin Mulcahy, adding: 'No one was allowed anywhere near where they were in the main living room. That whole section of the house was just cordoned off, there was no way anybody was going to hear anything.'

That evening, there was a formal banquet at the house featuring a quintessential Irish menu which wouldn't look out of place in the fashionable farm-to-fork menus of the twenty-first century. For starters, they could opt for Irish smoked salmon, Clew Bay oysters, Aran scallop soup, or consommé with sherry. Options for the main course were steamed Comeragh salmon with Hollandaise sauce, Cecilstown pigeon crust pie, boiled Limerick bacon and cabbage, Springhill lamb stew and roast contra fillet of Kilfrush beef. There were baked and boiled potatoes, tossed green salad, green spinach, deep-dish apple pie and a cheese board and Irish coffee. John A. Mulcahy even persuaded the US president to forgo his usual Scotch whisky for his favourite Irish Red Breast malt.

As part of the heavy security operation in the castle, Secret Service agents in the kitchen tasted all food that the president would eat before it was served up. At the banquet, two dining rooms were used for the occasion, with President Nixon in one with John A. Mulcahy and the US ambassador, John Moore, but Kevin Mulcahy believes he landed on the best table with Henry Kissinger keeping his companions in gales of laughter. 'Henry Kissinger was the funniest man I've ever met in my life,' he says definitively. 'He was hysterical at dinner. Kissinger just used accents to very good comedic effect. You would think he was a very serious and dour man, but he was actually very gregarious and very humorous.'

The evening was a very relaxed affair among the guests:

> The times when Nixon was in the living room in Kilfrush, and the people sitting around, it was very laidback. I remember we had a nice big roaring turf fire going, Nixon was saying how much he loved the fire and he used to turn the air conditioning on in the White House and light the fire. With all the pressure of negotiations with Vietnam, to be able to let your hair down, to use the old expression, to just relax among friends.

During the pre-dinner conversations, Kevin learned that First Lady Pat Nixon didn't have a good impression of Ireland from a previous visit in the 1960s with her two daughters, but was charmed by this state visit. 'She was kind of noting when they were here last, you would see a lot of the men hanging outside of pubs at midday and this sort of thing,' recalled Kevin Mulcahy. But he said the feel-good factor around this visit to the town of Hospital had led her to revise her view; she reported she was very taken with the warmth of the reception on her second visit with her husband.

Michael O'Sullivan believes the warm regard of the local people for John A. Mulcahy, who was known for his generous attitude to the townsfolk, would also have been a factor in their reception for Nixon. Then there was the glitz and hoopla surrounding the office of the

American president in a small town which had never hit the international headlines prior to this. US newsmen and TV crews, six busloads of them, streamed into the town, along with CIA and FBI agents, while the skies around the picturesque rural parish buzzed with helicopters during his two-day stay. In addition, more than one hundred diplomats were flown in from embassies all over Europe to cope with the logistics of the three-day Nixon visit. And the exhaustive search by diplomats for a distant Milhous cousin in the lead-up to the visit prompted the *New York Times* headline: 'Wanted for Nixon Visit to Ireland: One Millhouse.'

While a female relative was discovered in Dublin years later, she eluded diplomats in the autumn of 1970, but they did manage to produce a relative of Mrs Nixon. As the peace negotiations in Kilfrush House on Sunday were ongoing, Mrs Nixon took a flight from the Limerick estate to the town of Ballinrobe in Co. Mayo to call on her closest living relative, Katie Naughton. The helicopter frightened the cattle, sheep and chickens into a stampeding run across the stonewalled Mayo fields as it landed on the village green, but Mrs Nixon was still greeted with tears of excitement, a cup of Irish tea and homemade raisin bread. During her chat with Mrs Naughton that day, she discovered she had 'more cousins than I knew about', before she caught a flight to Ashford Castle for a lunch appointment.

On the morning of his departure from Kilfrush House, Nixon planted a redwood tree in the grounds before a roar of chopper blades from the back lawn took him away from Limerick. Less bucolic were the streets of Dublin, with anti-war protests visible, and the president narrowly escaping getting pelted by an egg as his car drove through the capital. On this last leg, President Éamon de Valera, a few days shy of his eighty-eighth birthday, hosted President Nixon at a reception in Áras an Uachtaráin in Phoenix Park. The

US president had referred to the iconic Irish leader as a 'giant of a man' in front of his press corps the previous day. In a state reception later that day, he told Taoiseach Jack Lynch how taken he was to hear he was a hurling champion. 'I understand that is one of the most rugged sports that we can possibly invent,' he said, before adding, 'so that impressed me.'

As Nixon prepared to jet out of Ireland, he made a light-hearted comment about the tendency of American politicians to try to trace their ancestry to Ireland. 'I can assure you that these days we will do anything that will help us win, and I think that helps us win,' he said. He added that he was very proud of his Irish ancestry, which goes back many centuries, making him keenly aware of the debt owed by America to Ireland and citizens of Irish heritage. He then name-checked his host John A. Mulcahy as among the Irish who have contributed so much to the United States.

And, in the final notes of his speech, Nixon exercised the well-honed charm which brought in millions of votes back home. 'I think politics is hard in our country, but in Ireland, when you have to run against somebody who is Irish all the time, it must be impossible. I have had some experience that way myself,' he said, in an apparent reference to his race against President Kennedy, before continuing:

> I sensed as I travelled through this land yesterday and today, a spirit that is very much needed in the world today, and particularly needed in our country with its responsibilities of world leadership, warm, friendly, with that ability to have a sense of humour even when things are very, very difficult. And the Irish have all of these capacities. They also have stamina, character, a deep religious faith. These are qualities that make a great people. These are qualities that have contributed enormously to America.

An enduring friendship

As the US president prepared to board Air Force One at Dublin Airport on the early evening of 5 October 1970, Taoiseach Jack Lynch referenced the centuries-old relationship between the two countries, speaking directly to Nixon:

> One of your ancestors, Mr President, Thomas Milhous, left this country as so many thousands of others did, and found in the New World opportunities and fresh horizons that were denied at the time to those who remained at home. You can appreciate, therefore, our special pride and satisfaction at having had you with us in a sovereign democratic Ireland in your capacity as leader of the world's greatest democracy.

The redwood tree that Nixon had planted before leaving Kilfrush was blown down in an Atlantic storm in recent years. But the stump of the tree and the plaque commemorating his weekend visit remain, and the estate has since seen visits from Princess Caroline of Monaco and President Ford. Mainly a cattle farm during its years in the hands of John A. Mulcahy, the stud has become a horse-racing powerhouse in the intervening years with eighty thoroughbred champions bred on its rich limestone soil.

The same Oval Office voice-activated taping system that captured the Timahoe-orientated photo op would prove to be Nixon's downfall in the Watergate scandal which resulted in his resignation in 1974. The infamous tapes proved the president's complicity in the 1972 break-in – linked to his re-election campaign – to the Democratic National Committee headquarters. Nixon might have resigned in ignominy four years after his Irish visit, but he would also go on to rehabilitate his image in what was seen as one of the greatest comebacks in American politics to become a celebrated author and a trusted advisor to American presidents.

The scandal didn't spoil his friendship with his Irish confidante. 'He very much regretted the Watergate incident, and he knew that he made a massive, massive mistake in what he did, and that he was probably also trying to help cover up some of the other people who might have been involved in the Watergate episode,' said Kevin Mulcahy, adding, 'But my father stayed loyal to him even after Watergate. He felt that Nixon had made a major, major error of judgement but that didn't affect the friendship.'

The tapes also captured phone calls from the president to Mr Mulcahy and a visit by the hotelier to the Oval Office in 1971. 'I remember him coming home and telling us that the president called him at his office and they spoke for a while and he was just saying, "I appreciate, Jack, everything you've done . . ."'

In fact, the Kilfrush visit cemented the friendship between Richard Nixon and John A. Mulcahy for decades to come. 'There really was a genuine closeness,' said Kevin Mulcahy. 'There was mutual admiration. Nixon didn't like phonies, people with posh accents who were trying to put on a bit of a show. I think the fact that my dad was a very straight shooter helped cement the relationship. It was a genuinely close warm relationship of two men who respected each other.'

One of his father's fondest memories was cruising down the Potomac River in Washington, DC, with Nixon during his presidency.

There was a small party of close friends on board with the president including my dad. Nixon spent about two hours verbalising his view on the world and on the presidency and what he was trying to achieve at this time. It was the height of the Cold War and one of the things he was saying was that the United States could outspend Russia and they could bring down communism by forcing Russia to overspend on military defence. He said the cocktails were flowing and it was absolutely fascinating to see the man's vision of where America should be going.

In a letter written by Nixon to his Irish friend on 29 July 1986, he passed on his best wishes for his eightieth birthday in the following weeks from himself and his wife, Pat:

> As we look back over the White House years, we cherish the memories of your very generous and loyal friendship, whether it was telling off a heckler at the White House dinner or hosting our fantastic visit to Ireland you were always there when it counted. Eighty would be old for some but not for you. Your Irish wit and charm will keep you forever young, Sincerely Dick.

Unlike Kennedy, Nixon never spoke of returning to Ireland, but he kept up his correspondence with his Waterford friend until they both died in 1994 within months of each other. And, as a host of the Nixon delegation, Kevin Mulcahy gained the sense that the US president did become more warmly disposed to the country of his forefathers. 'He got an appreciation of the warmth of the Irish people,' he said. 'I think he became much closer to Ireland because of the Irish people and what he experienced here. I do think it did help enhance his view of Ireland.'

Garret FitzGerald exchanges a 'Very Important' gift
with Ronald Reagan at the White House, 1984.

CHAPTER THREE

PRESIDENT RONALD REAGAN

———

Other presidents have airports and bridges called after them,
I have a pub back in Ireland, now that's class.

———

IT COULD HAVE BEEN ANY ONE OF the six bars in the rural Irish village of Ballyporeen, but the head man from Debrett's Peerage & Baronetage strode through the brown wooden doors of O'Farrell's pub with his companions.

It was November 1980, and the publisher of an annual list of the ancestral lines of the British aristocracy, a centuries-old form of *Who Do You Think You Are?* for the titled classes, had been digging into Ronald Reagan's family tree since he clinched the nomination to run as the Republican candidate in the US election months earlier. Instead of finding he was an English duke or marquis, or an honourable of some sort, the blue-blooded bible uncovered records showing he was a great-grandson of a labourer called Michael Regan, who had left his rural parish in Tipperary in the 1800s around the time of the Irish famine. While Reagan was crisscrossing the US on the canvassing trail, the Sherlock Holmes of the genealogy world, Hugh Peskett, was poring through nineteenth-century records to determine the Hollywood film star's long-lost Irish relatives.

When Peskett, along with an Associated Press reporter and two men from Hibernian Research in Dublin Castle, arrived at the mahogany counter of O'Farrell's pub on a cold November morning to deliver their startling intelligence they were taken aback by the response. 'I said, "Oh I've met him!"' said the landlady, Mary O'Farrell. 'It was a chance encounter.' An accidental meeting that took place a few years earlier when her brother, a parish priest in California, introduced Mary and her husband John to the then governor of California, when they bumped into Reagan in the company of mutual acquaintances at LA Airport.

Now, a week after the film-star candidate defeated incumbent President Jimmy Carter in a landslide election, baptismal and marriage certificates were spread out on the bar counter by the delegation for examination before they were taken by John O'Farrell to the graveyard where Ronald Reagan's ancestors were buried.

That afternoon, the couple paid a visit to their parish priest where they cross-checked the information with a Latin entry for Michael Regan's baptism on 3 September 1829.

'John and I sat down and said, "Now what are we going to do?" We knew it could be huge,' said Mary, whose husband has since passed away. 'O'Farrell's was over the bar, but we decided we'd get a sign made – The Ronald Reagan; a picture would tell a thousand words as they say.' The sign in green lettering, complete with the Reagan coat of arms, went up over the lounge by the end of November, and a letter was posted to the White House inviting the US president-elect to his namesake pub. The local county council and the community council also dispatched official invitations.

These events marked the start of a love affair between the movie star president-to-be and a tiny Irish village with an entrepreneurial streak. Cue a decade-long bonanza that would spawn Ballyporeen's first ice cream machine, Reagan bumper stickers, new roads, a state-of-the-art telephone system and busloads of American tourists.

Ballyporeen goes global

On the second day of December, a map of Ireland with two dots, one for Ballyporeen and one for Dublin, appeared on the front of the *Wall Street Journal* with a full column relaying the news of Reagan's Tipperary roots. One leading light on the New York stock exchange, who had left the Tipperary village decades earlier, was astonished to find his hometown staring him in the face as he read his morning paper at his desk in a Big Apple skyscraper.

The farming village tucked neatly into a fertile valley between the Knockmealdown and Galtee mountains was eight miles from the nearest big town of Mitchelstown in Co. Cork, although it was inside the Tipperary border. Suddenly the locals going about their business in this unassuming rural hamlet found themselves in the eye of a global media storm. 'It was mad,' said local man Neil Donovan. 'In Ballyporeen there are three hundred people. As we say, there are as many in the graveyard. It does not fluctuate. It goes up and down ten or twenty people every census.' Within months, the villagers became seasoned at giving interviews on every aspect of Reagan's family connection to day-tripping reporters from the national and local press along with a steady stream of journalists flying in from outlets such as the Press Association and Reuters.

Some, like the reporter and photographer from one of Germany's biggest weekend magazines, stayed for two weeks, distilling every detail of the unassuming village from its ivy-covered stone walls to the famine graveyard and vibrant greenness of the valley. The *Wall Street Journal* newsman, who spent the weekend, was a 'lovely fella'.

The Ronald Reagan sign over the lounge acted as a beacon to reporters who trekked into the pub as their first port of call. 'We did eight interviews a day from that November until April. It was extraordinary,' recalled Mary O'Farrell, musing that her role as a speech and language teacher helped her deal with the attention along with her widely read husband's business acumen: 'It would die down and then someone would say the president was coming to Europe on a summit and the whole thing would start again.'

The press also gravitated towards the sociable and long-standing county councillor, the late Con Donovan, who ran a small country shop that stocked everything from sewing needles to farming clothes to cakes of brown bread.

His son, Neil, still has books of business cards from jet-setting journalists from that time. 'They were amazingly interesting people who absolutely broadened our horizons. Being from a rural village, going to Cork was a big thing, this opened up a lot of us to a different kind of world, an exciting world.' A Japanese journalist caused much discussion when he hired a taxi to bring him on the four-hour journey to the village from Dublin Airport, leaving the meter ticking for hours before hopping back in to make the return journey to the capital with material for his story. Locals didn't want to contemplate the cost, even the taxi driver was muttering, but it emerged that the story made the Christmas Day edition of a Japanese newspaper. 'At the time it had the biggest daily circulation in the world, and they published a two-page spread,' explained Mary. 'There were a couple of photos of us here and there. All we could read on it was "O'Farrell"; it was very exciting.'

The hospitable village – with a newly awakened capitalist spirit – fully embraced their newfound fame, taking the publicity circus all in their stride. For Ronald Reagan's inauguration in January 1981 in Washington, Ballyporeen staged a parade through the village, which ended up being a rain-soaked affair. 'Most of these things happened to coincide with horrible weather,' observed Neil Donovan wryly. 'We had a parade up and down the village. It was the middle of January, lashing rain in Ballyporeen, but we made a point of doing it.'

But while Ballyporeen was busy dispatching invitations and braving downpours in front of the world's media to welcome the prodigal president to his ancestors' birthplace, they were unaware that the Irish government were already ahead of the game. In fact, the US ambassador, Seán Donlon, had already presented the presidential candidate with a dossier of evidence about his Tipperary relations two months before the election. As soon as Reagan announced his candidacy, the diplomat went to see the governor in California and, owing to his Irish surname, opened the conversation with the logical line, 'What part of Ireland are you from?'

'Well, lots of people have asked me that, but I've never been able to trace it,' replied Reagan. He went on to relay how he had been to Ireland twice. Once in the 1950s, in his role as the president of the Screen Actors Guild, staying in Dublin's Gresham Hotel where he was astonished to witness girls dressed in long ball gowns getting hoisted up on the crossbars of bicycles by their Irish dates to catch a lift home after the dance.

In 1972, he arrived back with his children on a grand tour of Europe. In his possession was a letter of introduction from President Nixon on White House paper to Irish president Éamon de Valera, asking him to 'receive Governor Ronald Reagan as my personal representative and friend . . . and friend of Ireland'. The letter goes on to say that Reagan is 'both an American and a son of Ireland'. In the note, Nixon expresses deep admiration for de Valera, adding: 'This admiration is shared by all the world's democracies, for you are our senior democratic leader.'

President Nixon might have referred to Ronald Reagan as a son of Ireland, but back in California in early 1980 he told Ambassador Donlon: 'I don't think we're Irish, I think we're English.' Nonplussed, the diplomat privately thought the former actor was cynically trying to keep on side of the WASP (White Anglo-Saxon Protestant) voters who dominated the American Republican Party. But Reagan did promise to get his brother, Neil, to send on the family's box of papers to the Irish Embassy in Washington.

Enlisting the help of the massive genealogical database of the Mormon Church in Salt Lake City – they famously keep a treasure trove of records for members seeking to baptise dead ancestors into their faith – Mr Donlon solved the confusion. Two months before the election, he went back to Reagan explaining his great-grandfather had come from Ireland but had stopped off in England on the way to America, an act which had muddied the genealogical waters. Although the governor appeared charmed by the discovery, he had one caveat. 'He did ask me not to go public on it at the time. He said, "People will think I'm playing politics,"' said Mr Donlon. Reagan's rationale was that he wasn't going to start suddenly identifying as Irish in the last few weeks of the campaign, but promised if he did get to the White House, he would acknowledge his Irish paternity.

'I presented him with his full family tree and frankly he seemed to be very pleased because he said he had never quite known where he came from,' said Mr Donlon. 'Obviously, there were some indications with a name like Reagan that it had to be Irish, but there were other indications that were English.'

The year of Reagan's inauguration was the same year John Lennon was murdered, the Prince of Wales announced his engagement to a doe-eyed Lady Diana Spencer and the Eurovision Song Contest was held in Dublin following a win in 1980 for Johnny Logan's 'What's Another Year'.

Barely two months after his inauguration, Reagan survived an assassination attempt on 30 March 1981 outside the Hilton Hotel in Washington, while six weeks later Pope John Paul II lived through a near-fatal shooting in St Peter's Square in Vatican City. Reagan, who made a remarkable recovery after having surgery to remove a bullet from his left lung, used his trademark humour to reassure the nation, famously telling the First Lady, 'Honey, I forgot to duck.'

Less than two weeks earlier, he had kept his pledge to Seán Donlon when he duly arrived for lunch at the Irish Embassy in Massachusetts Avenue, Washington, on St Patrick's Day. During a toast, President Reagan explained his delight at his Irish bloodline: 'My father was orphaned at age six, and I grew up never having heard anything or knowing anything about my family tree. I am delighted to now finally know what I've never known all my life – the line and the heritage and to where it goes in Ireland.'

Sunday Drive Capital of Ireland

At this time, Ireland was at the start of a decade of recession, unemployment and emigration, while the death of prisoner Bobby Sands and nine others in the political protest hunger strikes of 1981 caused deep unrest across the nation. Against this backdrop of a country in the economic doldrums, Ballyporeen was carving its own path out of the slump by becoming the 'Sunday Drive Capital' of southern Ireland. It was the era before televised Gaelic games would keep the Irish population glued to the hurling or football matches on their screens on Sunday afternoons, so they were indulging in another national pastime. 'It was quite common for people to throw the family in the car for a Sunday drive with a warm bottle of lemonade and a couple of bags of crisps,' noted Neil Donovan. 'Quickly Ballyporeen became the place around Munster. It was curiosity. We bought an ice cream cone machine for our shop and you couldn't keep them going out the door.' For many of the youngsters, the arrival of 99s to their village was the high point of the Reagan years.

The St Patrick's Day parade every year would reignite fresh interest in the Tipperary town from news outlets. A tape of recorded messages and songs from Ballyporeen residents played to the US president on the patron saint's day in 1983 could have been the deal clincher in copper-fastening Regan's four-day state visit in 1984.

But the official announcement of the long-awaited news of a presidential visit was pre-empted by Con Donovan making a prophetic proclamation to liven up a dreary council meeting in Clonmel in early 1984. Before he left his house that evening, the councillor had spotted an item on the new 24-hour news channel, CNN, on Reagan's impending attendance at Normandy, France, in June to mark the D-Day landings. 'As he was putting on his coat he said, "I bet you he will come to Ireland,"' recalled his son.

In a break between discussions on roads and drains at the meeting, the local reporter perked up when another councillor said, 'I believe Councillor Donovan has an announcement...' with a pregnant pause before Councillor Donovan stood up to declare: 'I'm not at liberty to say too much now but I believe we'll be making announcements in Ballyporeen quite soon.' In the coming days, the nationalist newspaper in Tipperary carried the headline: *Reagan Visit Imminent For Ballyporeen*. 'It was speculation from my father,' laughed his son. 'Maybe a week and a half later he got a call from the Foreign Affairs department wanting to know how he got wind that they were about to announce that Reagan was coming to Ireland for a three-day visit. Like a good politician, he said, "I don't reveal my sources."'

The Pope, the President and the Rock of Cashel

Following the announcement of the June visit, the flamboyant White House Deputy Chief of Staff, Mike Deaver, flew around Ireland on Black Hawk helicopters with former ambassador Seán Donlon, now back in Ireland as Secretary of the Department of Foreign Affairs, trawling for the perfect photographic backdrops for the Irish-American electorate who were set to vote in the presidential election at the end of the year. The showman aide was responsible for creating iconic photo ops that stood Reagan atop the Great Wall of China and filling sandbags to show concern after a Louisiana flood. And so he touched down in Kenmare, Limerick, Connemara, Ballyporeen and Dublin on the tour.

On the road to Reagan's ancestral village, Mr Deaver came up with one of his most ambitious plans when he set eyes on the Rock of Cashel, the majestic medieval cathedral where St Patrick is said to have converted the King of Munster. 'Deaver felt it would be a great idea if we could get the Pope to say Mass at the Rock of Cashel,' said Seán Donlon. But, as he also added in an amused tone: 'It had never occurred to me that during a visit by the American president, we would also deal with a visit by the Pope.' Deaver, the Californian image-maker, was surely struck by the symbolism of the Polish Pope saying Mass for the American president who was seeking to break down the Iron Curtain. Overtures were made by American and Irish ambassadors to the Vatican, but the message was relayed back that the Pope wasn't prepared to come to Cashel just to say Mass for Ronald Reagan.

However, in a nod to Reagan's passion for horses, Seán Donlon and Mike Deaver did pay a visit to the Ballydoyle Racing Stables in Tipperary, run one of Ireland's legendary trainers, Vincent O'Brien. Donlon remembers Deaver as more like a Hollywood producer than a political aide. 'He was great craic,' he said, but the manicured stud farm was ruled out as a venue as it looked too much like Kentucky, and not the image of traditional Ireland the White House wanted to broadcast to Irish America. From Ireland's point of view, the Department of Foreign Affairs were also interested in beaming picture-postcard images back to the US in order to boost tourism, promote American investment in Ireland and help deal with the political Anglo-Irish situation. Kenmare contested with Connemara to host the presidential party, but while they were on a par in terms of natural beauty, the west of Ireland won out thanks to the powerful sway of the Mayo Men's Association and the Galway Men's Association in the US.

During that reconnaissance tour, the villagers in Ballyporeen got their first taste of the American security machine with Deaver's dramatic helicopter landing in the local GAA field in February 1984. 'For us as young fellas, this was Hollywood stuff,' said Neil Donovan in an echo of Seán Donlon's thoughts. 'First stop was the parish priest and then on to O'Farrell's pub, with Deaver flanked by around thirty staff.'

'Mike Deaver came over to the counter and we spoke,' said Mary O'Farrell, 'and at the end of it, I said, "Is this going to happen, Mr Deaver?" and he said, "Oh yes, Mrs O'Farrell, you are well able for it."' In truth, at this stage, the O'Farrells had become more media-versed than many movie stars of the day after years of press interest.

Meanwhile, although Councillor Donovan had been putting in requests for various roadworks over the past three years, red tape melted away and the town underwent a transformation. There was fresh paint on every house, whitewash on every wall, newly tarred roads along with the arrival of pristine public toilets and Ballyporeen's first public telephone booth. Overnight, the townsfolk went from old-style crank-up phones to a state-of-the-art system.

Secret Service collar bumper catch of salmon

The head agent for the visit was Barbara Riggs. As one of the first women to be sworn into the Secret Service, she would go on to protect six US presidents, including Gerald Ford, Jimmy Carter, Ronald Reagan, George H.W. Bush, Bill Clinton and George W. Bush. In 2004, she would become the first woman in the agency's history to serve as deputy director of the Secret Service. On this occasion, she arrived in the town weeks in advance doing daily walk-throughs with local council workers, sealing manhole covers, making reconnaissance visits to the church and the graveyards. 'For three weeks before the visit, every morning six big black limousines used to pull up across at the parochial hall across the road from us,' said Mary O'Farrell, 'and the White House staff who arranged the visit got out. It was just something else.'

Simultaneous security operations were being carried out in the west of Ireland around Ashford Castle where the president would be spending two of his three nights while in Ireland. The thirteenth-century castle – complete with turrets, a moat and sumptuous suites – had already played host to luminaries such as King George V, Prince Rainier III and Princess Grace of Monaco, and Oscar Wilde. The Irish-American castle owner, John A. Mulcahy, a major Republican donor, who was hosting the president, had bought the property in the 1960s before adding a new wing with opulent new suites. Mulcahy, originally from Dungarvan in Waterford, had been a close friend of President Nixon while his relationship with Reagan was more like a close acquaintance. 'My dad used to holiday in California when Reagan was governor of California and they would have been at certain dinner parties together,' explained his son, Kevin Mulcahy. 'Throughout his term, I have a whole bunch of letters from Reagan to my dad congratulating him on his birthday and that sort of thing.'

Mr Mulcahy, who had helped host President Nixon in Limerick fourteen years earlier, remembers the security being much more intense for Reagan's visit. The staff living quarters in the castle had to be vacated, with employees moving out to the nearby village of Cong, while guests booked in for the dates of the visit were transferred to surrounding hotels. Every room was inspected by Secret Service agents before the doors were sealed.

Again, the Mayo village was catapulted into twentieth-century telecommunications as their old operator-facilitated phones were cast off for direct lines. An enormous switchboard was installed in the basement of the castle, which operated as the White House switchboard during the stay. A more unusual remnant of the visit is the result of a special request for an exceptionally large bed to be crafted to Reagan's precise height and length specifications. The bed remains in the hotel to this day. 'When the bed had been installed, four inches were sawed off the legs because it was too high – I presume for Nancy to sit on the side of it,' recalled hotel manager, Rory Murphy.

The key to two locked drawers in an antique sideboard in the presidential suite that dated back to the days when it was owned by the Guinness family had long been lost, but it was discovered after the visit that the ancient locks had been carefully unpicked by the Secret Service during the stay. 'They visited every nook and cranny of the place,' said Mr Murphy. He remembered a blue line of Gardaí, the Irish police force, numbering an estimated 1,400 men, surrounding the castle in the run-up to the visit. The five islands on Lough Corrib, the lake which cuts through the estate, were crawling with detectives. An Irish army tank was stationed in the farmyard of the castle, which had famously been one of the locations for *The Quiet Man*.

The minor embarrassment over the egging of President Nixon's car in Dublin in 1970 was one of the lesser reasons for the unparalleled security operation around Reagan's visit. The IRA were active in Ireland at the time, but threats were deemed to come from the Middle East in the Reagan era, not from Republican or Loyalist terrorists operating in the country.

Air Force One touched down in Shannon Airport on the first of June to a waiting delegation which included President Patrick Hillery and Taoiseach Garret FitzGerald. After briefly addressing the crowds in Irish as *A Chairde Gaeil*, translating to Irish friends, the US president went on to describe Ireland as an 'isle of wondrous beauty, with a countryside green as no other place seems to be'. He said, 'I want you to know that for this great-grandson of Ireland, this is a moment of joy.' And then he told the crowd:

> And from the beginning, when that first large party of your ancestors arrived at Newport News in 1621, your Irish blood has enriched America. No wonder we've been blessed all these years by what some call the luck of the Irish. Today, the sons and daughters of our first Irish settlers number forty million strong.

The white-topped helicopter then flew up the west coast and over the battlements of Ashford Castle before landing on the front lawn to the sound of a pipe band. 'What a fabulous-looking figure of a man, tall, elegant and fit,' recalled Rory Murphy, adding how the first couple made a beeline for the children lined up at the door before moving inside to greet the hotel manager and his wife along with the Mulcahy family and the Foreign Affairs Minister Peter Barry: 'They were lovely people, very natural, he had a great presence but a very friendly smile. He was a very affable man.'

Rory particularly remembers the White House press arriving shortly afterwards in a Black Hawk helicopter on the front lawn for a photo call with the president. 'This flap came down at the back and they came running out like they were under starter's orders.'

A few minutes into the press conference, the quick-fire questions were interrupted by a commotion at the water's edge. An anti-personnel steel net installed by the Secret Service in the river below to catch intruders began to shake, causing two rubber-suited US navy divers to investigate before emerging with a flapping fish. By the end of the visit, the net intended to snare would-be terrorists had landed a bumper catch of salmon.

Nancy and the Quiet Man . . . and the suspect Aran cardigan

On the first night, President Reagan and the First Lady dined quietly in a small group, but on the second night there was a banquet where they were served Connemara lamb, fresh seafood and local smoked salmon. 'They had their own chefs with them, but they just observed our chefs performing, they didn't partake in the actual preparation of food themselves,' said Mr Murphy. 'I remember Nancy took a great love of the brown bread and the apple tart and wanted the recipes for her chefs.'

On the second day, Mr Murphy escorted Nancy Reagan down to the farm to the spot where the scene was filmed of actor John Wayne famously dragging Nancy's close friend Maureen O'Hara along by the hair in their roles for the movie. 'We set up a little bar, similar to the bar scene in the movie. She was fascinated with the Maureen O'Hara scene because she's heard so much from her about *The Quiet Man*.'

The following day, in a radio address recorded in Ashford Castle after just returning from University College Galway, where he was conferred with an honorary degree, Reagan's film-star background came to the fore. He greeted his American listeners with a silver-voiced 'Top o' the mornin' to you', then went on to describe the Mayo estate as a place of 'spectacular beauty overlooking a large lake filled with islands, bays and coves'. In an aside about the beauty of Ireland, it's worth noting that Mike Deaver had also visited the University of Limerick, but he deemed the grandeur of the Galway college's ancient limestone quadrangle building much more repre-sentative of an old European university, leading to it being chosen for the presidential honorary degree rather than the nation's newest university in the neighbouring Munster county.

Addressing his fellow Irish Americans, possibly with an eye on the upcoming election in November that year, Reagan said: 'Those of you who, like me, can claim the good fortune of Irish roots, may appreciate the tug I felt in my heart yesterday when we saw the Emerald Isle from Air Force One.' On a more serious note, he touched on his visit to University College Galway earlier that day where he met its president, Dr Ó Eocha, who chaired the New Ireland Forum, which was seeking reconciliation in Northern Ireland. Reagan also alluded to Ireland's 'employment problem'. He said: 'By the strength of our economy, and by the presence of some three hundred US firms here, Americans can and will help our Irish cousins create jobs and greater opportunities.'

It wasn't surprising that he omitted to mention the thousand or so anti-nuclear campaigners, left-wing politicians, nuns and monks who marched in protest at his Galway visit but were kept away from the college by the Irish police. Two nuns reportedly carried a banner saying, 'We are mourning the 50,000 dead in El Salvador.'

In contrast to the unmarred joy of JFK's visit in 1963, the excitement at President Reagan's arrival was mixed with hostile demonstrations and calculated snubs from the Catholic hierarchy. The US government's support of the right-wing counter-revolutionary forces, known as the Contras, who were fighting against the Marxist Sandinista government in Nicaragua, was the cause of much of the protest. Reagan's policies in Central America, an area where Irish priests worked in missions, were judged to be the real reason behind the refusal of Irish Catholic bishops to attend a single official event, significant in a country where the hierarchy of the church still held waning but considerable sway.

In a televised interview with Brian Farrell of RTÉ at the White House library a week before the visit, Ronald Reagan said he believed Irish protestors were misinformed about his stance in Central America: 'All I can suggest to some of these people who are saying this in Europe and who have evidently been propagandised is – and

I don't mean this to sound presumptuous – but is there any one of them that has access to all the information that the President of the United States has?'

Seán Donlon, now back in Ireland as Secretary of the Department of Foreign Affairs, remembers significant protests in both Galway and during the Dublin visit to the Phoenix Park. The Taoiseach Garret FitzGerald walked the diplomatic tightrope of making his feelings clear on US foreign policy during his speech in Dublin Castle while not insulting his guest of honour.

In his carefully drafted speech, he spoke of the close emotional ties of Irish priests and nuns and lay helpers to the people of Central America. 'Our people's deep concern is that these problems be resolved peacefully by the people of the region themselves – in Central America, along the lines proposed by the Contadora countries,' said the Taoiseach in a gentle admonishment during his toast at Dublin Castle. He added:

> Many people in Ireland have been most heartened by the news of Secretary Shultz's visit to Nicaragua on Friday last and hope that this may lead to the restoration of normal relations between that small state and your great country, thus enhancing the climate for peace and democracy in that troubled region.

In fact, George Shultz, the Secretary of State, was en route from Nicaragua with intelligence for the president when he flew into Ireland separately from the White House party on the morning of Reagan's arrival on Ireland. He went straight to bed in Ashford Castle to catch up on his sleep before taking long walks with Reagan, briefing him on his dealing in the war-torn Central American country.

'Himself and George Shultz had their meeting outside on the garden seats out on the lawn... President Reagan spent his time walking around the grounds, he was very athletic. He often had a number of security men following him and I think a lot of them found it hard to keep up with him, he was so fit,' recalled Rory Murphy.

That night, Mr Shultz, having recovered from his flight from Nicaragua, attended the banquet and entertained guests with his piano playing, while Seán Donlon joined in with a duet with Mike Deaver on the piano. It was beneficial there were so many musical guests that night, as Ireland's most famous pianist, Phil Coulter, was refused entry at the gates by an Irish guard and two US Secret Service agents.

'Phil Coulter was very annoyed that he had gone to all the trouble of coming down especially for it and then to be turned away,' said Mr Murphy, who invited the Derry songwriter back to the castle a few days later. The Grammy-nominated musician, who has written hits for Elvis Presley and Cliff Richard, had flown in from London with his band after undergoing a week-long series of security checks, but his credential letters were rejected by the security staff without a word of explanation.

The piano player, famous for penning 'The Town I Loved So Well', decamped to Mellett's pub in the nearby village of Neale with his crew where he put on an impromptu music session – and indignant press conference – for delighted locals and the assembled news outlets, which had made the Mayo pub their unofficial headquarters. The incident made the nine o'clock news in Ireland and was splashed across the front pages of Sunday newspapers the next day.

Hotel manager Rory Murphy had his own brush with the Secret Service when he made his way down to President Reagan's suite to ask the Republican commander-in-chief to sign a booklet for the Mayor of Galway, which had been previously signed by President Kennedy more than a decade earlier. While waiting for the signature, he was standing next to a tall man next to a large black bag, which he presumed held the nuclear codes. During a jittery silence, Murphy asked: 'Is that the important bag with all the codes?'

'Then I said, "What would happen if I tried to steal it?" And he said, "Sir, I would have to shoot you." It was the first time he smiled; he was a very stern kind of guy. Amazing the things you say when you're nervous,' he added.

While significant anti-Reagan protests raged in Galway, a carnival atmosphere prevailed a hundred and ten miles away in Ballyporeen, where the party had been in full swing in anticipation of the president's visit for weeks before his arrival.

The day before the visit, Mary O'Farrell, who had given birth to her daughter Catherine Nancy at the end of April, was catering for siblings and in-laws of her extended family in the pub. It turned out to be a day that led to, in her words, 'a very funny story'. That afternoon, a local man arrived at the pub with a gift of an Aran cardigan knitted by his wife as a present for Mrs Reagan and stoutly refused to hear the landlady's advice that it couldn't be passed on as it hadn't been vetted by agents.

Could she just do her best, he insisted, placing it into her hands. Worn down, she put the wrapped gift on the piano. At three that morning, unable to sleep, Mary sat bolt upright in bed. In the kitchen were a couple from her extended family sleeping on a mattress not too far from an armed officer positioned at the end of the bar.

I said to myself, 'Mother of God, there should be anything inside that box for all I know, I'd better have a word with the detective.' I was coughing mad coming down the stairs in case he'd pull a gun on me. I explained my worries, he told me to get it immediately. 'Get it? What if there's something in it!' I said. 'Plus there's a pair asleep on the mattress!' and he said, 'Well you'll have to get it.'

Taking the retrieved package into the bar, the officer gingerly opened up the gift wrapping. On examination, it did turn out to be nothing more than a hand-knitted garment, which was duly packed off to America in the end. All the same, on the morning of the actual visit, sniffer dogs went meticulously through the O'Farrell kitchen and sitting rooms and bedrooms.

I have a pub called after me. That's class . . .

That summer day, one interspersed with rain showers, parishioner Neil Donovan remembers there being a smaller crowd than in the previous summer weekends leading up to the visit as only ticketed village residents were cleared for entry. A couple of hundred protestors were kept out of the village by security. There was a huge Garda presence, with one member of the force even positioned on the flat roof outside Neil's bedroom window. 'He was supposed to stay there all day but sure he was in having breakfast; he was frozen and wet.'

The grandstand erected at the crossroads in the previous weeks had turned the village into a hive of activity, attracting revellers from the parishes all around for one big street party. 'The Sunday before, the guards reckoned twenty thousand people were in the village; the pubs ran out of beer,' Neil recalled.

A huge white media tent was erected near the Church of the Assumpta, which was visited by the Reagans after stepping off their Marine One helicopter in the football field. The president prayed in the old stone church of his ancestors, where he was shown the ancient font where his great-grandfather, Michael Regan, was baptised and where church records list his baptism in September 1829. A few decades later, in the wake of the famine, Michael emigrated to London around the year 1850, where he married his Tipperary wife Catherine Mulcahey in 1852 before the family travelled to America in 1857, later settling in Illinois where President Reagan would be born on 6 February 1911. Father Murphy caused a few smiles when he bade Mrs Reagan farewell with, 'Good luck now, Missus.'

In his White House diaries, Reagan talks about meeting 'old Father Murphy keeper of the baptismal records'. He continues:

> There I saw the handwritten entry of Michael Regan's baptism in 1829 ... Our family line going back to Brian Boru has us related by way of Mary Queen of Scots to every royal family in Europe. I'm a 6th cousin of Queen Elizabeth of Eng ... We walked thru the town shaking hands with as many people as we could on our way to the pub that has been named for me.

On the platform at the town's crossroads, the president told the exuberant crowd of his delight that his ancestors had been found late in his life. 'I feel like I'm about to drown everyone in a bath of nostalgia.' He explained it wasn't a lack of interest but a lost family history which had left him unaware of his Irish relatives for most of his life:

> Now thanks to you and the efforts of good people who have dug into the history of a poor immigrant family, I know at last whence I came. And this has given my soul a new contentment. And it is a joyous feeling. It is like coming home after a long journey.

His speech touched on the very humble beginnings of his forebear who left during the potato famine. 'My great-grandfather left here in a time of stress, seeking to better himself and his family. From what I'm told, we were a poor family. But my ancestors took with them a treasure, an indomitable spirit that was cultivated in the rich soil of this county. And today I come back to you as a descendant of people who are buried here in paupers' graves.' He also delighted the elated crowd when he singled out the Gaelic Athletic Association, formed a hundred years earlier in Tipperary, stating: 'Some of you may be aware that I began my career as a sports announcer.'

After addressing the parishioners, he made his way in through the doors of his namesake pub to finally meet the O'Farrells after corresponding with them for a number of years. 'They took off the trench coats, she had a red one, he had a khaki colour, and threw them on the seat beside the door,' said Mary. 'You'd think they were coming in every night of the week.' The genial President and First Lady walked straight up to the counter, greeting John and Mary, then down along to shake hands with their relatives and three children.

A pint of Smithwick's was pulled for President Reagan, while Nancy was served a glass of the Tipperary-made Carolan's Irish cream liqueur. 'Everyone asks did he drink it, well, he went down almost to the bottom of the glass,' relates Mary.

The brand of stout in that pint glass had been the object of intense lobbying by Guinness and Beamish, but eventually Smithwick's won the day. The couple spent more than two hours with the O'Farrells chatting about America and the nearby Araglin ponies. 'You could see the Irish wit actually in him,' noted Mary O'Farrell. 'We settled down for a chat. He told yarns. He was just lovely and really calm, ever so nice, and we found Nancy great.'

He spoke about his friendship with film star Pat O'Brien, who was also connected to Ballyporeen, and urged genealogist Hugh Peskett, who was in the bar, to research the ancestors of his Treasury secretary, Donald Regan, to see if they were related. Before they left, the first couple were introduced to the newest addition to the O'Farrell family, Catherine Nancy, who had been born five weeks earlier, mindful of staff instructions that the president never held babies. The beaming First Lady put out her arms to hold the infant, who had been named after her, while her husband signed the visitors' book. 'He then turned to Nancy saying, "Honey, they'd like you to sign too,"' prompting Mary O'Farrell to spontaneously say, 'Why don't you hold the baby, Mr President?' She handed over the baby. 'It was such a fantastic photo because he was so astounded,' smiled Mary.

At one stage in the afternoon, staff asked the O'Farrells if they could leave the premises as the president was to have a summit meeting with staff, but when the landlady asserted she couldn't leave with her tiny daughter they relented and cleared the rest of the crowd minus the immediate family. Mary remembers, too, how the Reagans uncharacteristically broke their schedule by delaying past their allo-cated time in the pub. 'The protective men came in a few times and said, "You've got to go, Mr President, it's time to go . . ." But he wasn't inclined to go, he was having as good a time as we were.'

President Reagan eventually flew off that evening – and, in the following weeks, the tour buses started to arrive. Donovan's shop was ready with a big map of America behind the counter and James Last's orchestral records of Irish music playing on a loop to draw tourists in the door. 'My father wanted to know exactly where they were from, everyone got a conversation out of him,' said his son Neil, who recalled John spending long nights in their kitchen talking to journalists like the BBC's Fergal Keane, then a young reporter. 'He was quizzing them as much as they were quizzing him.'

Neil smiles as he recalls:

We managed to get *Reagan Ancestral Home* T-shirts, with an Irish flag and an American flag, a shamrock, and other T-shirts printed with *I'd Rather Be in Ballyporeen*. You could not keep them in the shop. There were pictures of Reagan on ceramics and car visors. It was a bit of craic. The shop was bananas for a couple of summers. There was so much demand.

The following day, the final one of the visit, President Reagan followed in President John F. Kennedy's footsteps in addressing a joint session of the Irish Parliament, as the Democratic president did twenty-one years earlier. Reagan calmly waited for three TDs to exit the chamber after a boisterous protest at his presence at the beginning of his speech before observing: 'I can't help but say I wonder if there is an awareness in some that there are counties in the world today where representatives would not have been able to speak as they have here.' In a sentimental address, he said:

> When I stepped off Air Force One at Shannon a few days ago and saw Ireland, beautiful and green, and felt again the warmth of her people, something deep inside began to stir. So, I hope you won't think it too bold of me to say that my feelings here this morning can best be summarised by the words 'home – home again'.

He invoked John F. Kennedy's poignant promise to return to Ireland in the spring at the end of his speech:

> It was a promise left unkept, for a spring that never came. But surely in our hearts there is the memory of a young leader who spoke stirring words about a brighter age for mankind, about a new generation that would hold high the torch of liberty and truly light the world. This is the task before us: to plead the case of humanity, to move the conscience of the world, to march together – as in olden times – in the cause of freedom.

The spy called Murphy

Owing to the passing of both of his paternal grandparents decades before his own birth, Reagan was in the dark about his Tipperary origins for most of his life, but in the aftermath of the discovery he would enthusiastically tap into Irishness during his weekly meetings with Tip O'Neill. The democratic speaker of the House of Representatives had a storied relationship with conservative champion Ronald Reagan, but while they regularly differed on politics, the larger-than-life politicians made a deal to end their weekly meetings trading Irish stories. In a diary entry in February 1981, Reagan alludes to this habit when talking about a White House dinner: 'It was a nice evening but maybe Tip & I told too many Irish stories.'

This practice led to regular phone calls to Seán Donlon from their aides in a quest for Irish stories. 'I used to get calls from Mike Deaver on the Reagan side and Kirk O'Donnell on the Tip O'Neill side saying, "Do you have any news stories?"' This could explain the origin of one of Reagan's most frequently repeated Irish jokes about a spy called Murphy, which was told at a Republican campaign rally in Columbus, Ohio on 19 October 1988, and then rolled out weeks later at rallies in California and Milwaukee.

During one of Deaver's phone calls, Seán Donlon had passed on this very story after hearing it on a stand-up record he had received of famous Irish comedian Niall Tóibín. Reagan would begin the story by saying:

It seems that they called in an agent, and they told him that he was to go to a little town in Ireland. And there he was to make contact with one of our spies named Murphy. Now, he said that the manner of recognition would be that he should say to Murphy – he should say that it was a beautiful day this morning, but it'll be a greater afternoon. So, he goes to Ireland and – in this little town – and he goes into the pub, and he sits up at the bar. And the bartender comes along, and he orders, and he says, 'By the way, I'm looking for a man named Murphy.' And the bartender said, 'Well, now, there's a Murphy across the street on the second floor. He's a bootmaker. And about a row down there to the left is a farmer named Murphy. And my name is Murphy.' And the agent said, 'Well, it was a beautiful day this morning, but it's going to be greater this afternoon.'

'Oh,' he says, 'it's Murphy the spy you want.'

Kevin Mulcahy, the son of Ashford Castle owner John A. Mulcahy, remembers the same story being repeated in 1986 by the real head of the CIA, Bill Casey, in a letter to wish his father a happy eightieth birthday. After his trip to Ireland, Reagan would regularly sprinkle his political speeches with Irish jokes, with a quip about an Irish builder and Lourdes told to laughter at a California Republican Party fundraising dinner in Los Angeles in 1985. He would also habitually reference his Irish ancestry in speeches. At a toast at a state dinner for Irish-born President Chaim Herzog of Israel in November 1987, he said: 'That you were born in Ireland and that my ancestors came from there may seem accidental, but it speaks to the history of both Israel and the United States.'

In the years after his visit, Seán Donlon said Reagan referred to the moment Father Condon in Ballyporeen brought him to the old baptismal font in the church and showed him the original baptismal record belonging to his great-grandfather more than once. The diplomat believed it was an emotional visit for the movie star, whose children returned to Tipperary on private visits in the following years. 'He seemed to have enjoyed himself and especially when he went to Ballyporeen. He loved chatting to people, he loved the visit to the pub.' His White House diaries reference his sentimental attachment to the song 'Danny Boy' on more than one occasion. After St Patrick's Day in 1987, he talked of his enjoyment of the celebrations, adding: 'By the time they were over I was talking with a brogue ...'

But in the case of Reagan's ties to Ireland, there was substance along with sentiment. In the aftermath of the visit, Reagan became more involved in Anglo-Irish relations. At a meeting at Camp David with President Reagan on 22 December 1984, six months after he was elected to his second term in office, he discussed Northern Ireland with the English prime minster, Margaret Thatcher.

In declassified notes of the meeting, Mrs Thatcher said that, despite reports to the contrary, she and FitzGerald were on good terms and were working towards making progress on this difficult question. The president said that making progress is important, telling Thatcher that Tip O'Neill had sent him a personal letter, asking him to appeal to her to be reasonable and forthcoming.

The following October, Thatcher's briefing cards for a meeting with President Reagan list 'an account of where you have got to with Garrett Fitzgerald [sic]' as no. 10 on the agenda, alongside talks on the Middle East and South Africa.

As former Irish ambassador to the US, Seán Donlon believes Reagan's interest in Anglo-Irish affairs was heightened by his deeply personal experience in Ireland. 'Every meeting that Ronald Reagan had with Margaret Thatcher, and they were very close, they discussed Northern Ireland, and they discussed Northern Ireland on the basis that the Irish government wanted a particular approach taken,' he said.

Nearly a year and half after the Reagan visit to Ireland, the watershed Anglo-Irish Treaty was signed by the Taoiseach Garret FitzGerald and the British prime minister Margaret Thatcher in Hillsborough Castle in Co. Down, the only royal residence in Northern Ireland. It stated that any change in the status of Northern Ireland would only come about with the consent of the majority in the six counties and, if there was formal consent for a United Ireland, the two governments would introduce legislation in the respective parliaments to give effect to that wish.

It was a defining moment. It was the first time London recognised that the Irish government had an advisory role to play in the affairs of Northern Ireland. Thatcher is widely thought to have signed after caving in to American pressure and regretted it soon afterwards. Several years later, she was remembered for exclaiming: 'It was the Americans that made me do it!' The landmark agreement which paved the way for the possibility of a United Ireland, with all sorts of caveats, could have been viewed as the heavyweight political capital from the whimsical return of one Ronald Wilson Reagan to the tiny famine-ravaged valley left behind by his great-grandfather over a hundred and thirty years earlier.

Back in Ballyporeen, the president's old-school charm and genuine emotion walking through the streets won over the three hundred or so villagers in the crowd for years to come. In the aftermath of the visit, everyone from Ashford Castle manager Rory Murphy to Mary O'Farrell received hand-signed notes from the Reagans thanking them for their Irish hospitality. 'A President's visit is something you cannot buy, that's the luck of it. It's a piece of history. They had a super time, and we had a super time,' said the former landlady.

Although there was talk that the visit might lead to the location of a US factory in the village, it never materialised. But in the post-visit 1980s, lots of B&Bs sprang up in the town along with two cafés called the White House and the Potato Kitchen. And it did bring a cosmopolitan dimension to the rural hamlet, changing the outlook of its younger population. For shopkeeper's son Neil Donovan, who had once been content to take over the store, it was life changing. 'The world was my oyster and I wanted to travel, it one hundred per cent broadened my horizons,' he said of the visit, adding: 'Reagan brought thousands and thousands of people to our village. He was one of our own.'

Ronald Reagan died nearly twenty years to the day after visiting

Tipperary in 2004. But before then, the O'Farrells kept up their correspondence with the Reagans. One of the last letters they received from the president told them he was starting to get Alzheimer's disease. In the end, a piece of Ballyporeen did end up lock, stock and barrel over in California. The week of Ronald Reagan's death, a friend of the president knocked on the door of the Tipperary pub and decided with the O'Farrells to have the rural bar sent across to America, where it now forms a central feature of the Ronald Reagan Presidential Library and Museum overlooking the Pacific Ocean. All the contents, including the pub quiz trophies and the bar stools used by Ronald and Nancy Reagan on their visit, are positioned right under the nose of Air Force One at the library.

It makes a fitting memorial to the president who had once written to the O'Farrells: 'Other presidents have airports and bridges called after them, I have a pub back in Ireland, now that's class.'

In the Rose Garden, 1999: a smiling Bertie Ahern with
President Clinton and the customary shamrocks.

CHAPTER FOUR

PRESIDENT BILL CLINTON

———

When are we playing Ballybunion?

———

A S PRESIDENT CLINTON STOOD on the sixth tee of the fabled Ballybunion golf course at the edge of the Atlantic, a steel-hulled Irish navy vessel patrolled in the distance.

Former Tánaiste Dick Spring nodded to the pebble-grey Corvette warship in the rolling waters below and wryly observed: 'Mr President, you can feel very secure today because twenty-five per cent of the Irish navy is looking after us . . .' As they walked along the links course, the Kerry politician and President Clinton deduced that the entire Irish navy fleet could fit inside one of America's super air carriers.

In the preceding weeks, every inch of the rugged course carved out of towering dunes had been combed by stern-faced agents, with dozens of golf balls retrieved from the tall grass and patches of gorse. The windswept course outside the seaside town of Ballybunion in North Kerry was one of the sport's best-kept secrets until US golfer Tom Watson stumbled upon it in the 1970s and turned it into the holy grail of links courses when he took to using it as a practice pit stop en route to his spate of British Open victories. Perched above the crashing surf of miles of deserted beach along Ireland's Wild Atlantic Way, its fast greens, whipping wind and treacherous rough along the contoured dunes combine to pose the ultimate golfing challenge.

This was 5 September 1998, and President Clinton, an avid golfer, was fulfilling his promise to play eighteen holes along the blustery Kerry coastline, the polar opposite of the sun-soaked manicured perfection of parkland country clubs in Washington. The journey to his afternoon round of golf had nearly as many twists and turns as the peace process he had helped to secure five months earlier. Dick Spring, a native of the nearby town of Tralee, had issued the invitation almost four years earlier when, as Foreign Affairs Minister, he flew into the US on 2 September 1994 and dropped in on Clinton during his Martha's Vineyard vacation a few days after the landmark IRA ceasefire in Northern Ireland to brief the president on developments. A round of golf in Ballybunion was duly put in the schedule for the first of his three visits to Ireland in 1995 but was removed days before Clinton arrived. 'I got a message that Jean Kennedy Smith wanted to see me,' remembered Mr Spring, 'and I knew as soon as I got that message, there was not going to be golf. So, she came in and she said, "I really feel bad about this..."'

'Don't worry, it's not your problem, not your fault,' was his reply to the then US ambassador to Ireland. 'President Clinton had decided to go to Germany instead of coming to Kerry, because the troops were being sent to Bosnia and with troops going to Bosnia, the President of America cannot be seen to be on the golf course in Ballybunion, which was understandable,' he recalled, 'But he did say to me that he would come back.'

Two grass sods, an Atlantic round of golf and a town square statue

The presidential resolve to visit North Kerry was undoubtedly bolstered by the charm offensive mounted by one of Kerry's most colourful characters, Frank Quilter. Shortly before President Clinton was set to make his electrifying speech to a crowd of tens of thousands of cheering supporters in Dublin's College Green on 1 December 1995, the Ballybunion hotelier marched through the barriers to the front of the stage with some fanfare. Quilter remembers:

> We did a banner that was about twelve foot long by two foot deep with *Ballybunion Backs Clinton – '96* to show our support for him in the subsequent election. It was like an All-Ireland that day and there was a big American influx around Dublin. We had an All-Ireland piper, Danny Houlihan, who was in a kilt, and we lined up at the top of Stephen's Green and paraded down by the Molly Malone fountain. There were only about twelve of us in it, but Americans in the crowd joined in. Danny played 'A Nation Once Again', and the Trinity students were all cheering.

As President Clinton and his wife, Hillary, came on the stage, the Ballybunion contingent lifted their placards, catching the First Lady's attention, who mouthed 'Ballybunion' to her husband as she pointed to the crowd. The US president did more than just notice the placards as he gave them a shout-out when he took to the podium minutes later: 'As a lot of you know, because of events developing in Bosnia and the prospect of peace there, I had to cut short my trip. But ... I will return to Ballybunion for my golf game,' he said to laughter from the crowd.

But that was only the beginning of the creative canvassing employed to entice the US president to the Kerry seaside town. Quilter, who ran the annual Ballybunion Bachelor Festival through the 1990s at his Atlantic Hotel, possessed lobbying skills that would put the wiliest Washington strategists to shame. After mingling with the US delegation to Dublin for the best part of a week during Clinton's 1995 visit, he had secured an invitation to the Democratic Convention in Chicago the following year with his friend, John Hannan. On arrival at the United Center, home to the Chicago Bulls, they ceremoniously presented the convention with two grass sods from Ballybunion golf course, which they had managed to get cleared through US Customs.

'We were invited by Senator Chris Dodd, who chaired the convention. We met Alec Baldwin, and a pile of other Democrats,' said Frank. 'There was a delegation from every state, and we got an award when we arrived for coming the longest distance. They had selected Alaska and then when they heard about us coming from Ireland, it ended up being a joint award. We were telling them we came because Clinton was after stopping a war in Ireland going on for seven hundred years.' He then added, 'I met Hillary and Tipper Gore, we went to a pile of parties. We wanted to keep Ballybunion in the news.' During the convention, the Irish networker handed out business cards for his local hotel, with the strapline: *Atlantic Hotel, only 3,720 miles from Chicago.*

On his return from Illinois, one of the more unusual schemes dreamed up by the hotelier – who had once shared a flat with former Irish Taoiseach Enda Kenny – was holding a contest to kick one hundred Gaelic footballs printed with *Ballybunion Backs Clinton* into the Atlantic. The first American to find one on the east coast of the US would win a free holiday to Ireland ... but it would later emerge that local tides conveniently ensured the balls simply circled before popping up right back on the Kerry side of the Atlantic.

Unknown to the Kerry campaigners, their small town in the south of Ireland was cropping up regularly at high-level security meetings in the White House between 1994 and 1997 when Dick Spring held the twin posts of Tánaiste and Minister for Foreign Affairs.

When I used to go to Washington, I would have a formal meeting with Al Gore. I wasn't going to get a meeting with the President of America, protocol being what it is, but the President of America always came in for my meeting. When he would come into the room, the atmosphere would change completely, and the first thing he would always say is, 'When are we playing Ballybunion?' I would say to him, 'It's twenty minutes away from me. Anytime you're available. I can be there in twenty minutes.' Then he always sat down for fifteen or twenty minutes, and we talked about Northern Ireland. That was the main preoccupation. He would actually have been a lot more interested in Northern Ireland than Al Gore. I don't think there was much interest in Texas in Northern Ireland.

*

When President Clinton returned to Ireland for his second state visit in September 1998, two years after he was elected for his second term, the political landscape had changed dramatically since his first historic trip in 1995, which took in Northern Ireland. Clinton was instrumental in brokering the Good Friday Agreement five months earlier, but back in America he was embroiled in the fallout from the Monica Lewinsky affair, which had broken on news channels that January and mushroomed into the biggest political scandal in Washington since Watergate. In the Dáil, Dick Spring was on the opposition benches as leader of the Irish Labour Party after the Fianna Fáil Party led by Bertie Ahern swept into power in the 1997 election in a coalition government with the Progressive Democrats. This all added to the intrigue behind this much-anticipated game of golf in the county referred to as 'The Kingdom' in Ireland because of its natural beauty. Mr Spring recalled:

The word came that he was going to come to Ballybunion. By then, of course, I was out of office, and the one thing you discover very quickly when you're out of office is you have to ask people for things rather than tell people, so then it becomes a negotiation about who's going to play. The only request from Clinton was that I was going to play, and they could fix up the rest of themselves. Fianna Fáil of course at the time weren't going to stand back and see Dick Spring walking down the first fairway in Ballybunion with his arm around Bill Clinton, so they said that Charlie McCreevy could play, the Minister of Finance, which was fine by me, because we were good golfing buddies.

After a bit of back and forth, it ended up becoming a five-ball, as opposed to the traditional four-ball where players would pair off in teams, with Ballybunion's captain, Brian McCarthy, and professional player, Christy O'Connor Snr, widely regarded as the patriarch of Irish golf, joining the trio of politicians.

In early August, just after Sunday Mass, startled Ballybunion residents got their first thunderous inkling of the preparation for a presidential game of golf when six low-flying helicopters in formation roared over the town. It would later emerge they were photographing the street and casing out possible sniper locations. With the game on the official agenda, one of the first orders of business was the commissioning of a life-size statue of the US president to stand on a plinth outside the navy blue door of the town's Garda station in the middle of Ballybunion. Sculptor Sean McCarthy was signed up to mould the bronze figure. 'But the problem was that he would not have it done by Saturday 5 September, a mere three weeks away, so it was decided he would do a plaster-of-Paris version ready for the day,' said Mr Quilter.

Two weeks before his arrival, in a primetime television address, a grim-faced President Clinton had admitted having an inappropriate relationship with former White House intern Monica Lewinsky, further intensifying the spotlight on his private life. With his Irish trip among his first public appearances since the admission, news crews from CBS, NBC, CNN and the BBC all camped in Ballybunion in the days before his arrival, along with dozens of other international outlets. Frank Quilter and Jackie Hourigan, chairman of the town's development committee, were left exhausted by last-minute preparations on top of endless rounds of interviews as the chief spokespeople for the town. 'Those four or five days before President Clinton came there were camera crews and journalists from everywhere ... Spain, Sweden, France. We were getting maybe five or six phone calls a day, the BBC were ringing. We were played out, the two of us, from taking phone calls,' remembered Jackie, who ran the thriving Harty Costello pub and guesthouse on the main street, with his wife Davnet, who has since sadly passed away.

Much was made of a sign for Monica's on Ballybunion's main street, a local hairdresser's salon which had been closed for several years. The sign was removed and the name above the door changed to The President's Shop just days before the visit. 'Monica had retired, and actually the sign was taken down but as it was up for maybe twenty-five years, the MONICA letters were still visible,' explained Jackie. 'Somebody went in then a couple of days before the visit and they were selling souvenirs of President Clinton's visit so that was that. But, of course, all the journalists took it up then that the people in Ballybunion took down the sign MONICA just because the president was coming. That wasn't true at all, as Monica had retired, but of course they made a great story of it.'

Back in Washington, the day before Clinton's arrival in Ballybunion, Democratic Senator Joseph Liberman took to the Senate floor in a significant break with his leader to condemn the president's behaviour as immoral, disgraceful and damaging to the country. In Dublin that day, in a press conference with Bertie Ahern, he had fielded numerous questions about the senator's eviscerating criticism across the Atlantic. That night, the Ballybunion organisers had their own, more mundane, troubles when the lumpy plaster-of-Paris arm from President Clinton's statue, now painted in a bronze hue, fell off, resulting in a frantic call to the sculptor. 'The night before Clinton came, we were in a garage here in Ballybunion fixing the arm,' laughed Jackie Hourigan.

On the morning of his Kerry visit, President Clinton stopped off in Limerick city after spending the night a few miles away in the finely manicured surroundings of Adare Manor, a seventeenth-century Tudor castle-turned-hotel owned by his American friend, Tom Kane. Despite the intense political pressure back home, the US leader exuded all the star quality of a rock legend as he received a rapturous welcome from tens of thousands in the midwest city. At the podium, the president spoke with barely a glance at his notes to crowds stretching back for blocks and blocks down the main O'Connell Street. Referring to the Good Friday Agreement, he told the throng:

> Because of what you have done in Ireland in 1998, you have made it possible for me, on behalf of the United States and the cause of peace in the world, to tell every warring, feuding, hating group of people trapped in the prison of their past conflicts to look at Ireland and know there can be a better day. Thank you for that.

In a light-hearted aside on the novel *Angela's Ashes* by Frank McCourt, which described rain-soaked winters in the city, Clinton told the crowd: 'I'll have to go home and tell Frank McCourt, "You know, Frank, you made a lot of money writing about the old

Limerick, but I like the new one better, and I think you would, too."'
He namechecked another of the country's favourite writers, too:
'George Bernard Shaw once quipped that he hoped to be in Ireland
on the day the world ended, because the Irish were always fifty years
behind the times,' before adding to much laughter, 'Well, Ireland has
turned the tables on poor old Mr Shaw, for today you are in the
forefront of every change sweeping the world. This island is being
redefined by new ideas, bringing prosperity and an increasingly
international world view.'

As the president made his way to Ballybunion by road from
Limerick, he stopped off outside Katie Nolan's pub in Lisselton, the
town which produced another Irish writer – Maurice Walsh, author
of *The Quiet Man*. Four hundred giant colour posters of Clinton
with the words *Ballybunion Backs Bill Clinton* hung from every telephone and electricity pole leading into the town, while the streets
were festooned with stars and stripes. As President Clinton emerged
from a black limousine at the clubhouse for his long-promised
appointment after a torrid summer in the White House, he declared,
'I'm so delighted to be here.' Before he'd ever set foot in the Kerry
club, he'd played the historic course in his mind with the aid of
photographs and an old course guide lent to him by an English
friend.

Before setting off for the first tee, the president was shown to a
dressing room where the club laid out a choice of club caps and
T-shirts in an array of colours. They were delighted when he decided
to take the lot – and even more thrilled in the following years when
they became a staple part of his golf attire. 'We saw him several times
afterwards on golf courses in America wearing the Ballybunion
logo,' said Brian McCarthy, a local schoolteacher and captain of the
club. Brian encountered the full force of Clinton's personality when
they were first introduced:

I don't think I ever met anyone in my life that would have the same charisma. If he put his eye on you when you were facing him, you were the only one in the world. He had that ability and he transferred it obviously to the next person in line. He made a huge impression, and it was a huge occasion in Ballybunion. It was a carnival atmosphere.

A bank of photographers trained their lenses on the president as he walked to the first hole, which might have added to the intimidation he would later recall feeling as he took his first shot. 'He was a very keen golfer,' said Brian. 'We were on the first tee ready to go, and Dick Spring offered him three shots on his handicap, and he said, "No way!" He was going to play off his handicap, which was thirteen. There was a nice lively breeze but as long as it was dry, we didn't mind.'

His first shot veered off, landing in a nearby cemetery, which would later prompt droll observations from commentators that it was a metaphor for the intense speculation that the president might be facing a political graveyard in the US. But neither his political woes on Capitol Hill nor the historic peace accord were conversation topics in between shots.

'It was serious golfing stuff and golfing terminology, and the language was the same as anybody else out in a four-ball playing golf,' recalled the club captain light-heartedly. 'It was very relaxed. At the time we were playing, he had a bit of controversy at home. It must have been a worry to him, but you wouldn't know it. He was totally down to earth, an exceptionally nice guy, a great sense of humour. Michael Scanlon caddied for him, and they had great exchanges.' The club captain was also struck by the agility of the US president: 'He was superbly fit at that stage, very athletic-looking, and he had no bother running around the eighteen holes.'

Agents were dotted around the course, but they were also tailed by a slow-moving truck with an open back. 'There was something in that that was covered all the time; we assumed it was a gun of some description, it was very close to us,' remembered Brian. 'There were agents, but they were unobtrusive; they didn't bother us in the slightest. He was out to enjoy himself and that was it.' The Secret Service had spent weeks casing out the course in advance of the game. 'They walked every single blade of grass. Up on the hills, everywhere, I don't know how many dozen golf balls they found.'

Publican Jackie Hourigan had been astonished the night before to see dozens of uniformed Gardaí pacing the course from the window of his house across from the fifth fairway.

Dick Spring, who has regularly golfed with Clinton over the last few decades, has a theory on the president's love of the game. 'It was a challenge for him personally. I got the feeling from playing with him all these times that when you are the president of America, you don't do an awful lot for yourself. But when you're standing on the first tee, you've got to hit the ball yourself,' he said before remembering another story: 'We were in the Old Head of Kinsale one time, and we were getting into the buggy. And I said to President Clinton. "I'll drive." He said, "No you won't, I haven't driven anything for about twenty years, buddy." He wanted to drive the buggy and genuinely got a bit of a kick out of it.'

Being the most powerful man in the world did not exempt Clinton from landing in the rough at one stage in the blustery course, but this was away from the lenses of the press corps. 'Christy O'Connor acted like a consultant all the way around and definitely gave Bill Clinton a few tips on how to play golf in the wind,' recalled Dick Spring. 'The round itself was quite fun, we had the place to ourselves. Playing the sixth hole in Ballybunion, he got stuck in the marram grass, but otherwise he enjoyed it, he played well. It's just one of those super golf courses.' Brian remembers how his game obligingly came good in front of the camera lens. 'I wouldn't say he had played anything like Ballybunion. There were a couple of holes he found particularly hard . . . but the cameras were on him on the first hole, and it was getting dark when he played the 18th, and he had a birdie putt. He played those two holes like a professional would play them, it worked out perfectly.'

A stop-off in the town to see the cast of the statue the village had commissioned was not on the official schedule that day. Thousands who lined the streets were left disappointed when his cavalcade went straight to the course. But Jackie Hourigan credits the intervention of one of the president's aides, Kevin O'Keeffe, who had been staying in his guesthouse in the town, with his eventual unscheduled arrival to the square as he personally told Clinton of the waiting crowds. The light was fading when the presidential limousine pulled up in front of the statue. A young US solider in full uniform was dispatched to Jackie Hourigan's packed pub sixty yards away:

> He stood in front of me, and he clicked his heels and he saluted me, and said, 'Mr Hourigan, the president wants to speak to you at the statue,' and lifted me out over the barrier. President Clinton was standing at the door of the car when I arrived and one of the officers walked over to me and frisked me a little and he took me over and introduced me, and we shook hands.

'I want to welcome you to Ballybunion, we're delighted to have you,' said the beaming chairman of the town council.

'I've heard an awful lot about Ballybunion,' Clinton replied.

Then Jackie Hourigan added earnestly, 'The main thing in this town outside agricultural and farming is tourism, and the Troubles in the North have cost us a lot. People in Ireland and Kerry, exceptionally, they love you and they are so taken by you, you've done so much for the peace process. I know the Irish people love you and they love your family.' As he came to the end of his impromptu speech, the chairman saw tears in Clinton's eyes. 'He got very emotional actually, he really did, he nearly cried, and I got emotional as well. The next thing the two of us caught one another and we hugged.'

He was later told how President Clinton's spirits had been boosted by the Kerry reception in the aftermath of the political blow of Joe Liberman breaking ranks in the Senate.

> He told friends of his in the White House that when he saw the four hundred posters all over the town that it gave him a fierce lift. He said that day, 'I just love the atmosphere in this town. I've never had a statue put up for me,' – and it was because of the way it was decorated. He looked a picture that day. He was on a high at the stage because the golf club had lined the entrance as he was going in and going out and all the ex-presidents of the club and captains were in their blazers.

Then the president asked the publican to accompany him to meet the waiting crowds. As they walked, a tall American man called out, 'Mr President, I'm an American citizen and I've never seen you and I have my passport – I can prove it.'

President Clinton laughingly said, 'That's okay, you don't have to give me your passport,' and they had a chat over the heads of people. Two years later, the same man walked into Jackie Hourigan's bar and showed him a Christmas card he had received that year from President Clinton.

That day, further down the line in the crowd, the US president spotted the Kerry politician, Senator Dan Kiely, who lives in Ballybunion. 'Senator Kiely,' he greeted him. 'Hi!'

He shouted back, 'Hi, Mr President, I'm wearing your cufflinks,' referring to a pair of cufflinks he had been gifted during one of his visits to the White House.

Darkness was falling as he got back into his limousine and headed out of the town, but Clinton motioned to his driver to halt when he spotted the Arkansas flag flying from one of the houses on the main street. The press corps were gone when he got on to the footpath and solemnly saluted his state flag before driving to a nearby field to board a helicopter to Shannon Airport where Air Force One was waiting to bring him back to the White House.

Oxford college, Dublin weekend and introduction to the Troubles

Bill Clinton's connection with Ireland had begun three decades before his love affair with his favourite golf course. As a fresh-faced graduate in international affairs, he was settling into postgraduate studies at the University of Oxford in the autumn of 1968 as the first stirrings of civil rights unrest were rumbling across the Irish Sea. William J. Clinton was among the latest crop of elite Rhodes Scholars, a beneficiary of a bursary bequeathed to the college from the will of nineteenth-century imperialist Cecil John Rhodes in 1902, making it the oldest, and one of the most prized, international scholarship programmes in the world. The future president of America would spend nearly two years in the English seat of learning at Rhodes House, a 1920s building with a magnificent domed Great Hall, oak-panelled libraries and walled gardens. The cosmopolitan scholars engaged in earnest weekly debates on global conflicts as part of their studies, but just a few hundred miles away in Ulster, one of the bloodiest conflicts of the twentieth century was brewing in real time.

Peaceful protests to challenge what was perceived as anti-Catholic discrimination on the markers of wealth such as jobs and housing took to the streets of Northern Ireland in the summer of 1968. The banner-waving marchers were not seeking a united Ireland but

simple fairness in the nuts and bolts of everyday life, such as aboli-
tion of the rule which only allowed homeowners – who tended to be
middle-class Protestants and not their poorer Catholic neighbours –
to vote in local elections. There was deep anger among the minority
Catholics towards the allocation of public housing and public jobs;
the protestors perceived the system as skewed in favour of
Protestants. Gerrymandering, the practice of manipulating election
boundaries, was blamed for the situation in which Protestant coun-
cillors took up the majority of seats on Derry Corporation despite
the majority Catholic vote among the local electorate. By 5 October
1968, the marches became headline news when TV footage flashed
around the world of the Royal Ulster Constabulary baton-charging
a civil rights march in Derry, actions which left many people injured.

Meanwhile, in a letter home to a pal in Arkansas, Bill Clinton, then
a gifted young scholar fresh from Georgetown University, described
his new English home as a 'triumph of man and nature'. During his
first term, he would take a trip over to Dublin with three friends in
late 1968. Around the same time, the future Irish Foreign Affairs
Minister Dick Spring was studying law in Trinity College.

'I said to him, "I searched every pub in Dublin to see if anybody
remembered you ... Nobody remembers a bearded Bill Clinton,"'
recalled Mr Spring with a smile, adding:

> But he came over to Dublin in the company of three friends. It was
> nothing to do with politics or otherwise, he was in Oxford, and they
> decided to take off for Dublin, and I got the impression it was, you
> know, do a few museums and the National Library, and have a few
> free drinks and enjoy Dublin. He told me that many years later, when
> he was on the presidential campaign, he was speaking at the hustings
> down in Texas, and he looked down at the audience, and lo and
> behold, there was a lady staring up at him, who was one of the two

ladies who had been in Dublin for the weekend with him. They'd gone their different ways after Oxford. He obviously met her then and they [ended up] chatting about the old times.

Former Irish Taoiseach Bertie Ahern believes Clinton tuned into Northern Ireland during his two years at Oxford in '68 and '69. By 1969, Ulster was regularly flashing up on international news bulletins as riots raged in the streets with the British Army deployed to the boiling-over province at the end of that summer. 'It was on TV all the time. Some of the college debates were about the north. I know he did follow it; he got a grip of the early days of John Hume and Seamus Mallon and Paisley and unionists and nationalists. It came from that period . . . he understood the difficulties from that period.'

In 1996, halfway through his first term in the White House, Clinton recalled those student days in a speech to Irish Americans in the ballroom at the Plaza Hotel in New York. 'I was a young student in England when the Troubles began. And as an American acutely aware of his Irish roots, I was deeply interested in it and troubled by it.' One Irish diplomat would later note the irony that the Oxford scholarship founded by Cecil Rhodes to promote the closeness of the sister democracies of England and the United States was what first stirred the US president's interest in Northern Ireland.

Certainly, Clinton's awareness would have made him more informed on the nuances of the conflict in the six counties in the north of Ireland, which dominated world headlines with bombings, hunger strikes and sectarian violence: a hotbed of deep human suffering on a par with war zones such as Beirut throughout the 1970s, 80s and into the 90s. The Troubles was the black term coined for the near-constant stream of assassinations, explosions and political violence which killed an estimated 3,600 people, many of them civilians.

The Irish roots Clinton regularly referenced are thought to date back to the early 1800s. His father, William Blythe, died a few months before he was born, and he took the name of his stepfather Roger Clinton after his mother, Virginia Cassidy, married the car dealer when he was four years old. On his paternal Blythe line, evidence points to two or three of his great-great-grandparents coming from Ireland. His great-grandmother, Hattie Hayes, was born either in Florida or at sea, according to two differing US census records. One of the census documents logs that she had two Irish parents, but there are no confirmed names for them. The paper trail also suggests that Hattie's husband – President Clinton's great-grandfather – Simpson Green 'Dick' Ayers, who was more than thirty years her senior, had a father who came from Ireland.

Clinton spoke about feelings of 'great honour' in respect of his maternal Irish connections at a Democratic National Committee Dinner in Baltimore just before St Patrick's Day in 2000. He said:

> My people are from Fermanagh ... which is right on the border of Northern Ireland and the Irish Republic. And I have a little watercolour in the Residence at the White House of the oldest known residence of my mother's people, the Cassidys. It's an early eighteenth-century farmhouse that still is in existence. I've never been able to trace my roots, beyond speculation, back before that. And it has been a great honour.

Bertie Ahern remembers President Clinton being pleased about the inference that his ancestors hailed from the border county of Fermanagh. 'He always thought that was a big plus because he was on the border.' Just before his first state visit in August 1995, a White House memo listed the pros and cons of going to Roslea in Fermanagh to visit the ancestors of Lucas Cassidy, who was 'supposedly President

Clinton's fourth great-grandfather'; in the end, the visit was decided against because of the imprecision of the ties.

After leaving Oxford, Clinton entered Yale Law School in 1970 where he met his future wife, Hillary Rodham. Three years after leaving Yale, he was elected the state attorney general for Arkansas in 1976 before becoming governor at the age of thirty-two in 1978. Crucially for Ireland, he then met Bruce Morrison, who would go on to become a key Irish-American lobbyist, and the congressman behind the Morrison Visa Programme, which allotted thousands of visas to Irish people in the late 1980s. 'Bruce Morrison has been a friend of mine for more than twenty years since we went to law school together,' Clinton would reveal during his '92 campaign.

Outsider candidate who shook up decades of US policy on Northern Ireland in a late-night meeting in Manhattan

Like President Carter before him, Bill Clinton was an outsider when he entered the race to become the Democratic candidate in 1992. Although he had two terms as the governor of Arkansas behind him, he had never served in Capitol Hill. He was viewed – positively – as someone who was unhindered and unfettered by the manoeuvrings of favour and fealty running through Congress and the Senate. Irish ambassador to the United States, Seán O'Huiginn (from 1997 to 2002) saw this quality in the brilliant lawyer. 'I think there was a little bit of the anti-establishment in him, a little bit of distance perhaps vis-à-vis the existing power structures, and I suspect he found that among his Irish-American friends, and in college, and identified with it as a choice almost.'

In the run-up to the '92 presidential election, this outsider candidate found himself in a meeting in the Bronx, the heartbeat of Irish America, talking to some of the most influential heavyweights of the Irish diaspora. 'When he was coming to New York, a group of Irish

Americans or Americans with Irish interest, including Bruce Morrison, asked to have a meeting with him,' recalled Dick Spring. 'Basically, the deal was that if Clinton undertook to take an interest in Irish politics, in Northern Ireland in particular, then in return for that, this group of people would work for him, and get the Irish American Coalition behind Bill Clinton, without which you probably couldn't get elected.'

In a 1996 speech to Irish Americans, Clinton expanded further on how this friendship helped reintroduce him to Northern Ireland's issues during the presidential election, decades after leaving Oxford:

> Time took me in a different direction. I went back home, I lived a different life, I missed a lot of what happened between then and four years ago. My second Irish journey really began here in New York City, and at least three of those who took me on it are here tonight, and I'd like to thank them for what they did: my law-school friend and long-time friend former Congressman Bruce Morrison, Congressman Tom Manton, and Paul O'Dwyer.

Bertie Ahern also remembers President Clinton speaking to him about the importance of Irish-American members of the grassroots political machine in Arkansas. 'He would name you people that were involved, his place wasn't the most Irish of places, but still, there would be Irish people there and Irish people active and people who would have been supportive and helpful.' Key members of the Clinton team were also going back and forth to Ireland before his election. 'Nancy Soderberg understood Ireland, she'd been up to Donegal and Derry; the first time I met her was up in Donegal with John Hume way back thirty years ago,' remembered Mr Ahern. Clinton's understanding 'came from individuals, it came from Tony Lake, it came from Nancy Soderberg, and they were the people keeping him briefed on it and interested in it and then of course he had great friends on the Hill, Richie Neal and [Jim] Walsh and guys that were big backers of his'.

Back in Ireland, in the run-up to Clinton's election, Sinn Féin leader Gerry Adams was looking towards the global anti-apartheid movement for inspiration in garnering backing from the international community – namely America in Ireland's case – to help end the sectarian conflict which had paralysed Northern Ireland in a bloody cycle of death and destruction. Gerry Adams told the Miller Center's oral history project:

> As part of Sinn Féin's peace strategy, and as part of trying to reshape the republican struggle to a certain extent and to grow a Sinn Féin organisation – the dominant organisation in republicanism had been the IRA – a group of other activists and I wanted to develop a popular political party. Sinn Féin existed, of course, but it was mainly a protest movement, which was a very good thing for it to be, but we wanted to develop it into something else.
>
> We had embraced electoralism, particularly following the hunger strikes of 1981. So, as part of looking at everything that we needed to do to get better at what we were trying to do – which was to end British rule in our country – we looked at other struggles, and clearly, every other struggle had an international dimension to it. We were very influenced by South Africa, which was the big anti-apartheid movement. I was a member of it, it was global, and it influenced us. The strong place that we had in the world was Irish America. We also had a number of organisations there, and other groups of people who were active on Irish issues, justice issues, calling for an end to British rule and so on.

Although President Carter was the first president to lay down a marker of US interest in the North, and President Reagan had helped coax a reluctant Margaret Thatcher into signing the Anglo-Irish Agreement, American administrations had been traditionally reluctant to disgruntle one of their closest allies on Northern Ireland. Bertie Ahern noted Ireland repeatedly failed to get support for outside help with the North. As he said, 'If you go back to when the Troubles started, if you go back to 1969 and 1970, when President Paddy Hillery went over to try and win support in the States for UN involvement, we got nowhere because the British lobbied extensively and they won the day saying this was an internal matter. We were totally pushed out.' He didn't feel the Reagan era was much more fruitful. 'While Reagan might have been helpful in some ways, the Thatcher–Reagan thing prevented us from making progress.'

In early April 1992, this was all about to change during a late-night meeting with fifty or so Irish-American leaders and the two leading contenders for the Democratic Party presidential primary in New York, Governor Bill Clinton and Governor Jerry Brown. Sitting, arms folded, at a desk at the top of a brightly lit function room in the Sheraton Hotel in midtown Manhattan, the young Arkansas governor caused a sensation with his clearly thought out, very precise answers to a whole raft of probing questions at the Irish American Presidential Forum. Boston mayor Raymond Flynn outlined his deep concern about the situation in Northern Ireland after a recent trip to the province, and the concerns of the forty-three million Americans of Irish ethnic origin which he referred to as 'perhaps one of the largest constituencies a president will have in the United States'. Standing up, he put a loaded question to Clinton:

> What we're looking at here is a situation in Northern Ireland that has been allowed to go on for such a long period of time, Governor Clinton, and we feel betrayed by the United States policy that has really not dealt with the issue of bringing all parties together and

dealing with the issues of justice, discrimination, unity, peace. Would you, as President of the United States, appoint a special peace envoy to bring all sides of the conflict to the table so we finally see the kind of end to the violence and the unity and end of the discrimination that the Catholic population suffer greatly in Northern Ireland?

The governor answered: 'The short answer to your question is *yes.*' In those eight words, he U-turned centuries of US policy on Ireland.

A few minutes later, Clinton would go a step further. From the floor, Martin Galvin, from New York's *Irish People* newspaper, directed this question to the governor:

Sinn Féin, the oldest political party and the political party which is opposed to British rule, which would be most vigorous in seeking Irish reunification, has their prominent members denied the opportunity to come to the United States to do what you are doing now, taking questions and stating your polices and defending your views; this has been extended most specifically to Gerry Adams, the president of Sinn Féin and an elected member of the British parliament. My question is: if you were elected president would you direct the State Department to allow a visa to Gerry Adams and other prominent members of Sinn Féin to allow them to come to the United States and state their views and defend them before the American people?

Governor Clinton didn't hesitate as he answered:

I would support a visa for Gerry Adams, and I would support a visa for any other properly elected official, who was part of a government recognised by the United States of America. I think that I understand the United States' historic position with regard to Sinn Féin and the advocacy of violence as opposed to non-violence, but I think that Adams is an elected member of the British parliament, and as government we recognise that that government recognises his legitimacy and right to serve. I think it would be totally harmless to our national security interest and it might be enlightening to the political debate in this country about the issues in Ireland.'

At the end of the meeting, Clinton emphasised to the assembled mayors and Irish-American leaders the importance of getting those forty-three million members of the diaspora to vote. 'I hope you will do what you can in November to ensure the highest possible voter turnout among Irish Americans, old-fashioned emigrants who share the values of family and work and the idea of progress,' he said before he went around the room shaking hands with those gathered there. At the Empire State Building, two nights later, Governor Clinton defeated Governor Brown in the New York primary, which was considered a must-win for Clinton after his campaign was rattled by his loss to Brown in the Connecticut primary a few weeks earlier. In the election that November, he went on to beat the incumbent President George W. Bush, ensuring the Republican was only a one-term president.

Envoy, Kennedy ambassador and desk officer in path to peace

In the inaugural year of his first term, President Clinton fielded questions about the promised special envoy and visa for Gerry Adams at press conference after press conference. Just over two months after his inauguration, at the St Patrick's Day ceremony with Taoiseach Albert Reynolds, he spoke of 'the continuing tragic conflict in Northern Ireland that has cost three thousand lives over the last two decades'. He added: 'The United States stands ready to do whatever we can to help in bringing peace to Northern Ireland.'

The presidency of John F. Kennedy also loomed large over Clinton when it came to the Irish question. It's a connection that began, famously, when a sixteen-year-old Bill Clinton shook hands with JFK in the Rose Garden during his attendance there as one of two Arkansans picked for Boys Nation, a summer vacation civics programme for outstanding high-schoolers. As JFK moves on to the next boy, a second even more interesting photo captures the artless moment in which Clinton looks down at his hand in wonder. 'That's just an electric moment,' notes US presidential authority Professor Russell Riley in reference to the handshake, 'and I think that for Clinton himself anything that he could do to emphasise his similarity to the Kennedys was a benefit.' Indeed, at his first St Patrick's Day in the White House, one of his first acts was to nominate JFK's sister, Jean Kennedy Smith, as ambassador to Ireland, noting she was 'as Irish as Americans can be'.

Sean Reidy, the CEO of the JFK Trust who forged a close bond with American's fabled political dynasty towards the end of the twentieth century, believes Ted Kennedy was the 'main architect of the peace process'. He said:

> He was the man behind the scenes pulling all the strings because Clinton depended on him. I got to know his foreign affairs secretary at the time, Trina Vargo, and I remember having lunch with her around the time of the Gerry Adams visa and she asked, 'What do you think? . . . What do people in Ireland think about Gerry Adams?' They agonised over it, and that was the key. Ted [Kennedy] pushing for Gerry Adams to get the visa was the key.

In the north of Ireland, another of the principal architects of the peace process, John Hume, leader of the Social Democratic and Labour Party, had been having back-channel talks with Gerry Adams when Clinton was sworn into office. 'Now bring in Father

Alec Reid. He is the thread that binds all of this together because he had been tick-tacking between me and John Hume. He'd been talking to anybody on the British side he could talk to,' Gerry Adams recalled in his oral history interview to the Miller Center in the University of Virginia in 2019.

> He was talking to the Irish government. He was talking to me and listening to all of us. He presented himself to Jean Kennedy Smith, and the two of them hit it off and developed a really close relationship. The sagart, as we called him – it's the word for priest – the sagart, Father Alec, nicknamed, or code-named, Jean Kennedy Smith a *spiorbhean*, which is the Irish word for 'spirit woman'. She was wonderful; she was down-to-earth, very straight, and very prepared to push out the boundaries. She knew John Hume through her brother Teddy. They clearly didn't know me, but they wanted to endorse the work that John was doing, and I presume if I was good enough for John, I was good enough for them.

In December 1993, Albert Reynolds and John Major made the Joint Declaration – or the Downing Street Declaration – which was laid out as a framework for peace in Northern Ireland to be facilitated by the two governments. A month later, President Bill Clinton – much to the anger of the British government – kept that New York election promise by granting Gerry Adams a visa to briefly attend the National Committee on American Foreign Policy in New York City. 'Obviously, that caused a great deal of disturbance in Westminster,' recalled Dick Spring. 'It was difficult, but it was the right thing to do. It had to be done, you had to have him inside the tent, otherwise an agreement would have been worthless. Gerry Adams had to go to America. They had to be convinced that there was a deal to be done and the war was over.'

But by February 1994, the rift between the US and the UK was smoothed over, at least on the surface, as President Clinton welcomed Prime Minister Major to America at the Air Force Reserve base at Pittsburgh International Airport. Northern Ireland was once again at the top of the agenda. Clinton said:

> We're going to discuss the political courage and the vision shown by Prime Minister Major and Prime Minister Reynolds of Ireland in working toward peace in Northern Ireland together. Their historic joint declaration offers new hope for that goal of peace. And as the president of this country, a country full of Americans of British descent and full of Americans of Irish descent, I again urge an end to the use of violence as a means of solving political problems and achieving political aims. It has no place in that effort.

Later that year, in August 1994, he heralded the 'watershed announcement by the IRA that it has decided to end the 25-year campaign of violence and pursue the path of peace'. Then, on 13 October, he welcomed the announcement by the Combined Loyalist Military Command in Northern Ireland that declared an end to its campaign of violence. The twin statements, he said, 'present the best hope for peace in a generation in Northern Ireland'.

The following year, the president kept the second late-night election promise he made in that New York hotel in 1992. He appointed former senator George Mitchell of Maine as a special envoy to help navigate the painstaking path to peace. 'There was an awful lot of toing and froing on that. The British detested the idea,' remembers former Irish ambassador to the US, Seán O'Huiginn. Still, Bertie Ahern believes this appointment was pivotal to Ireland finally making progress in solving the conflict. He explains, 'George Mitchell was put there by the American president and with Ambassador Jean

Kennedy put in, that was very much the Americans putting a big stamp on it, without the British having any kind of a veto on it.'

The intellectual brilliance which had carried Bill Clinton to Oxford and Yale, coupled with his attention to detail, astounded Irish politicians during this time. 'I remember one White House aide saying to me, on Ireland, the president has his own desk officer,' observed Mr O'Huiginn. 'It was perfectly true; everybody who met him came out awed. President McAleese, when she visited him in the White House – and she would be perhaps a severe enough critic in that sense – was simply gobsmacked by the amount of local knowledge he had of the Irish situation.' Clinton's open-door policy and the sheer number of hours devoted to the conflict in one tiny corner of the world were striking. His 'involvement was highly operational', recalled the Irish diplomat.

> It was at the level of being available to a quite extraordinary degree. Given that he was president of the United States, [it was] being available to the protagonists of the Irish peace process. I was joking at one stage that there wasn't a county councillor in Tyrone that didn't expect to be received by the president if he sashayed up to the White House. Irish people tend to lose perspective of the scale of the American operation and its ramifications, but Clinton was extraordinarily generous in that sense.

Bertie Ahern remembers fellow Europeans showing open amazement at Irish access to the Oval Office. 'Nearly all the European leaders would say, during the Clinton period and Bush period, which was my two periods, they would say, "Jesus, you've had the American president in Ireland four times, he's been in Europe twice and he hasn't been in our country at all.' I did ten Paddy's Days, and I did fourteen Oval Office meetings in my time. When we were in the early years of the Good Friday Agreement, not only did you have a meeting with the president and vice president, but you probably got six or seven of the secretaries of state coming to the Oval Office as well. It was phenomenal.'

By 1995, Clinton made history by becoming the first US president in office to visit Northern Ireland. After touching down in Belfast on Air Force One, he went on two informal walkabouts on streets synonymous with the worst sectarian violence of the Troubles. Mindful of a cable from the American Consulate in Belfast to the Secretary of State on unionist concerns that President Clinton's visit would have a nationalist slant, he first stopped off at the Shankill Road, which had been the scene of numerous terrorist attacks by the Provisional IRA. On the mostly Protestant street, locals gave the first couple a warm welcome to Belfast with the highlight being a stop at Violet's Fruit Shop. Then he travelled to the mostly Catholic Falls Road, a place which had been repeatedly on news bulletins over the decades as the scene of violence. Upon exiting his limousine, Clinton paused to shake hands with Gerry Adams in what was a controversial photo opportunity.

Earlier that day President Clinton had been deeply moved when two children told of their hopes for peace. Ten-year-old David Sterrett, a Protestant, explained from the podium at Mackie metal plant that he lived in a mixed area of Protestants and Catholics. He read: 'I want to thank you for coming to Northern Ireland to help with the peace process. I think peace is great because there is no shooting or bombing. It means I can play in the park without worrying about getting shot.' Then nine-year-old Catherine read: 'My first daddy died in the Troubles. It was the saddest day of my life ... My Christmas wish is that peace and love will last in Ireland forever.'

In the preceding months, White House speechwriter Carter Wilkie had sent a memo suggesting Clinton would be treated to a hero's welcome in John Hume's hometown. He was not wrong. Although it presented numerous logistical difficulties, President Clinton insisted on paying his respects to John Hume in Derry's symbolic Guildhall Square. Since Derry lacked an airfield suitable for Air Force One, the President and the First Lady took a cold and turbulent hour-long flight aboard a US Marines Blackhawk helicopter to the city. The glamorous commander-in-chief was at the height of his powers, in the ascendency of his presidency, when he walked out to a sea of waving stars and stripes. At the end of his speech in the late winter afternoon of 30 November, he recited the often-repeated phrase from the town's Nobel prize-winning poet, Seamus Heaney, of when 'hope and history rhyme'. To cheers from the crowd, he said:

> Well, my friends, I believe. I believe we live in a time of hope and history rhyming. Standing here in front of the Guildhall, looking out over these historic walls, I see a peaceful city, a safe city, a hopeful city, full of young people that should have a peaceful and prosperous future here where their roots and families are. Have the patience to work for a just and lasting peace. Reach for it. The United States will reach with you. The further shore of that peace is within your reach.

That evening, thousands of ecstatic supporters gathered to watch a black-Crombie-wearing William Jefferson Clinton switch on the Christmas lights in Belfast's City Hall. It was an electric moment of hope and goodwill for a city torn apart by bombs and bullets in the preceding decades. The crowds chanted 'Bill, Bill' – which sounded more like 'Bull, Bull' in their Belfast accents. The city, used to being flashed regularly across international news bulletins amid grim scenes of devastation, was now beaming a powerful statement of light and hope as its citizens basked in the reflected spotlight of the world's most powerful leader. With his parting words – 'Blessed are the peacemakers' – President Clinton encouraged the citizens of Belfast to keep up their efforts. The following day in Dublin he stopped off in a smoke-filled Cassidy's pub to mingle with well-wishers before he gave his memorable address to a crowd of an estimated hundred thousand people in Dublin's College Green. It was a carnival-style forty-eight hours, crammed full of engagements on both sides of the border.

In the wake of the euphoric '95 visit, Dick Spring remembers receiving the shocking news that the IRA had ended their ceasefire by detonating a bomb on London's docklands in February 1996:

> I was in Washington. I had a particularly good meeting with Clinton, where he was, I think, confirming that they would be very involved in any peace process talks we got going, which would have been a first. We were on our way back across the Atlantic when we got a phone call to tell us that a bomb had gone off in Canary Wharf. So, after all the good work, we felt we were looking at the starting line and all of a sudden back into the bunker. Now in 2021, it's sometimes actually difficult to comprehend how difficult the circumstances were back in the 80s and the 90s.

Hanging on the telephone: president's persistent push for peace and the right thing to do

Declassified documents over the following three years show the US president displaying a relentless resolve to push the peace process over the line. Northern Ireland cropped up in almost every conversation he had with Tony Blair and Bertie Ahern. Dick Spring said he simply made himself available to Irish politicians:

> Once he started getting involved in the Northern Ireland peace process, he was very determined that this was going to be one of the things that he was going to leave as a legacy. All through his

presidency, the two terms, he went way beyond what one would have expected. Clinton obviously took on the British government, took risks in relation on Northern Ireland, took risks with the state department in terms of policy.

But Dick Spring believes it could not have been done without Clinton persuading his friend, Senator George Mitchell, to act as a mediator to help steer the parties to the Good Friday Agreement.

He must have been involved for three or four years, at huge personal sacrifice, but he was just one of those exceptional people. I'm not sure I can think of another President of America, who would have been as involved as Clinton. We were just very fortunate that the combination of Clinton and Mitchell and, effectively, Sinn Féin and the Provisional IRA realising that they weren't going to win this one with bullets and the British government likewise looking for a settlement. So, you put all that chemistry together and it's time to move on.

The alchemy of personality, timing, backchannels and ceasefires all steamrollered into ensuring hope and history did rhyme in those words of Seamus Heaney. On 10 April 1998, the historic Good Friday Agreement, also known as the Belfast Agreement, was signed. The accord established rules for power-sharing between the Protestant and Catholic communities in the governing of Northern Ireland as well as establishing mechanisms for conflict resolution involving both British and Irish governments. The Good Friday Agreement is generally regarded as marking the end of the Troubles. On 22 May, the day the Republic of Ireland and Northern Ireland voted to pass the Good Friday Agreement, President Clinton made a round of congratulatory calls from Camp David to Bertie Ahern, David Trimble, Gerry Adams and John Hume.

After the euphoria of the summer when the majority of Republican paramilitary had laid down their weapons, the fragile peace process was rocked with the Omagh car bombing, which killed twenty-nine people in a busy shopping area on 15 August 1998. The Real IRA, a splinter group of Republican paramilitaries, claimed responsibility. Just over two weeks later, the US President and the First Lady returned to Ireland for their second visit. During a walkabout with Tony and Cherie Blair, the Clintons placed flowers at the Market Street site in the town where so many innocent civilians had lost their lives, before meeting some of the victims in person. In Armagh later that day, he made a spine-tingling speech at a stage emblazoned with the words *A Gathering For Peace*. Clinton said:

> The bomb that tore at the heart of Omagh was a blatant attack on all of Northern Ireland's people who support peace. The prime minister and Mrs Blair and Hillary and I just came from Omagh; we met with the families whose innocents were slaughtered. We met with those who were terribly wounded. We saw children scarred, some of them for life. Because of the madness. That if someone could just set off a big enough bomb and kill enough Protestants and Catholics, kill enough men, women and children, including two pregnant women, kill enough people from Northern Ireland, Ireland and foreign countries. That maybe everybody would walk away from peace, but it backfired. Out of the unimaginably horrible agony of Omagh, the people said it is high time somebody told these people that we are through with hate, through with war, through with destruction, it will not work anymore.

Before Clinton left the podium to cheers and applause, he said he had come in person to thank the people of Northern Ireland for choosing peace:

When I go now to other troubled places, I point to you as proof that peace is not an idle daydream for your peace is real and it resonates around the world. It echoes in the ears of people hungry for the end of strife in their own country. Now when I meet Palestinians and Israelis I can say, 'Don't tell me it's impossible. Look at Northern Ireland.' When I met Albanians and Serbs in Kosovo, I can say, 'Don't tell me it's impossible. Look at Northern Ireland.' When I hear what the Indians and Pakistanis say about each other over their religious differences I say, 'Don't tell me you can't work this out. Look at Northern Ireland.' Thank you for the springtime of hope you have given the world. Remember you will be tested again and again, but a God of grace has given you a new beginning.

The following year, Clinton's administration papers reveal him making a slew of phone calls from the Oval Office, Camp David and even Air Force One to David Trimble, Gerry Adams, John Hume, Bertie Ahern and Tony Blair to help them implement the Good Friday Agreement. From the easy, casual tone of the conversations, it's clear the US president is deeply familiar with all the men. He asks David Trimble if he is about to undertake an all-nighter, while he tells Gerry Adams that his daughter, Chelsea, has written a term paper on him in Stanford College. In the call he good-humouredly tells Adams: 'She called me, and I sent her some stuff, and they gave her a little grief. The professor said while her father is certainly authoritative, he is not really an academic source; you need to be a little more balanced. So, I drummed up some articles, finding one mildly critical of you; it was really fun.' The call is made on 30 June 1999, and he's trying to broker a solution on the decommissioning of arms which is still a thorny issue in the aftermath of the Agreement. Clinton signs off by telling Gerry Adams: 'If you need me, wake me up.'

In another call to under-pressure Unionist Party leader David

Trimble on 2 July 1999, he opens the call with: 'How are you keeping? Are you still standing?' He goes on to say: 'Look, I wanted first to thank you and second to say I tried to issue a helpful statement. Thirdly to ask what can I do to help?' Trimble, who won the Noble Peace Prize with the SDLP's John Hume in 1998 for the pragmatism he showed in taking risks in negotiating peace, would eventually take another gamble in November 1999 in going into government with Sinn Féin on the understanding that the decommissioning of IRA weapons would follow. From the phone calls, President Clinton's great empathy with the Unionist Party leader, who had the most to lose from the high-wire political negotiations, is evident.

On the last St Patrick's Day at the Clinton White House in 2000, nostalgia and sentimentality flowed among the politicians and poets. Seamus Heaney recited his Nobel Prize-winning words while Nobel Prize winner John Hume broke into a verse of 'Danny Boy' in front of a delighted Hillary and Bill Clinton, who were looking down at the assembled Irish guests like indulgent parents with their arms around each other. During his speech, Bertie Ahern joked that most of the guests never dreamed they would get to the White House, never mind 'having the run of the place'. But, on a serious note, he thanked President Clinton for devoting hours and days and months of paperwork and middle-of-the-night phone calls and meetings to one small country out in the middle of the Atlantic with 'five million souls' when there were so many other conflicts around the planet.

On 12 December 2000, during his final visit to Ireland as president, Clinton ruminated on how his interlaced Irish roots were perhaps some kind of a DNA marker for peace-making:

> When I started to come here, I got a lot of help in rooting out my Irish ancestry. And the oldest known homestead of my mother's family, the Cassidys, that we've been able to find is a mid-eighteenth-century

farmhouse that's in Rosslea, Fermanagh. But it's right on the – literally right on the border. And in my family, all the Catholics and Protestants intermarried, so maybe I was somehow genetically prepared for the work I had to do. Maybe it's because there are forty-five million Irish Americans, and I was trying to make a few votes at home. The truth is, it just seemed to me the right thing to do.

The return – Ballybunion proved to be more than just a photo call

In the end, Ireland – and Ballybunion – also proved to be much more than a photo opportunity for the diaspora back home in America. The course would be namechecked by President Clinton as his favourite in the world in the fiftieth anniversary issue of *Golf*. The politician, who started playing at the age of twelve, said of the course, 'I love it. It's perfectly Irish: beautiful, rough, and a lot like life – you get breaks you don't deserve, both ways. You just have to keep swinging and know it will all even out.'

In 2001, a year after he was out of office, Clinton arrived back to Ballybunion. Brian McCarthy remembered him walking straight over in the clubhouse and addressing him by name. 'He asked how I was and asked how my daughter was,' he said. This time Clinton did thirty-six holes. After playing eighteen holes of the old course, he turned to Dick Spring after lunch saying, 'I understand you got a new course right here. Should we have a look at it?'

'Let's play the back nine,' suggested Dick Spring hopefully, mindful of his own long-standing back injury. 'Coming up to the 18th, one of the Secret Service guys says to me, "Boss, what's happening now. Are you finishing?" I said to President Clinton, "Some guys are getting restless around here, are we going in?" He replies, "You guys want to go drink beer that's fine with me. I'm going to play the front nine." So of course, we all played the front nine!' laughed Mr Spring.

At the end of the marathon thirty-six holes, he turned to the former Tánaiste saying, 'We gotta go down and see the statue. Some of my guys don't believe there's a statue of me in this town.' At the statue, a few hundred local people who had gotten wind of the visit had gathered in the hope that the ex-president would view the bronze sculpture of himself taking a golf swing. The request did not surprise the former Tánaiste. 'You see,' he explains, 'Clinton is so happy with people. He just lights up. There is no way he would have wanted to have left Ballybunion without meeting people.' But even the seasoned Kerry politician was struck by the Clinton effect. 'I was absolutely astounded watching this one particular woman, she had to embrace Bill Clinton. The parish priest had to shake hands with him. He came over the fence [saying], "Dick Spring, introduce me to this man . . ."'

And finally, at the statue in 2001, Clinton got to meet Frank Quilter, who arrived with Jackie Hourigan at the town square after a hasty phone call from Dick Spring. 'Dick said, "Jackie, are you at home? The president wanted to see the statue." I said I'd be up, I'm only sixty yards away. Frank had never met the president in person, so I rang Frank, and he came up.'

When Clinton arrived at the sculpture he said, 'I didn't realise it was as big as that!' before noting that there was a 'lot of storms in Ballybunion'. Jackie assured him, 'You needn't worry, there's iron gone down into the feet under the cement.' He also drew a smile when he told him the youngsters in the town had taken to sitting up on the statue while they waited for the school bus. 'So, I'm being introduced to the young people as well?' said Clinton. 'You are,' confirmed the publican solemnly.

The statue improved business in the town as it brought visitors into the square, but not all Americans were thrilled to see the Democratic president staring down at them. 'You know, the Republicans, they hated Clinton,' said Jackie, 'they'd say the wrong person is up on the statue.' But over the years in his restaurant, he noticed how the Democratic Clinton was not always so unpopular with the spouses of the Republican golfers. 'The meal would be ready upstairs and I'd often walk up with the women and the men would be finishing their drinks, and several of the women would just tip me and they'd say, "Jackie, we voted for President Clinton, but we didn't tell our husbands." Honest to God that happened several times.'

The Clinton visit certainly ended up bringing tourists and golfers into the town. 'There's no doubt about it, we got worldwide publicity. And we put it in the town so people would come and see the town and it worked, everyone who comes gets a photo with the statue!' said Jackie.

When a new Democratic president was elected to the White House just before Christmas 2020, the town decided to decorate their Clinton statue with pictures of Joe Biden and Kamala Harris to celebrate. When Jackie Hourigan and his neighbour Joan O'Connor, who runs Kilcooly Country House in Ballybunion, took a photo and turned it into a Christmas card, one was dispatched to Bill Clinton, who sent a touching letter, complete with the presidential seal, in the post to the pair the following January. He wrote:

Dear Jackie and Joan, Thank you very much for the terrific Christmas card. I *love* it and your thoughtfulness means more than you know. I cherish the memories of my visit to Ballybunion and remain grateful for your support, kindness and hospitality. I hope you and your loved ones are staying healthy and safe during these challenging times and I'm sending my very best wishes for the years ahead. Sincerely Bill.

Ceremonial laughter in the White House for St Patrick's Day 2007.

CHAPTER FIVE

THE BUSH PRESIDENTS

---

*I'm witnessing such an occasion with the arrival of
Reverend Paisley and Mr Martin McGuinness here to the
White House. These two men have dedicated themselves to
bettering Northern Ireland through their courage and conviction
and desire to put aside the past and focus on a hopeful future.*

Y O BONO!' OPENED PRESIDENT GEORGE W. BUSH in his handwritten letter to the Irish rock star. Dated 1 June 2007, the Texan
president's informal note on White House paper in scrawling black
pen tells the singer: 'I'm proud to be in the trenches of justice with
you.' The text, indicating the familiarity of the pair, went on to compliment Bono's editorship of *Vanity Fair* that summer before ending
with a PS: 'All the Bush chicks send their best', in reference to his twin
daughters, Jenna and Barbara, who were big fans.

The alliance of the U2 frontman and the Republican president
over their work with AIDS in the first decade of the twenty-first
century was an improbable political partnership. Bono had become
the darling of left-wing politicians in America in the 1990s and
during the Clinton administration had enjoyed a bromance with the
saxophone-playing Southern president. In stark contrast, George W.
Bush was far from popular with the Democrat-leaning music world,

with Tom Petty famously asking him to stop playing his hit song 'I Won't Back Down' during his campaign prior to his highly contentious win over former vice president Al Gore in November 2000. Gore won the popular vote by 543,895 votes, but the presidency hinged on Florida's electoral votes with recounts, disputed ballots and lawsuits going all the way to the Supreme Court. In the end, by just a few hundred votes, Bush took the state of Florida and with it the presidency.

Following the huge success of the band's Grammy-winning album *All That You Can't Leave Behind*, their diametrically opposed politics didn't dissuade Bono from rolling up to the White House in 2002. By this time, in the wake of the terrorist attacks on the World Trade Center on 11 September 2001 that killed nearly three thousand Americans, Bush had become a wartime president. Still, Bush's mission statement was one of 'compassionate conservatism', and that did tie in with the Irishman's agenda.

Driving around Washington with the Texan president in a motorcade, the Dublin singer would later recall how he had not expected the new White House incumbent to make him belly laugh with a quip about crowds waving to him with one finger when he first got to Washington. Good humour aside, the singer had a deadly serious mission: to get the president on board with the worldwide fight against HIV/AIDS, which was then engulfing Africa.

At the Inter-American Development Bank in Washington in 2002, the US president stood at a podium flanked by the rock star, who was wearing his requisite dark glasses. The Republican leader laid out his proposal for a $5 billion plan to help the world's poorest people in the developing world. Referring to the incongruous presence behind him, he said, 'As you can see, I'm travelling in some pretty good company today: Bono,' he quipped to laughter and applause. 'We just had a great visit in the Oval Office. Here's what I know about him:

first, he's a good musician; secondly, he is willing to use his position in a responsible way. He is willing to lead to achieve what his heart tells him, and that is that nobody – nobody – should be living in poverty and hopelessness in the world.'

Turning to the singer he added, 'Bono, I appreciate your heart. To tell you what an influence you've had, Dick Cheney walked in the Oval Office and said, "Jesse Helms wants us to listen to Bono's ideas."' President Bush's reference to the deeply conservative Republican senator, known as a beacon of right-wing politics, drew even more laughter.

At the start of 2003, President Bush surprised his detractors by launching the President's Emergency Plan for AIDS Relief or what became known as PEPFAR, a five-year, $15 billion initiative to combat AIDS in a hundred and twenty countries around the world, an initiative which would go on to avert a huge number of deaths.

The growing closeness of Bono's relationship with the US president can be seen in a letter written from his ocean-facing Temple Hill home in the Dublin village of Killiney on 29 December 2004.

'December is cold, but days are bright here in Dublin this Christmas,' he begins before getting straight on to political matters. 'In Ireland they say, "Peace comes dropping slow..." Your phone calls to Paisley and Adams are greatly appreciated.' The singer had famously held up the hands of Nobel Peace Prize winners, the Catholic leader of the moderate Social Democratic and Labour Party, John Hume, and the Protestant leader of the Ulster Unionist Party, David Trimble, on a Belfast stage as he urged thousands of Belfast teenagers to vote 'Yes' for the Good Friday Agreement and bring an end to decades of bloodshed.

He goes on to compliment the president on his PEPFAR plan, calling it a 'historic AIDS initiative'. In free-wheeling prose, he compares it to the Marshall Plan rolled out by President Harry

Truman in 1948 to help Europe rebuild after the devastation of the Second World War. And, in typical pulpit-bashing vein, the activist frontman urged the president: 'Next year is critical, your leadership is vital. Somebody needs to bang the table and say this doesn't have to be so ... History belongs to people who refuse to accept norms.' He implored Bush to continue with his spending in Africa: 'It is God's work.' He ended the letter with: 'Thank you for taking the time with me ... I know you don't have to,' before writing out a note saying, 'Special hello to your girls Barbara and Jenna.'

Ten days earlier, George W. Bush had been named *Time*'s Person of the Year for what they termed his ten-gallon-hat leadership style, which had won him a second term in the White House. America had rocket-launched its controversial 'shock and awe' war on Iraq on 19 March 2003, a move which had seen the president's popularity see-saw during his first term, but at the end of 2004, he was preparing to be sworn in for his second after winning the election against Senator John Kerry.

Six days before the war on Iraq stunned the world, the US president took a day out of his military preparations to welcome Irish leaders to the White House, accepting the obligatory bowl of shamrocks. 'This annual gift symbolises the deep and enduring friendship between our two countries,' he told Irish Taoiseach Bertie Ahern.

The president obviously had covert operations on his mind as he referenced how an Irish-American woman named Lydia Darragh had provided valuable intelligence to George Washington's troops during the Revolutionary War, which had helped to prevent a planned British offensive. He added: 'We've stood together in Afghanistan, in Kosovo, in Bosnia and beyond, to stop aggression and to alleviate suffering. Ireland is a valued member of the coalition against global terror.' He also referenced the American people's appreciation of Ireland's work on the UN Security Council to help secure passage of Resolution 1441.

That resolution demanded that Iraq disarm itself of all weapons of mass destruction. We appreciate our own support for ensuring that the just demands of the world are enforced. The responsibilities of freedom are not always easy to bear, but Ireland and America are joined by a common commitment to freedom's defence against tyranny and terror.

Bush then moved on to their joints efforts to achieve a lasting peace in Northern Ireland.

Recent years have seen historic progress thanks to the tireless efforts of Prime Ministers Ahern and Blair and many other people who long for peace. Now, all parties can, and must, build on this progress, so that the people of Northern Ireland can replace old resentments with new cooperation and new hope. America has long supported this vital work, and today that support endures and continues. We will help where we can.

In December 1998, after people across Ireland voted in favour of the Good Friday Agreement, the Northern Ireland Assembly was formed to give Northern Ireland self-government led by First Minister David Trimble, but after much in-fighting it was suspended in 2002 and its powers reverted to the UK government.

The Dublin Taoiseach had been to the Oval Office twice in 2001, once for the patron saint's day celebration and another private visit on 8 November of that year, while the country was still reeling from the 11 September attacks. The former Irish leader remembers giving his American counterpart a 'Who's Who' of European leaders during their first meeting:

> President Bush had hardly ever been out of America and the first year I met him on Paddy's Day, he spent over an hour with me. He was coming to Europe a few months later, and it was 'Who's this guy? Who's this guy? What makes him tick?'

In fact, Ahern had ten private meetings at the White House with President Bush over the eight years they were both in power, with two two-day trips scheduled in the US president's diary in 2007 when the Northern Ireland Assembly finally got up and running after a five-year impasse under the joint leadership of Ian Paisley and Martin McGuinness. Mr Ahern remarked:

> Often, they would say about Bush, 'Ah he wasn't interested.' I always found him very engaging, I got on really well with him even though Clinton was my buddy and still is. I found Bush a very interesting guy and interested in Ireland, he knew about Ireland. He was here a number of times. He was up north with Tony [Blair] and myself, and during the EU presidency he came to Clare and stayed in Dromoland Castle. So, we had a lot of engagement with him.

Ireland's cool welcome for wartime president

In stark contrast to his predecessor's rapt reception, when Air Force One touched down in Shannon Airport with President George W. Bush on board, he was met with open hostility from an Irish public who tended to greet US presidents like returning sons. The summer downpour which met him as he walked around the grounds of Dromoland Castle, where President Kennedy's ancestors once worked as servants, was in tune with the squally mood of the protestors marching down the road out of Shannon Airport that day. The sixteenth-century Clare estate was heavily guarded at all entrances for his whistle-stop visit in one of the biggest security operations ever seen in Ireland.

Anti-war protestors at the American occupation of Iraq made their presence known as picketers thronged the main road to the airport as the presidential plane landed. In Dublin, ten thousand marched while thousands more gathered for protests in Galway, Sligo, Waterford and Kerry. Their anger had been inflamed by the recent publication of photos from Abu Ghraib prison in the war-torn country showing Iraqi detainees stripped naked and humiliated by American soldiers, some wielding snarling dogs at terrified prisoners.

The unfriendly treatment to the incoming US president was in striking contrast to the arms-wide welcome afforded to Presidents Clinton, Reagan and Kennedy, with even President Nixon attracting plenty of stars-and-stripes-waving supporters on the streets amid the Vietnam War protests. Before leaving Washington, Mr Bush sat through an interview broadcast with Ireland's national television station, RTÉ, where he lost patience with the volley of no-holds-barred questions from reporter Carole Coleman, repeatedly raising his hand and telling her, 'Let me finish . . .'

The tense interview broadcast on RTÉ began with Mr Bush being asked how it felt to come to Ireland knowing that the majority of the public did not welcome his visit as they were angry over the Iraq War and graphic photographs showing mistreatment of captives by US soldiers in the notorious Abu Ghraib prison.

'I hope the Irish people understand the great values of our country, and if they think that a few soldiers represent the entirety of America, they don't really understand America,' Mr Bush replied, referring to the scandal. 'There have been great ties between Ireland and America, [we've] got a lot of Irish Americans here that are very proud of their heritage and their country . . . but, you know, they must not understand if they are angry over Abu Ghraib, if they say this is what America represents, they don't understand our country, because we don't represent that.'

He added in the interview with the national broadcaster:

> We are a compassionate country. We are a strong country, we'll defend ourselves, but we help people and we've helped the Irish and will continue to do so. We've got a good relationship with Ireland. People don't like war but what they should be angry about is the fact there was a brutal dictator there that had destroyed lives and put them in mass graves and had torture rooms.

At the European Union–United States summit, hosted by Ireland in Dromoland Castle thanks to their EU presidency at the time, the Taoiseach Bertie Ahern, stressed, at the time, the ties between Europe and the US. 'It's a relationship that generates twelve million jobs on both sides of the Atlantic,' he said. 'We discussed and have issued joint declarations on Iraq, as well as on counterterrorism, on non-proliferation, the fight against HIV and AIDS, Sudan, and partnerships with the Mediterranean and the Middle East. So the European Union and United States share, ladies and gentlemen, a common set of values based on the unshakeable commitment to democracy, to human rights and the rule of law.'

The US president, who would be in Ireland for less than twenty-four hours, appeared unruffled by the protests around his arrival. 'Taoiseach, we – Laura and I – thank you for your hospitality,' he said to the press pool. 'And we appreciate the people of this great country for welcoming us, as well. I want to thank the people who work at this beautiful resort for their warmth, and their great service.

It's a wonderful place. Not only is it beautiful, but the people who work here are really fine people.' He went on to talk about working with the EU in defeating the forces of terror.

At the end of his speech, Bertie Ahern asked: 'Mr President, do you want the first question?' He drew laughter when he answered, 'I have to?'

Most questions revolved around the ongoing conflict, but when asked whether he shared President Clinton's passion for peace in Northern Ireland, Bush gave an insight into his view on the peace process as a beacon of hope to other warring nations:

> I do view it as a model for resolution of conflict, whether it be in the Middle East or elsewhere. And we view this issue as a very important issue in my administration . . . I'm fully aware that the prime ministers of both Great Britain and Ireland are going to advance the process this early September. And we stand ready to help. I wish them all the best. Because when this conflict is resolved, it will be an example for others that long-simmering disputes can be put behind them and free societies, and peaceful societies, can emerge, for the interest of the peoples which have been involved in those disputes.

When put on the spot by Charlie Bird, one of the Irish reporters, over whether he had expressed the concerns of the Irish people over the Iraq conflict and the prison abuse, Bertie Ahern said he had raised the issues with Mr Bush.

> The answer is, I did, Charlie – and not on the first occasion. When I had the opportunity of meeting the president on St Patrick's Day, as he kindly does every year for us, we raised these issues. We discussed these issues at the G8 meeting. How prisoners have been dealt with in some of the – in one of the prisons, what has happened – from

Afghanistan to Guantanamo, that that's been an issue . . . The president is concerned about his own troops and some of the issues that happened as much – as much as I am, or anybody else in this country, and we've discussed that issue. And I think it is a great thing that – where we have such good relationships with the United States, where we have so much cooperation, where today we can clear eight declarations, but still, we are all interested in progress, we're all interested in human rights and the dignity of the person, that we can raise these issues. That is a good thing.

At the Irish press conference, Mr Bush confirmed that the Irish president, Mary McAleese, and Mr Ahern had raised the issues:

I told them both I was sick with what happened inside that prison . . . And so were the American citizens. The action of those troops did not reflect what we think. And it did harm, because there are people in Ireland and elsewhere that said, 'This isn't the America we know, this isn't the America that we believe exists.' And both leaders, of course, brought the issue up, and they should. And I assured them that we'll deal with this in a transparent way – which stands in stark contrast to how a tyrant would deal with it.

He gave a typically straight answer to another questioner who observed that he didn't 'appear to be a very popular fellow here in Europe':

I don't like it when the values of our country are – are misunderstood because of the actions of some people overseas. As far as my own personal standing goes, Hutch, my job is to do my job. I'm going to do it the way I think is necessary. I'm going to set a vision, I will lead, and we'll just let the chips fall where they may.

The playing of the Irish card

It is telling that President George W. Bush is one of the few US leaders of the twentieth or twenty-first centuries – with Irish ancestors in their family tree – who didn't claim the link. Certainly, when he visited Ireland twice during his two terms, there was no mention made of his genealogical tie to the country.

His nearest ancestor was a great-great-great-great-great-grandfather, on his mother's side of the family: an emigrant called William Holliday from Rathfriland in Co. Down. This number of 'greats' indicates, coincidentally, the same number of generations separating President Nixon from his ancestors in Co. Kildare. William Holliday was born in Ireland in 1755 but, following his move to America, died in Kentucky in 1811 or 1812.

Leading presidential genealogist Gary Boyd Roberts also uncovered blood links to the south of Ireland. Bush's great-great-great-great-great-great-great-great-grandfather William Shannon was born in Cork in 1730, before travelling across the Atlantic where he is recorded to have died in Mercersburg, Pennsylvania in 1784; he was also Dorothy Walker's ancestor, the mother and grandmother of the Bush presidents. Records also linked the Bush presidents to King Henry II in twelfth-century England and King Robert II of Scotland. Locally in Co. Wexford, the home of the Kennedy ancestors, the story has been told that the Texas presidents were related to notorious twelfth-century warlord, Richard de Clare, Earl of Pembroke, known in the eastern county as 'Strongbow' for his skills with a bow and arrow.

Bertie Ahern recalled that President Bush had 'some very far back relations', but acknowledged that unlike President Clinton, 'Bush didn't seem to have the same connection with the Irish people.' He added:

Texas probably wasn't our strong spot but himself and his wife got [into] St Patrick's Day. They did all the functions; he went to the speaker's lunch. He'd be at the meeting in the morning, he'd do the shamrock bit and then he'd do the detailed meeting. He used to do a meeting with me first before we did the formal press with the shamrock, which was really a thing for the press, and then he would come to the lunch and then the evening. So you know, he joined fully in it. The other thing was that they were good at inviting all the Irish on the Hill from both sides.

Irish ambassador to the US from 1997 to 2002 – which spanned the end of the Clinton administration and the start of President Bush's first term – Seán O'Huiginn, described Bush's pragmatic approach to Ireland's peace process:

> He was correct... as the Germans would say. He accepted it as a good thing, that American support should be available. He did all the right things The onus had passed back to the politicians in the island at that stage to make a go of it. There was lots of goodwill... But whether you have gone to him with the kind of heavy lifting that Clinton did, no, it's no reflection on him, that wasn't the kind of person he was, and that wasn't the kind of politics he did. In terms of political ability and charisma, Clinton had it in spades, Clinton was one of the youngest presidents elected in the States which also gave him a degree of a glamour. George Bush was correct in doing his duty. But horses for courses, he wasn't seen as a horse for gladhanding things in Derry.

While President Bush appeared unenthusiastic to play the Irish card, Ambassador O'Huiginn had an amusing encounter with Vice President Dick Cheney that centred around his apparent reluctance to claim Celtic ancestry. 'There was a rumour in Kerry that Dick Cheney had Kerry ancestors. There are a lot of idle moments in these White House events,' O'Huiginn remembered. 'I think we were waiting for five or six minutes at the threshold of the White House for the cars to come up. So, I mentioned this to him and asked him was there any truth to it. "No," he said, "English all sides from 1608!"' Ambassador O'Huiginn observed wryly.

Three years after President Bush's overnight trip to County Clare, the Northern Ireland Assembly was given back power and, in 2007, the British army officially ended its operations in Northern Ireland. A few weeks before Christmas that year, Bush hosted former sworn enemies First Minister of Northern Ireland Reverend Ian Paisley and Deputy First Minister Martin McGuinness at the White House. The bitter adversaries – one a Catholic former IRA commander and the other a pulpit-beating Protestant minister – would earn the nickname of the Chuckle Brothers owing to the forging of a confounding friendship which was pickled with the pair dissolving into fits of laughter to the bemusement of onlookers.

At their White House visit, which marked the end of one of the world's bloodiest sectarian conflicts, President Bush told the two men:

> One of the great experiences for me during my presidency is to witness historic occasions, and I'm witnessing such an occasion with the arrival of Reverend Paisley and Mr Martin McGuinness here to the White House. These two men have dedicated themselves to bettering Northern Ireland through their courage and conviction and desire to put aside the past and focus on a hopeful future... I'm looking forward to hearing about how the United States can help Northern Ireland move forward. I know one way we can help, and that is to encourage our business leaders to take a good look at the economic opportunities that Northern Ireland presents.

The first minister said in response: 'Well, Mr President . . . we want to say from the people of Northern Ireland: Thank you. Thank you to the American people for all they have done for us in the past. We did a lot for you in the past, too.'

'That's right,' answered President Bush to laughter.

Mr Paisley, a strident preacher, and once one of the most defiant voices of hard-line Protestant opposition to power-sharing with Catholic nationalists, added: 'We have had our political squabbles and fights. I think we have come to the end of that. I think that peace has come, there will be a fight for peace. You don't win peace; you have to fight to keep it.'

His deputy first minister added his thanks for the help they had received in the peace process from the Clinton and Bush administrations: 'We're hugely appreciative of both of you for all of the tremendous support that we have received. Up until 26 March this year, Ian Paisley and I never could accomplish anything about anything,' he said to laughter. 'And now we have worked very closely together over the course of the last seven months and there hasn't been an angry word between us.'

*

The following year, President Bush visited Stormont to double down on his support for the peace process. 'I'm excited to be here in Northern Ireland,' he said on the steps of Stormont Castle in 2008.

> The world is impressed by the progress being made toward peace and reconciliation. And that obviously takes a commitment by leadership . . . The interesting thing about the progress being made here is that it's attracted the attention of societies around the world that wonder whether reconciliation is possible for them. And Martin was

telling me about his talks with some of the Iraqi leaders ... sharing his stories about how folks can reconcile. Northern Ireland is a success story.

Martin McGuinness spoke of the key role America had played in the ending of the violence.

Beginning with the work of President Clinton, the contribution of Senator George Mitchell, the envoys that were sent by President Bush, such as Richard Haass and Mitchell Reiss and now Paula Dobriansky, all of whom have played a very important role in contributing to our process, which I do believe is, as the president has identified, a real model for how other conflicts can be resolved in other parts of the world.

The senior Bush, the MacGillycuddys of Ireland and the Walker Cup

The president's father, President George H.W. Bush, had a much more distant role in Irish affairs during his term in office. While his son was the target of anti-war protestors, it is generally acknowledged among Irish politicians and diplomats that he diligently took up the ball from Clinton when it came to the Northern Ireland peace process. Behind the scenes there were encouraging phone calls to leaders in the north of Ireland while he was magnanimous to the visiting parties from Ireland every year on 17 March.

His father only hosted Irish Taoiseach Charles Haughey once in the White House on St Patrick's Day 1989, two months after he was sworn into office. The Irish leader flew to America the following year at the end of February on a two-day working visit in his role as president of the European Council, but there were no Irish visits to Washington in 1991 or 1992.

When he met Mr Haughey in 1990, Bush Snr noted that 'nine

signers of the Declaration of Independence proudly claimed Ireland as their ancestral home'. Yale-educated President Bush – a decorated navy pilot in the Second World War – was deeply familiar with European issues as he had served as ambassador to the United Nations under the Nixon administration. The 41st president told Haughey of his concern over the Northern Ireland situation, one which his son would help to resolve, declaring: 'In a time when all things seem possible, all Americans hope for an end to the conflict that has brought such sadness to your beautiful land and your wonderful people.'

Later that year, he held up Ireland as an example of the success of immigration in a speech to a joint session of the congress in Montevideo, Uruguay, which he called a nation of immigrants like the United States:

> The history of our republics is told in the history of our families. One such family was the MacGillycuddys of Ireland, who left the shores of Europe in the last century. One went north, and one went south. Both worked hard, prayed to the same God, learned the language of their adopted countries. And today their grandchildren are the children of the Americas: Eduardo MacGillycuddy, Uruguay's ambassador to Washington, and Cornelius MacGillycuddy, better known in my country as United States Senator Connie Mack – common dreams, common bonds, common families.

In another speech in 1991 to mark Irish American Heritage month, Bush praised the contribution of Irish immigrants to American popular culture:

> American literature has been greatly enriched by the contributions of gifted Irish-American writers such as Eugene O'Neill and Edwin

O'Connor. Throughout the arts – and throughout education, government, business, science, and agriculture – talented men and women of Irish descent continue to merit the honour we give to them and to their ancestors. Indeed, in recent years, renewed immigration from Ireland and the revival of interest by all Americans in their roots have led to an increasingly vibrant Irish-American culture. The dramatic expansion of university courses in Irish studies and the countless annual St Patrick's Day parades held throughout the United States all attest to the continued vigour of the Irish-American heritage.

Before Bush Snr was sworn into office, his grandfather, George Herbert Walker, had forged his own links with Ireland – on the golf course – when he dreamed up the Walker Cup in 1922 while he was the president of the United States Golf Association. The Walker Cup is golf's oldest international match pre-dating the Ryder Cup by five years. The biennial tournament is a ten-man amateur golf competition contested by a team from the United States of America and a team from Great Britain and Ireland.

Bono and Bush: the abiding friendship of an unlikely duo

But the most enduring link President George W. Bush has with Ireland is undoubtedly his friendship with the country's most famous rock star. The Dubliner became the first recipient of the George W. Bush Medal in Dallas in 2018 for his work combatting AIDS. The pair dressed in black – the 43rd president in a black tuxedo and the singer in a Johnny Cash-style black suit – sat in a book-lined library during the ceremony.

Bono joked that he had stolen away from a U2 tour in Montreal so as to receive the 'huge honour'. 'I'm here to honour your leadership on the greatest health intervention on the history of medicine, no less,' he said. 'That's what I'm not sure people understand, that there's thirteen million lives saved thanks to PEPFAR. And if you add the global fund, there are probably about twenty-one million lives that have been saved by this work that you began.'

President Bush intervened:

> Actually, Bono, it's the work we began, and the truth of the matter is, it never would have made it out of Congress had you not been engaged. The first time I met you, you knew more statistics, it was like you were from the CIA, one of these analysts. That's the thing about Bono . . . he's the real deal. This is a guy who's got a huge heart, obviously a talent, but cares so deeply about the human condition that he spends an enormous amount of time and capital on saving lives.

Whichever way the credit is carved up, these two men from either side of the Atlantic, who shared a love for wearing cowboy hats, moved past politics to help millions fight one of the most devastating pandemics of recent times.

President Obama is thrilled with his gift of shamrocks
from Taoiseach Brian Cowen.

CHAPTER SIX

PRESIDENT BARACK OBAMA

*My name is Barack Obama of the Moneygall Obamas.
And I've come home to find the apostrophe that we lost
somewhere along the way.*

D RIVING DOWN MASSACHUSETTS AVENUE in the back of the
presidential limousine, Henry Healy found himself listening to
Barack Obama explaining the peculiarities of parenting in the White
House.

The president's eighth cousin had climbed into the armoured
Cadillac – known as the Beast – a few minutes earlier with his uncle,
Ollie Hayes, after exiting the Obama family's private quarters in the
White House. It was 2012 and nine months on from their first meeting
with their long-lost relative, the 44th president of the United States,
at the tiny village of Moneygall in Co. Offaly. The impossibly cool
commander-in-chief and his equally magnetic wife, Michelle, had
popped into Ollie's pub the previous May, where they got along
famously over the pouring of pints of Guinness. Obama affectionately christened his Irish cousin Henry the Eighth and teased him
about possessing the family trait of big ears.

Cue a reciprocal invitation to the Obamas' pad for the annual
St Patrick's Day shindig in Washington, which would take place

between dozens of green-tie-wearing Irish and US politicians on Tuesday 20 March 2012, three days after the actual saint's day. Henry had taken in one trip to New York previously, but as it was Ollie's first visit to the States, they flew into JFK Airport the week before to catch some sights. But plans to ascend the Empire State Building and join one of the Offaly delegations in the city's St Patrick's Day parade on Saturday were swiftly cancelled when they got a call from Washington.

A White House aide had come through on Henry's Irish mobile asking if they would mind coming to the US capital on Paddy's Day for a private meeting with their cousin. Before getting off the line, they were cautioned not to tell a soul about their new itinerary, not even family members, and to dress informally.

They booked out of their hotel, organised an Amtrak train to DC, and pulled up at a specified gate at the White House in a taxi. Secret Service agents screened them before they were met by a staffer who led them into the West Wing, explaining he would take them on a tour while their presidential relative wrapped up some business. 'We were taken into the Oval Office and got to lean on the Resolute desk,' remembered Henry. Their chatty staffer motioned to a door at the side of the office. 'I've never been through here,' he explained. 'This is the president's private dining room and private office, so this is a big deal for me as well.'

As they walked down the west colonnade in front of the Rose Garden towards the family quarters, their guide pointed to a lawn beside the swimming pool where President Nixon used to throw horseshoes. Gardeners were busy planting trees to ensure the Obama daughters, Malia and Sasha, would have privacy when friends came over for pool parties. The newfound Irish relatives were told to order snacks off a menu while they waited. 'The Marines come in and cook in the White House on Saturday, it's just something different, so there's a little menu there,' explained Ollie.

Windswept and interesting conversation in the Beast

A few minutes later, President Obama arrived, dressed down in a khaki bomber jacket and a white polo shirt. 'Hi, guys, you're welcome,' he said with a smile after hugging his Irish visitors. 'Thanks so much for coming up on Saturday. Would you join me for a pint?' It was clear – as a staffer had earlier confided – that the president wanted to return the hospitality shown him in Ireland.

Before they left, his Irish relatives presented Obama with a jersey sported by their local Gaelic games club. It bore the inscription *Is Féidir Linn*, which translates to his election slogan: 'Yes, We Can.'

'All this sort of thing was pretty surreal to be taking in,' recalled Henry. 'We walked out, and the president got into a car, and I started to walk towards the car behind, assuming there was no way we were travelling with the president. I was pulled back by an aide saying, "No, no, you're travelling with the president," so myself and Ollie sat in the back seat with him.'

Secret Service agents had handed them a pin to wear on their shirts to ensure they would be included in the inner cordon of protection around the president in the event of an incident, and the White House gates swung open to allow the 28-car cavalcade to move in unison down the shutdown streets of the capital. In the back of the car, the commander-in-chief broke into casual conversation about his trip to Ireland. 'It started about his visit to Ireland and about how he genuinely loved it,' recalled Henry. The president mentioned how he was struck by the bracing Irish winds in Dublin Airport, which knocked one member of his staff clean off her feet, causing her to sprain a wrist. The same gusts had repeatedly played havoc with the First Lady's hairdo during photo calls despite her best efforts to keep it in check.

As Ireland is a nation perhaps uniquely obsessed with the weather, this conversation opener put his relations at ease as they listened, while taking in the gadgets in the back of the presidential car. Obama also told his cousins that he had just received David Cameron, then prime minister of the United Kingdom, to the White House for a state visit and how the Irish golfer Rory McIlroy had been a guest at one of the functions, before filling them in on family news. Henry stated:

> He started then to tell us that Malia was in Mexico doing some charity work. He was explaining that Marian, Michelle's mother, was living with them and the reason they do that is because the kids need to remember where they came from and what they came from. They are quite privileged now, but they need to know how the real world is. He explained that his daughters made their beds and had to do chores and that as a family they were trying to keep life as normal as possible.

At one point Obama leaned across to ask the pair: 'What do the people of Ireland really think of Enda Kenny?' It was 2012, Ireland was starting to claw its way out of the deep economic downturn which had followed the spectacular collapse of the famed Celtic Tiger. The gravy train fuelled by a bullish run of bankers lavishing loans on big-spending builders had come shuddering to a halt in 2008 around the time that Obama had come to power in America. For most of Obama's first term, Ireland was knee-deep in recession with strict austerity measures installed to get the nation through one of the worst periods since the potato famine. The country was saved from bankruptcy by a multibillion-euro bailout from the so-called troika comprising of the International Monetary Fund, European Commission and European Central Bank. Regular headmaster-style visits from grim-faced European troika officials ensured there wasn't the slightest hint of a return to the unbridled spending spree of the previous decade when half the country seemed to have a leg in a racehorse while the other half clocked up air miles like they were going out of fashion.

The new Taoiseach, Enda Kenny, had swept to power with the largest majority in the Republic's history in March 2011 just in time to jet over to the US to present President Obama with the customary bowl of shamrocks. As Henry Healy and Ollie Hayes cruised around Washington a year later, they paused at the question about the Irish premier from their American cousin before conducting a bit of off-the-cuff diplomacy. 'We were quite reserved in what we said, conscious he was going to be meeting him,' Henry said with a smile, 'and we explained to him that Kenny was doing the best he could with the restrictions at the time. He had the troika pretty much dictating to him what he could and couldn't do.'

In a country scattered with ghost estates and half-finished buildings abandoned by developers, the issue of new charges for septic tanks had become a hot topic on news shows back home. Buried under most rural gardens in Ireland, these large drums gather toilet waste. In 2012, the EU had issued an order saying all these tanks – an estimated half a million of them – had to be inspected to ensure they were environmentally friendly, which in turn led to the state charging a fee to the tanks' disgruntled owners. Not the sexiest of subjects, but when President Obama asked about Ireland's recovering economy, the furore over human waste charges for the country's rural population popped into Henry's head:

> He began to ask us about the economic crisis in Ireland and the different ways that it had affected people. At the time there were septic tank charges being brought in and that came up in conversation and Obama began to explain how the system works in the States – that is,

you pay for everything, and you get nothing for nothing. He felt it was the right approach by the government at the time.

As the motorcade arrived outside the Dubliner Bar, Ollie remembers Washington's first citizen catching his arm before they emerged. 'Ollie, keep an eye on the agent, if anything happens,' he cautioned.

The stunned St Patrick's Day crowd spontaneously burst into chants of 'four more beers', punning on Obama's election slogan 'four more years' as they entered, surrounded by agents. 'The pub is packed with revellers on St Patrick's Day 2011. No one was expecting him. He just loves doing that. The publican was only told hours beforehand. In we went and the crowd went wild; they couldn't believe it,' remarked Ollie. It turned into a twenty-minute stop-off, during which Obama took time out to glad-hand the customers and the Irish owners.

'There were three pints of Guinness put in front of us,' explained Henry, adding how a waiting pool of press began to snap their photo on the most Irish day in the calendar. As Obama turned his back to the press he remarked to his guests: 'I won't be finishing this pint. It's not that there's anything wrong with it, but the Republicans would have a field day that the president was drinking on the job.'

Back in the car, Obama requested the driver to slow down – causing the entire cavalcade to brake to a crawl – before asking: 'Is this your first time here, guys?' to an answering nod from Ollie. Pointing to a park, where a man slept on a bench, the president told them they would see a lot of homeless people in the city. 'He said, "Although it's the capital and the powerhouse in America, we've got a homeless problem here and a big one." He wasn't just saying don't look, drive on,' observed Ollie. 'He wasn't hiding, he said it out straight.'

As they neared the White House, Obama asked about their plans.

'I'll be going back to work,' he told them, before quipping with a grin, 'I can open any door you want in DC. My name is good around here.'

He agreed to organise a tour of Capitol Hill for them and, as Ollie remembers, 'We got back to the White House and, basically, we were in shock.' Before he departed, President Obama handed over two prized military coins to his Irish guests. 'Every commander-in-chief has a coin, and he gave one to me and Henry,' explained Ollie – who would later receive presidential golf balls and cufflinks during subsequent visits. 'The agent said they'd never seen this happen before [and told us] *mind them coins.*'

Just before they left, Henry remembers the president saying he'd see them on Tuesday before turning to add: 'It's Paddy's Day, but maybe whatever you do tonight, don't return to the bar we were in, not today, go another day.'

'We didn't ask why,' Henry mused. 'We just did what we were told.'

As they were debriefed by White House staff, the Offaly men were to discover that even a casual chat over a pint between cousins is not straightforward when you are the president of the United States. 'We had to discuss what the president had discussed with us; we weren't allowed to discuss, obviously, that Malia was in Mexico, that was not known by anyone and it was a Secret Service issue,' Henry recalled. Unfortunately, the following Tuesday there was an earthquake in Mexico, and so her trip did become public knowledge and the White House had to issue a statement confirming the first daughter was safe on her school trip.

As they left the White House, stunned, Henry and Ollie found themselves wandering into a nearby McDonald's. 'We got two Cokes and sat down and looked at each other and just said, "What's just after happening?"' Then their phones started buzzing: the White

House press pool had released photos from the bar. 'None of our family had known what we were up to. I had a cousin in New York, waiting to meet me. When I got the photograph, I just sent it on to him and said, "Sorry, I was busy with another cousin!"' Henry laughed. 'It was a strange, strange, surreal thing to happen.'

In the intervening days, they attended a reception thrown by the Irish ambassador, appropriately named Michael Collins, before returning to the White House with Henry's mother, Mary, and Ollie's sister for the shamrock-giving ceremony. Having been let in through a special side entrance, 'We were met by a member of staff and we were sort of skirting through the West Wing and next thing: "Hey, you guys, hold tough." The president walks out, and I can still see my mother's jaw drop. She wasn't expecting him to appear like that,' said Henry.

'I'll walk with you,' said President Obama, striding along and asking what they had seen during the last few days in DC. Then he turned to the Irish guests and offered them the presidential box in the Kennedy Center that night, for a performance by the Russian ballet. 'We said, "Thanks, but the Irish ambassador has invited us to his residence,"' said Henry with a grin. 'And he said, "That's no problem, you can have it the next time you come." Then he hopped into an elevator and said he'd meet us in a while.'

In the queue to meet the Obamas at the shamrock ceremony, they reached the top of the line where Michelle Obama greeted them with: 'How are my cousins?' and warmly waved off their address of 'Hallo, Mrs Obama' with, 'No, we're relatives, it's Michelle.'

Shortly afterwards, at the podium, the president started with formalities by welcoming, 'My good friend Taoiseach Kenny; his extraordinary wife Fionnuala; First Minister Peter Robinson; Deputy First Minister Martin McGuinness of Northern Ireland.' He then noted: 'As you may have noticed, today is not, in fact,

ARRIVAL AT NEW YORK

Immigrants disembark at New York, circa 1880.

© Fotosearch/Stringer

ANNIE MOORE & HER BROTHERS

This waterfront statue in Cobh, Ireland, commemorates Annie Moore and her brothers. She was the first person to be admitted to the USA through the new Ellis Island immigration centre on 1 January 1892.

© Glyn Genin/Alamy stock photo

NEW BEGINNINGS

The Old Wagon Road was used by early settlers as they headed into the southern United States. It's shown here in the Prairie in Theodore Roosevelt National Park, North Dakota.

© wildnerdpix/Alamy stock photo

DE VALERA IN THE US

President Éamon de Valera of Ireland addresses Congress on 28 May 1964. The 81-year-old ended his speech: 'I confess this is an outstanding day of my life.'

© Harvey Georges/AP/shutterstock

**MEETING THE KENNEDY FAMILY
AT NEW ROSS**

President Kennedy visits the farm at Dunganstown,
New Ross, Co. Wexford, where his great-grandfather lived
before emigrating to the United States.

THE START OF A DYNASTY

JFK's great-grandfather John 'Honey Fitz'
Fitzgerald at the Treaty Stone monument
in Limerick with his daughter, Agnes,
on 5 August 1908.

**ST PATRICK STREET CORK,
28 JUNE 1963**

JFK is driven through St Patrick Street on the way to
City Hall for his official welcome to town.

**GREENPARK RACECOURSE,
29 JUNE 1963**

Greenpark Racecourse on the outskirts of Limerick
was JFK's last stop before leaving Ireland. Although
not originally on the itinerary, Lord Mayor Frances
Condell campaigned tirelessly to have it included –
and succeeded.

**BUMPER-TO-BUMPER
CAVALCADE IN HOSPITAL**

A jubilant President Nixon glad-hands the crowd in the
town of Hospital, Co. Limerick, 1970.

A DOG CALLED KING TIMAHOE

President Nixon, a teenage Marian Scully
and an Irish setter puppy. King Timahoe
shares a name with Timahoe, the village in
Co. Kildare where Nixon's forebears lived.

VISIT TO TIMAHOE, 5 OCTOBER 1970

President Richard Nixon visits his ancestral graveyard, where he is greeted by Olive Goodbody.

ASHFORD CASTLE, 3 JUNE 1984

President Reagan and his wife Nancy pat the head of three-year-old Feargal O'Brien. They'd just visited University College Galway, where Reagan received an honorary degree.

A GLASS OF STOUT IN BALLYPOREEN

Reagan raises a pint of Smithwick's as he stands with Nancy at the bar of O'Farrell's pub in the village of Ballyporeen, 3 June 1984.

A PUB NAMED AFTER ME . . .

A president and his namesake bar, which was later transported lock, stock and barrel to the US where it was rebuilt as a key attraction of the Reagan Library.

COLLEGE GREEN, 1 DECEMBER 1995

President Bill Clinton with the crowd in Dublin after his address to the people of Ireland.

© Independent News and Media

A PRESIDENT CHARMED

Bill Clinton on the golf course at Ballybunion on a Saturday afternoon in 1998 after finalising the Good Friday Agreement.

© PA Images / Alamy stock photo

STORMONT CASTLE, 5 MARCH 2014

Northern Ireland First Minister Rt. Hon. Peter D. Robinson (R) and Northern Ireland Deputy First Minister Martin McGuinness (L) meet with Bill Clinton at the place where the 1998 Good Friday Agreement was signed. Clinton played a key role in the peace process.

© Handout

BUSH AND BERTIE AT DROMOLAND CASTLE

President George W. Bush with Irish Prime Minister Bertie Ahern at the start of the
European Union/US summit meeting on 25 June 2004.

PLACARDS IN PROTEST

As President Bush arrived at Shannon
before the EU/US summit, a crowd made
their displeasure known.

THE ROCK STAR AND THE PRESIDENT

Bush and Bono in the Oval Office on 19 October
2005. Bono, in town for a U2 concert, was invited
to a presidential lunch at the White House.

RAISING A GUINNESS TOAST

President Obama at the bar in his ancestral home of Moneygall alongside First Lady Michelle Obama on 23 May 2011.

© Pool

THE PRESIDENT AND HIS LONG-LOST COUSIN

Obama celebrates St Patrick's Day in Washington, DC, enjoying a pint in the Dubliner Bar with Henry Healy, his ancestral cousin from Moneygall.

© Brendan Smialowksi

A COLLEGE GREEN MEET AND GREET

On 23 May 2011, Barack and Michelle Obama greet well-wishers in College Green, Dublin.

© Peter Macdiarmid

WHERE IT ALL BEGAN

Side by side in an obscure Ohio cemetery, the tombstones of William and Joseph Kearney held the key to the puzzle of Barack Obama's lineage.

© Megan Smolenyak

CONTEMPLATION AT THE CILL MHUIRE GRAVEYARD

Local parish priest, Fr Malachy Conlon, with President Biden at the ancient Cill Mhuire graveyard.
Dating back to the fifth century, this is the cemetery where Biden's ancestors are thought to be buried.

A CARNIVAL ATMOSPHERE AT LILY FINNEGAN'S

The publican of this picture-postcard pub is convinced that Biden's long-ago relatives would once have patronised the Cooley hostelry.

'I DON'T WANNA GO HOME'

Just as for so many American presidents on tour, Biden found the conviviality, warmth and humanity of the Irish people irresistible.

St Patrick's Day. We just wanted to prove that America considers Ireland a dear and steadfast friend every day of the year.' Then, with a glance over at the Offaly contingent, he gave a broad smile and said, 'Everyone, please welcome my new friends from Moneygall. My long-lost cousin Henry; his mother Mary is here as well. And my favourite pub keeper, Ollie Hayes, is here with his beautiful wife. In return, I did take them out for a pint at the Dubliner here in Washington, DC, on Saturday. That's right, I saw some of you there,' he joked. 'And I've asked them to please say hello to everybody back home for me.'

The president then told the crowd of his homecoming trip back to Ireland nine months earlier:

> Michelle and I received absolutely the warmest of welcomes, and I've been trying to return the favour as best I can. There really was something magical about the whole day, and I know that I'm not the only person who feels that way when they visit Ireland. Even my most famously Irish-American predecessor was surprised about how deeply Ireland affected him when he visited in his third year as president. 'It is strange,' President Kennedy said on his last day in Ireland, 'that so many years and so many generations pass, and still some of us who come on this trip could feel ourselves among neighbours, even though we are separated by generations, by time, and by thousands of miles.'
>
> I know most of you can relate to that. I think anyone who's had a chance to visit can relate. And that's why Jackie Kennedy later visited Ireland with her children and gave one of President Kennedy's dog tags to his cousins in Dunganstown. And that's why I felt so at home when I visited Moneygall.

Such strong emotions of familiarity and connection found voice, too, earlier in the day, at the Friends of Ireland luncheon, where

Obama had deadpanned: 'I met my eighth cousin, Henry, who has my ears, I might point out.'

Dreams of Ireland – Kearneys leave markers on the frontier pointing back home

The president had been in the dark about his maternal Irish family ties for most of his life. Born in 1961 in Honolulu, Hawaii, to an American mother, Stanley Ann Dunham and his Kenyan father, Barack H. Obama Snr, his beautifully penned memoir, *Dreams From My Father*, tells of his journey to find his identity across continents.

He was twenty-one when he received a call on a crackling line from his aunt in Nairobi to his New York apartment telling him his father had died in a car crash. The call was a death knell to any hope of reconnecting with the charismatic Kenyan who had swept his mother off her feet when he married her in 1960 after arriving as the first African student at the University of Hawaii. Barack was just two years old when his bright father won another scholarship to Harvard, and the ensuing separation was made permanent when his father returned to his homeland to help forge a new Africa with his American education.

When he wrote the book in the mid-1990s, as the first African-American president of the *Harvard Law Review*, he mused over his maternal grandparents' liberal attitude to the marriage of his white mother to his Black father, at a time when interracial marriage was still a felony in many American states. Their easy approval puzzled the young senator. He remembered an old black and white photo of his maternal grandmother's Scottish and English grandparents in Kansas and surmised their pioneering temperament could have been what informed the open-minded attitude of the grandmother he called Toot.

Toot had grown up in Augusta, Kansas, and Obama's grandfather,

Gramps, had grown up in El Dorado less than twenty miles away, raised by his grandparents after he found the body of his 26-year-old mother, Ruth Lucille Armour, after she tragically took her own life, when he was just eight years old in 1926. Obama, as a Harvard University graduate, did not yet know that his grandfather's people also had a frontier spirit – around the time of the Irish famine they had crossed the Atlantic from an outpost in Co. Offaly in Ireland to America.

Moneygall, with a population of around three hundred, and located eighty-six miles outside Dublin, is a typical Midlands farming village with one main street, a few shops, two pubs, a church, a school and a fire station.

This tendril-like tie between Offaly and the US was lost over the years, as emigrant generations fought to eke out a living in the sun-baked centre of America, but handwritten records dating back over two hundred years remained in Ireland.

It was late March 2007 when Reverend Stephen Neill remembers emails pinging in from the US inquiring about his parish records for the Kearney family, one of the many ancestor-checking requests from Americans, Australians and – less frequently – the English, thanks in part to the popularity of the TV show *Who Do You Think You Are?* The email was sitting in the inbox of the busy Church of Ireland clergyman when he got a call from Salt Lake City, from a researcher from ancestry.com called Kyle Betit, who was working for one the world's top genealogists, Megan Smolenyak. 'He told me that this Kearney family were potentially connected to the then-presidential candidate Barack Obama,' said Reverend Neill:

> I got very excited at that stage because I had actually read his first book; he was very much on my radar. My ears perked up and I was asked to check through our parish records. The sad thing was our

parish treasurer, who had been the custodian of the records for many years, had died only a couple of weeks previously and she would have loved the story. But her son passed them on to me and we discovered references to the Kearney family which definitively proved the link between Barack Obama and Moneygall.

It would be another month before the details were released. 'I sent various photographs of our records. I had to keep it quiet until they got their ducks in a row, so to speak. It was a very long month. Although as clergy, I suppose we're used to keeping secrets in the best sense of the word,' he surmised. 'But on 3 May 2007, ancestry.com issued a press release to virtually every news agency in the world.'

The release confirmed baptism and probate records linking the Obama family line back to Moneygall had been unearthed, with the assistance of Canon Stephen Neill, in the Templeharry rectory records. It was found that Obama's third great-grandfather Fulmoth (or Falmouth) Kearney had sailed from Ireland to New York aged nineteen in 1850 aboard the SS *Marmion*.

The records also revealed that other Kearney family members had in fact been in America since the 1790s. Fulmoth's paternal uncle, Francis, had bequeathed land to his brother – Fulmoth's father – Joseph, with the condition that he emigrate to inherit. He did so along with his wife Phoebe Donovan and four children, including Fulmoth, who made the journey at various times in the mid nineteenth century. In earlier generations, Irish genealogist Fiona Fitzsimons had discovered his family had been very successful wigmakers, while Joseph was a shoemaker. Megan Smolenyak commented: 'This research will once and for all put to rest any perceptions that Barack Obama is a first-generation American – like most of us he has an interesting mix of ancestry, including some impressively early all-American roots.'

After arriving in New York, Fulmoth Kearney went out west to

Ohio, where he married a woman called Charlotte Holloway and they resettled eventually in Tipton, Indiana, where Kearney worked as a farmer, with their children, one of whom was one Mary Ann Kearney, President Obama's grandfather's grandmother. With the 3 May announcement of the Irish link to the US's first African-American president, the world's press descended on Moneygall. 'On that day, I did about thirty or forty press interviews including the *Today Show* on Sky News and various UK radio channels and RTÉ, it just went absolutely mental,' remembers Reverend Neill.

Henry Healy was watching the nine o'clock news with his mother Mary later that evening when he heard his village namechecked on the bulletin. Unlike Stephen Neill, he'd never heard of Senator Barack Obama, but his mother sat up when RTÉ reporter Bethan Kilfoil relayed the Obama connection to the Kearney family. 'We used to have a field, it was always known locally as Kearney's Garden,' commented his mother. 'I wonder, has that got anything to do with it?'

Picking up the phone to her brother, who had recently completed the Healy family tree, she said: 'Have you seen the news?' He had. 'Was that the field we would have had? Kearney's Garden?' Thinking aloud, he deduced they were possibly related to the presidential candidate – as he had been contacted by a Roger Kearney from Ohio a while back. A bit of digging revealed their connection with Barack Obama came through his seventh great-grandparents, Joseph and Cicely Kearney, who had four sons. One of the sons, Joseph, born in 1730, married Sarah Healy, the ancestor of the Moneygall Healys. 'It was a falling-together of another piece of the jigsaw or an extension to another branch of the tree,' commented Henry of the link, 'and Megan Smolenyak was satisfied because my uncle, who was in our family homestead, which has been in our family since the 1700s, had old documents such as wills witnessed by Kearney family members.'

Moneygall gets a Dulux makeover – and a security shakedown

With all their paperwork confirmed, the villagers became some of the Chicago-based senator's loudest cheerleaders: 'We immediately jumped on the bandwagon and were supporting Senator Obama over Hillary Clinton,' said Henry, explaining how it felt like exactly the connection the ordinary Midlands village needed to lift it out of the doldrums of the economic depression in 2007. 'It was our way of putting our heads above the doom and gloom. Now we were following an inspirational individual with a sense of hope and change,' added Henry. However, no one was more surprised than Barack Obama at this newfound Irishness. Indeed, he would often quip afterwards that it would have elevated him to the front of the St Patrick's Day parades in Chicago instead of the back.

After years of 'Will he? Won't he?' speculation, the Obama visit was given the green light on St Patrick's Day 2011, after the annual White House meeting with Taoiseach Enda Kenny. President Obama announced his upcoming 23 May visit to Moneygall and Ireland by joking: 'Joe Biden is envious because he wants to go first,' then somewhat prophetically added, 'But my expectation is that I'll just be laying the groundwork for what I'm sure will be an even more wonderful trip by him.'

At that same conference, Enda Kenny used his White House platform to stress how his newly elected government would continue to build on the very strong traditional links with the United States, in business and in politics and in culture. 'Ireland is open for business,' he declared in front of the White House press pool, 'and we continue to be open for business to the United States. We appreciate the investment of so much foreign direct investment from the US to our country. But, unlike previous centuries, we come bearing gifts as well. There are many Irish companies now operating in the US, with at least 80,000 American jobs created out of Irish firms here.'

That night, at the counter inside his bright red-and-black-fronted traditional pub, Ollie Hayes was watching the Sky News report on the impending visit. Although he is Henry Healy's uncle, there is no family tie to President Obama, as Henry Healy is related to the president on the maternal side of the family while Ollie Hayes is on his paternal side. But when US Embassy officials first arrived in Moneygall to survey Obama's ancestral village, they met with Henry Healy at Ollie Hayes's bar.

It was early April 2011 when a US-plated car pulled up outside the bar. At the counter, a White House official told the publican he oversaw the president's flight routes. 'The helicopters were his remit,' explained Ollie.

'I'm looking for some landing spots around the area,' said the official. 'Would you come with me in the car?'

They visited the local hurling field, before going back to the pub for a coffee. When he left, the official gave Ollie a metal pin souvenir of Marine One, the presidential helicopter. 'We'll be talking to you soon,' he said on his way out, before adding, 'By the way, the Secret Service will arrive here in the next hour or two.'

Within an hour the phone rang. 'It was the *Sunday Mirror* in London,' recalled Ollie. 'They asked me did I hear anything from any Americans about the potential visit in May. I said, no, I didn't. But, he said, you were seen getting out of a car in the Moneygall area, an embassy car with American plates. I denied it; sure, I'm only a pub, why would they contact me?'

A few hours later, a busload of the 'president's men' arrived in the pub. 'The whole place was covered in them. One of the men said, "I'm in charge of the visit," and we became great friends. They trusted me after that,' said Ollie. 'I suppose the call from London was a test. But I don't know, I'll never know.'

A committee was set up to deal with the advance team of thirty or forty US officials looking after the visit. They batted away lots of overtures from companies looking to attach themselves to Moneygall, but the offer from Dulux to paint the entire village was happily accepted. 'Everyone was out painting, people were pulling in to see the village that was going to get this visit, it was nonstop, we had interviews all around the world.' The *Offaly Independent* got caught up in the hoopla, briefly changing its name to the *Obama Independent*, while a local group of dancers renamed themselves the Obama Stepdancers.

In the weeks leading up to the president's arrival in Moneygall, Ollie's pub became the hub of operations, with his kitchen given over as the White House communications room for the fortnight before the visit. 'There was a big desk down the middle of the kitchen with sixteen phone lines in there. The equipment was unbelievable. They were measuring mobile activity for two weeks before the visit so they knew that if on the day it went above that bar there would be something going on.'

Continued Ollie: 'That was their control room inside the kitchen. So, if anything happened that day in Moneygall, where he had to make a decision or ring the Russian president or whoever, it would have been done in our kitchen.' The family took their meals in the sitting room over the pub. 'We managed,' said Ollie good-humouredly. 'But when I went to America, a senior Secret Service guy said to me, "We never forgot what you did for us in Moneygall, you gave us the key to your house."' He was also visited by the president's food and beverage person.

They would be watching the filling of the pint from a distance. Rumours went out that the barrel was brought down from the brewery, specially tested and checked. That's not true at all. The night before the president came, the bar was open to people within the inner circle in the village. That barrel was pulled [opened] that night. When the president ordered pints, I just filled it straight out of that barrel.

Unlike the Reagan visit, there was very little lobbying over Obama's choice of beer. 'I didn't care if he had a pint of Guinness or a bottle of Coke,' said Ollie. 'That was never prearranged. He just asked for a Guinness!'

A more obvious security issue meant that all legally held firearms were handed in to the local Garda station, while one household were stumped what to do with unlicensed gun in their family going back to a relative's IRA days in the Civil War of the early 1920s, but in the end, it was spirited out of the village for the duration. Every house in Moneygall had the addition of a Garda detective for the day along with an inspection by a sniffer dog.

On the morning that President Obama was due into the pub, Ollie confessed to his newfound friend in the White House administration that he was feeling nervous. 'He pointed his finger at me and said, "Ollie, he gets up out of bed, he eats breakfast, he showers, he shaves, and he does something else the same as you do. Treat him like a normal person because that's what he wants."'

Emotion of snatched private visit contrasts with euphoria of College Green 'O'Bama' address

With the Obama visit timed just five months before his successful re-election, the Harvard lawyer, who started off as a community organiser, could have been forgiven for thinking there was nothing more grassroots to the forty million Irish-American voters than paying a visit across the Atlantic to the very green countryside and pulling an obligatory pint of Guinness.

But that doesn't tell the whole story of the young lawyer who wrote a powerful memoir at the age of thirty-three exploring his roots across the continents of America, Africa, where his father was born, and Asia, where he spent part of his childhood in Indonesia with his mother and stepfather. Here in one of the most northern parts of Europe was another piece of the puzzle in his genetic make-up.

That puzzle was one which local musicians, The Corrigan Brothers, had fun with, earning lots of airplay out of their skit song 'There Is No One More Irish Than Barack Obama'. It drew easy smiles and a few good-natured eye rolls, but everyone was in on the joke on their bit of tuneful – or maybe not so tuneful – blarney. 'One of the great gems of Irish culture,' laughs Reverend Stephen Neill, 'it was good craic.'

In a press briefing on 20 May 2011 in the White House, three days before the visit, Ben Rhodes, deputy national security advisor for strategic communications, described the meeting as a 'homecoming of sorts for President Obama'. Mr Rhodes continued, 'I've seen reports about the bloodlines that extend across the town.'

On the day when Barack Obama walked into the Kearney homestead to the hearth, where his great-great-great-grandfather had sipped tea and warmed his hands on the open fire, he seemed visibly affected. The cameras were not rolling; it was the only private part of the visit. 'One thing that still strikes me, and it was never captured on camera, was when he walked into the ancestral home President Obama pounded his foot on the timber floor, and I can still hear the echo of his foot banging on the floor,' recalled Henry. 'He looked up and said, "This is where my grandfather's grandfather left from."'

The president walked around looking intently at two sketches on the wall, one depicting the streetscape of the mid-nineteenth century when Fulmoth would have left Moneygall, and listening to the owner of the house, John Donovan, talk of the home's history. 'You could see his eyes were kind of watering up,' recalled Henry. 'The First Lady was a few minutes behind coming in after him and he shared all that information back to her verbatim. He really had taken it in.'

The sun had shone throughout April and May when villagers were painting and preening their shopfronts for the international spotlight, but the heavens opened as the Obamas determinedly shook every outstretched hand in the streets of Moneygall.

'The President and the First Lady were exceptional,' said Reverend Neill. 'It was the wettest, most miserable day I remember for many a year, and they literally worked the entire crowd: there wasn't a person who didn't get to shake their hand or see them at close quarters.' Plus, he remembered, 'When they came into the pub afterwards, they were literally dripping wet, they had to give them towels to dry off.' It was said to be the longest line of meet-and-greet the President and the First Lady ever did together.

Reverend Neill, who has now moved on from Moneygall, handed over the records dating back two centuries to the Obamas. 'I must say I was nervous enough waiting to meet them but when it came to it, they were the easiest people to talk to, no airs or graces, just straightforward and approachable.' He remembers the president receiving a few Irish lessons from people in the pub for a speech he was due to make at a star-studded College Green concert in Dublin city later that evening. 'He was getting various advice on how to pronounce his Irish. He had a great sense of humour,' added Neill before observing, 'One thing I noticed was the electricity between him and Michelle Obama; you could just see it between them, they had great banter between them, and they had time for everybody.'

'You're keeping all the best stuff here,' Obama declared at one point, referring to how Guinness tastes better in Ireland than anywhere else.

For Henry, who was effectively their host, there was a surreal feeling over the whole afternoon. 'I always remember describing when I saw him get out of the car here in Moneygall; it was like watching someone come out of your television screen.' But then he added: 'I always felt relaxed with him because he seemed so ordinary. I wasn't intimidated by him or the office, but it was always a pinch-me moment after he had left.'

When the press pool departed that day, the Obamas lingered in the bar, prompting the publican to ask if they wanted to pull a pint of Guinness. 'I'd love to,' said Michelle before going inside the bar where she was instructed on how to slowly fill the black liquid into a slanted glass before leaving the creamy head to slowly settle to the top. 'The cameras had left, and they loved that. She filled two pints and we had good banter. Barack liked those off-the-cuff moments. He was very witty, good fun, a real gentleman,' said Ollie Hayes with a smile.

Meanwhile, earlier that day at Farmleigh House in Dublin, Enda Kenny had handed Obama a book of children's stories based on Hawaiian legend, written by Trinity College professor Pádraic Whyte. It prompted President Obama to try to put his finger on the Irish-American relationship. He said, 'It is not just a matter of strategic interest, it's not just a matter of foreign policy. For the United States, Ireland carries a blood link with us.'

And then, at a podium in College Green just hours after his Moneygall trip, he told a crowd of 60,000: 'My name is Barack Obama,' adding, to huge applause, 'of the Moneygall Obamas. And I've come home to find the apostrophe that we lost somewhere along the way. Now, I knew that I had some roots across the Atlantic, but until recently, I could not unequivocally claim that I was one of those Irish Americans. But now, if you believe the Corrigan Brothers, there's no one more Irish than me,' he joked to a burst of laughter from the crowd.

In his speech, he gave further insight into why he found it so emotional to enter the house where his ancestor was born.

> Standing there in Moneygall, I couldn't help but think how heart-breaking it must have been for that great-great-great-grandfather of mine and so many others to part, to watch Donegal coasts and Dingle cliffs recede, to leave behind all they knew in hopes that something better lay over the horizon.
>
> When people like Falmouth boarded those ships, they often did so with no family, no friends, no money, nothing to sustain their journey but faith: faith in the Almighty, faith in the idea of America, faith that it was a place where you could be prosperous, you could be free, you could think and talk and worship as you pleased, a place where you could make it if you tried. And as they worked and struggled and sacrificed and sometimes experienced great discrimination to build that better life for the next generation, they passed on that faith to their children and to their children's children, an inheritance that their great-great-great-grandchildren like me still carry with them. We call it the American Dream.

The Irish tricolour flag fluttered alongside the stars and stripes on the podium, as his stirring speech wowed thousands of Irish spectators in the same spot where President Clinton had delivered an electric speech in 1995. He went on to tell the crowd, which included acting superstars Stephen Rea, Saoirse Ronan and Daniel Day-Lewis, that, 'Irish signatures are on our founding documents. Irish blood was spilled on our battlefields.' Bringing the focus back to the twenty-first century, he told the recession-hit crowd of Irish men and women that America would stand by them. Making excellent use of those Irish lessons from the pub, he declared to rousing cheers, 'Remember that whatever hardships the winter may bring, springtime is always just around the corner. And if they keep on arguing with you, just respond with a simple creed: *Is féidir linn*. Yes, we can. Yes, we can. *Is féidir linn*.'

And the following St Patrick's Day in 2012, President Obama was still reminiscing about his pub visit. He joked with guests at the White House celebration about how Ollie 'was interested in hiring Michelle when she was pouring a pint. I said, she's too busy, maybe at the end of our second term'.

At that same gathering, he recalled how his great-great-great-grandfather had attended the first annual banquet of the St Patrick's Society in Brooklyn shortly after he arrived in America. And a toast was offered to family back home who were enduring what were impossibly difficult years. His ancestors never lived to see one of their ilk rise to the highest station in the New World, but over 160 years later, in his own toast, President Obama called out the tenaciousness of the race that would leave forty million of its descendants in the US.

> For all the remarkable things the Irish have done in the course of human history – keeping alive the flame of knowledge in dark ages, outlasting a great hunger, forging a peace that once seemed impossible – the green strands they have woven into America's heart, from their tiniest villages through our greatest cities, is something truly unique on the world stage.

With Irish ears keenly listening in the White House, he echoed his *Yes, We Can* rhetoric to a nation tired of the hangover of debt and austerity. 'This little country that inspires the biggest things, its best days are still ahead.'

When it came to superlative days, Reverend Neill still wonders at the sequence of events that brought the Obamas to a rural pub in

Moneygall in 2011. 'The whole thing was bizarre. Looking back on it, I'm not saying it was the best day of my life, but it was certainly the most extraordinary day of my life.'

Van Morrison famously sang about 'Days Like This', a song which became the theme tune to the lives of Henry Healy and his uncle Ollie Hayes over the next six years. They were to find out a presidential cousin was an utterly different proposition from a run-of-the-mill Irish-American relative scattered in Irish enclaves like Brooklyn or Scituate in Boston or Chicago's Edison Park. It was certainly much harder to arrive in the country under the radar.

Rumbled by the Secret Service in Washington, DC

The pair flew into Washington on 20 January 2013, planning to join the crowds streaming into Washington to see Barack Obama inaugurated for his second term. They didn't want to trouble him on his big day and so, as Ollie explained:

> We were going on the street like Americans to see what the inauguration was like. So we're in America, maybe ten or twelve hours, in our hotel and contact was made again. 'What brought you over to America without telling us?' The White House staffer continued his good-natured scolding: 'At 18:00 hours, be at the coffee shop near Pennsylvania Avenue, I want to see you.' The agent continued: 'The president knows you are in town and can't believe you came over. And he said you're going to meet him tonight.'

At the coffee shop, they were handed tickets to the pre-inaugural celebrations, front row tickets to the inauguration in front of the Capitol, and tickets to the official inaugural ball. 'We had a great time of it. There was a party in Washington that night for people close to the president at the White House and we were taken there.

Henry and myself met President Obama and Michelle, and Joe Biden and Jill Biden.'

While they were posing for a photo with the Obamas and Bidens, Joe Biden tapped Ollie on the shoulder: 'Ollie, do me a favour, ask the president, can I go to Ireland, to see my ancestors?' Ollie obligingly pokes his head out of the line-up calling down: 'What are the chances of the vice president going to Ireland to see his ancestors?'

The president smilingly answers, 'No, Ollie, tell him we're too busy. Second term ahead,' in an echo of his St Patrick's Day quip about the First Lady being too busy with the second term to take up Ollie Hayes's offer of a job in his bar.

The following night, after President Obama was sworn in for his second term in front of an estimated million people on the mall, the two watched the tuxedo-clad President and First Lady, dressed in a floor-length scarlet gown, sway together while Oscar-winner Jennifer Hudson belted out Al Green's 'Let's Stay Together', as they mouthed the words 'so in love with you' to each other.

It was an iconic popular culture moment – a slow dance that sent Twitter into meltdown – and the Moneygall contingent of two had a ringside seat. It might have been the perfect ending, but the glittering ball wasn't the finale of their White House adventure.

Later in 2013, when President Obama touched down at Belfast International Airport for the G8 summit, he kept up his running joke about Henry sharing his big ears during a mischievous shout-out to his cousin. The First Lady, and daughters Sasha and Malia, visited Dublin's Trinity College, where genealogist Fiona Fitzsimons gave an illuminating talk on the Obama Irish ancestors, and went to a *Riverdance* performance in the city's Gaiety Theatre. A member of the White House administration met Ollie and Henry beforehand in a coffee shop in Nassau Street – he'd been told they did a tasty croissant – and brought them into a side door to Trinity College where they were the surprise first-in-line guests to meet the Obama family. 'They said, we just want her to meet someone she knows,' said Ollie, who remembered Michelle's delight at seeing them again.

White House favourites, the Obama Plaza and the 'Yes, We Can' village motto

Around this time the germ of an idea to create a permanent monument to the 44th president of the United States was taking root. By 2014, a gleaming petrol station – The Barack Obama Plaza – had risen out of the Offaly skyline outside the town of Moneygall. One of only a handful of pit stops off the new motorway from Dublin to Cork, this is truly the Rolls-Royce of filling stations. A life-size cut-out of the smiling Obamas – taken as they exited Marine One in 2011 – has new customers doing a double-take as they enter the glass building. Inside, the dining options range from Supermacs – Ireland's answer to McDonald's – a pizza joint, a traditional carvery with roast dinners, plus sandwiches and assorted salads. The Plaza was the brainchild of Supermacs' boss Pat McDonagh, but he convinced Henry Healy to step into the role of business development manager.

Obama was informed about the building of the station named in his honour during one of their St Patrick's Day visits. 'It was in 2013, or 2012,' said Henry. 'We were in the White House and Ollie started to tell him about this place that was going to be built and was going to be called the Obama Plaza. I remember he looked at Ollie and said, "Are you drinking the beer, or are you serving the beer back home?"'

While it lacked the grandeur of a bridge or an airport, the Plaza was a sorely needed source of employment in the area, which pleased the president when they gave him an update on progress in 2015. 'We explained that it had opened and the jobs it had created, and he was delighted, again conscious that there was a recovery needed in Ireland. At the time there were about a hundred or so jobs, but it went to 170 or 180,' said Henry. An upstairs visitor centre showcases the history of Irish emigration, in particular the journey of one Moneygall descendant whose children's children would end up in the White House. The service station – situated halfway between Dublin and the famous Cliff of Moher in Co. Clare – is a mecca for tour buses, crowds of GAA supporters and drivers taking a stop-off on the motorway. 'During the summer months you could have anything up to fourteen buses with fifty passengers in each,' said Henry.

There are mixed feelings in the village on the futuristic service station, as its arrival coincided with the closure of small independent grocery shops, but this is a fate that has befallen small villages all over Ireland over the last decade. The departure of the local shops could have also been accelerated by the new motorway, which bypasses the village while also leading off to the service station. Some see the closure of the shops as a sad loss to the village's character; others see their demise as an inevitable cost of progress.

The Plaza is certainly a nationally famous landmark, one which gives much-needed employment, especially to college students in the area. 'The Plaza keeps the connection and people are reminded of it because this is a service they need on the commute every day. It will always keep Moneygall and the connection with President Obama alive. For the locals it's brought an economic boost and it's keeping our Obama story alive,' said Henry. 'Who knows? Maybe one day he'll be over and have his Supermacs.'

Henry is as aware as anyone that his link to President Obama is somewhat distant. 'You would have had some naysayers and begrudgers, and people making a skit of the connection,' he says amiably but adds, 'what it did for our community can never be underestimated, it really brought back a sense of community spirit and it's still here today. It implanted the *Yes, We Can* attitude in the community.'

During the Obama presidency, the village became an Irish microcosm of the White House with their own Moneygall spin in adopting Michelle Obama's 'Let's Move' approach by building a playground, children's activity park and walking trails, along with creating a community garden to twin with the First Lady's famous White House Kitchen Garden, initiated to promote healthier eating.

On a personal level, the visit changed the direction of Henry's life, as his new national profile saw him being offered a job as a tourism ambassador for Ireland in 2012 before being offered the role in the Obama Plaza two years later. 'I was working as a business development manager in construction, so that was the polar opposite to what I was doing. When I think back to that time, so many of my friends had emigrated. Who knows? I could have been an illegal alien over in the United States if this had not happened or I could have gone to Australia or further afield,' mused Henry.

While Moneygall experienced the star wattage of the Obamas just once, Henry and Ollie continued their annual trips right up until the president's final year in office. 'Until 2016, we were invited to the White House every year with a personal audience with Obama every time,' said Ollie, explaining how they would wait for 'the nod' from a Secret Service agent while they were in the audience at the St Patrick's Day events in the White House.

In 2016, their friend in the White House staff pulled them back at the door before their annual meeting, saying: 'Ollie, ask the president will he go for a pint with you? Michelle is out of town tonight, and he might go with you and we'll be listening and if he does, we'll get everything ready.'

As they went into the room Ollie recalled: 'We're chatting away, fist-pumping and messing and hugging.' He pauses and says: 'Mr President, do you want to come for a pint?'

'Where are you going?' asks President Obama.

'An Irish pub in Dupont Circle,' replied Ollie.

'Ollie, only I'm on the podium at 8 a.m. in Detroit otherwise I would be in that car with you,' Obama answered. 'Thanks for asking.'

On their last meeting, he did express a desire to return to Moneygall post-presidency, but such a visit has yet to happen. The American dream that President Obama referred to in his College Green speech evoked the survival of his ancestor as he crossed the Atlantic in a coffin ship to forge a new life in the US. But there was a very modern strand to the dream, too – and that was in the uncle and nephew who found themselves with an access-all-areas pass to the highest echelons of Washington, because of a long-lost blood tie that went back hundreds of years. And because the most powerful man on the planet wished to repay the hospitality he received in a tiny Irish village one rainy afternoon early in his presidency.

As Ollie said, 'If you wrote it down, they would say it's a fairy tale.'

The first virtual shamrock ceremony took place
owing to the Covid-19 lockdown in 2021.

CHAPTER SEVEN

PRESIDENT JOE BIDEN

Remember, Joey Biden, the best drop of blood in you is Irish.

THE ADVERT APPEARED IN THE PAGES of the *Irish American* newspaper on 24 March 1866. The nineteenth-century US publication carried news from the old country, but it also regularly printed pages of personals, among which were pleas for information from relatives back in Ireland who had lost all track of loved ones after they had crossed the Atlantic. The poignant advertisement was placed by two women looking for their stonemason father, John Ward, their sister, Mary Hanafy, and her husband.

At just eighty-nine words long, it reveals a lifetime of separation and sorrow for the scattered family who had crossed continents to seek out a better life around the time of the famine. The advert explains that Mary and her husband were originally from Ballinacourty, near Oranmore in County Galway but that they had crossed the Irish Sea to England before leaving for America. 'When last heard from, 5 years ago, they were in Milleboro, Kentucky,' states the ad. It asks for information to be sent to an address in Rockingham, Massachusetts, indicating that her sisters had also made the move across the Atlantic. This short article simply titled 'Galway' would lead famed *Who Do You Think You Are?* genealogist

Megan Smolenyak on a paper trail to President Joe Biden's lesser-known Irish paternal ancestor, his great-great-grandfather, John Hanniffy, more than a hundred and fifty years after it went through the printing press.

It is unknown if the sisters were ever reunited with their relatives, but fast forward to Ballinacourty in the twenty-first century and the advert did eventually come to the attention of the Hanniffy family, three generations on. Sitting in his back porch looking across a rolling deep-green field running down to Galway Bay, Liam Hanniffy tells how his links to President Biden came as a bolt from the blue in 2014 when his long-lost cousin from Atlanta, Robert D. Walt, turned up on his doorstep to tell him he was related to Vice President Joe Biden. Following the visit, another Tennessee cousin, JoAnn Birmingham, sent on a slew of documents showing his great-grand-uncle John Hanniffy on the 1870 US census, along with the personal ad posted by his sisters indicating his origins in this rugged farm facing the sea.

At the top of a narrow boreen, edged by winding stone walls, stands the centuries-old two-roomed cottage where John Hanniffy was born. Amazingly, it is occupied by his family today. While JFK's homestead still survives in Wexford, it is very rare for a nineteenth-century cottage to be in use by the same family nearly two hundred years on. Galway's legendary oyster beds lie just a few hundred yards away. The seafood, along with a native seaweed called carrageen moss, which grows on rocky outcrops of the Atlantic, would have kept the Hanniffy family alive in the fishing parish during the famine. Across the bay is Eddy Island, lying in the shadow of the Clare Hills, where the youngsters would have eaten periwinkles along its shore. In the present day, just a mile or two up the road, the oysters which were the staple diet during the potato famine are served up as a Galway delicacy in the famed restaurant Moran's Oyster Cottage.

While John Hanniffy was the relative in the wanted advert, his older brother and Liam Hanniffy's great-grandfather, Timothy or Thady, stayed behind in the whitewashed thatched cottage, now roofed with tiles, where generations of his family were born. From the family plot, Liam reflects on his relative's journey across the Atlantic around the time of the famine, pointing to the field edged by west of Ireland stone walls. 'He would have picked potatoes in that field in his youth,' he says, gesturing the sloping plot before explaining how they would have rented a few fields where they would have kept cows and hens and tended to vegetable and potato crops. The harvests along with plentiful varieties of shellfish and seafish and seaweed in the bay would have ensured they were pretty much self-sufficient. 'They were able seamen . . . Back then there was a pier in Ballinacourty named Lynches, which was a trading port.'

The daughter of Liam's great-grandfather's brother, Mary, married Joseph Robinette, Joe Biden's great-grandfather, making him by his deductions a third cousin, once removed, to the president. His Irish descendant has a theory that seafaring John Hanniffy first went to Britain from his home on Dunbulcawn Bay before working his way across to America on a boat from Liverpool, a journey which could explain the lack of records detailing his entry to the United States.

The advert and census records point to the Galway family being Biden's blood relatives, but in the absence of local church records these weren't enough to confirm the link. And so Megan Smolenyak began looking into the case. Joe Biden contacted the professional genealogist after she'd spent time digging into his family tree years earlier, and she had been flooded with claims of lineage to the vice president. 'Strangers come to me saying they're cousins with him,' she explained, 'but nine out of ten times they're not – they just have a surname in common.'

But when the Hanniffy family produced the 1866 ad, she went searching back through the original records. 'It doesn't happen all that often, but it is really cool when a case turns on a smoking gun. The Hanniffy family dug out the initial ad, and I had to go to the original source.' Although the spelling of the family name had changed from Hanafy, those eighty-nine words would prove to be a signpost to a family line that extended from a boreen in Galway Bay to the railroads of Ohio and on to an Indiana cemetery and finally to the White House itself.

After sifting through ads and census records, she turned to a very 21st-century method to confirm the Galway link with President Biden, using DNA to confirm what missing Irish records failed to do.

> I looked for any Biden connections I could prove. I was concentrating on fourth cousins or closer. I did it very much the same way that people do forensic genealogy these days to solve all these cold cases. You can build up a family tree of any potential matches and you hope to find some overlap. The newspaper ad really bolstered my confidence but without the DNA I wouldn't have been certain.

Although Joe Biden has yet to acknowledge his newly confirmed bloodline to Ireland, his relatives celebrated his inauguration in the middle of the pandemic with stars and stripes flying over his Hanniffy homestead and a wreath of flowers laid at the simple headstone that marks the grave of John and Mary Hanniffy in a graveyard in Indiana.

The US president, the All Blacks and his Irish try-scoring cousins

On the maternal side of Joe Biden's family, one of his recently discovered distant cousins would become part of the Irish rugby team which made history with a maiden win over New Zealand's All

Blacks in November 2016, shortly after their first meeting. It was a David and Goliath rugby rivalry that Joe Biden had witnessed up close and personal decades earlier when he followed the Kiwi legends on a tour of Ireland as a young senator with his brother Jim, watching the South Pacific visitors notch up victory after victory.

Five months before Ireland's first-ever win against New Zealand, David Kearney, the father of Rob and Dave Kearney, the powerhouse siblings who played side by side on the national rugby team for a number of years, received an intriguing call to inform him that the vice president was his fifth cousin. It came just before the US leader made an official visit to Ireland while at the end of his time in office in the Obama administration. 'We had no idea at all,' said Rob Kearney. Towards that trip's conclusion, the Irish rugby-playing brothers were invited to meet their American cousin at a farewell dinner in Farmleigh House in Dublin hosted by Taoiseach Enda Kenny.

At the dinner, Mr Biden and his brother Jim decided to return the Irish hospitality by inviting the siblings over to the White House a few weeks later. President Biden's niece Caroline Biden, who is Jim's daughter, took her newfound Irish cousins on the tour as her uncle was out the country – in New Zealand on official business, as it happened. 'It was very surreal,' remembered Rob of the White House visit:

> We were standing outside the Situation Room, which was pretty incredible when you consider some of the biggest moments in history that would have gone on down in that room. The walkway through the Rose Garden was quite cool. It was a real nice intimate culture there among the staff, it was all quite relaxed, as if it was a very close tight knit family . . . all the same, there was a huge amount of security guards around the place.

Although they missed their chance to visit the Oval Office owing to a delay at the front gates when his brother Dave had to dash back to the hotel for his passport, they were ushered into the vice president's office. 'Dave was sitting down as his table and we were taking some photographs and he went to pick up the telephone and one of the staff was like, "Sir, do not touch that telephone, please do not touch it," which I think put him back in his box a little,' he laughed. 'It is quite incredible,' he said of the visit. 'I suppose it shows how highly Biden thinks of the bond between the Americans and the Irish people.'

On his return to Ireland, a handwritten note in a big brown envelope, mysteriously without postage stamps but with the seal of the vice president's office, arrived at his Dublin home. It read: 'Really sorry I missed you guys when you were Washington, hope you had a good time.' Then the president explained where he was during their July trip. 'By the way, when I was New Zealand, when you were in DC, and I mentioned the two of you to the All Blacks, that we had two cousins who played for the Irish team, and they immediately said "the Kearney brothers". I said we were related. Again, sorry I wasn't in town at the time.' It was signed 'Joe'.

In fact, when he was in Government House in Auckland in July 2016, Mr Biden spoke of his own rugby-playing past to Prime Minister John Key.

> Four hundred years ago, I played rugby when I was in law school . . . and I was telling the two representatives of the All Blacks that came to see me this morning, Mr Prime Minister, that my brother was a rugby player, as well. And one day when I was a young senator during a recess period, he said, 'The All Blacks are playing four matches in Ireland.' And so we packed up, and we followed them all through Ireland. There was nothing but carnage left behind . . . But I am a real fan.

Just a few months after that speech in Auckland, Ireland eventually ended a 111-year wait for a victory at Soldier Field, Chicago, with a 40–29 win against the All Blacks on 5 November 2016 in a stunning upset. Rob Kearney was playing in his full-back position. Celebrating with the team in New York afterwards his phone started buzzing with a call from a private number. 'I don't normally answer private numbers so I didn't, because after that game your phone would be going absolutely ballistic. Then I got a text message from Jim to say, "That's the president calling from the private number." Rob answered immediately when the next private call came through. 'We were chatting for about five minutes or so after the All-Blacks game in Chicago.'

Since his election, the president has kept up his interest in the Irish team with his now-retired cousin receiving a call from his brother Jim on the day before Ireland were to face the All Blacks – the world's top-ranked side – at the Aviva Stadium in Dublin on 13 November 2021. 'Jim said, "Listen, the president wants to wish the Irish team good luck the night before the game,"' said Rob. 'They were trying to set up a video call, but they couldn't align times for one reason or another and then he sent them a letter the morning of the game just wishing them the very best of luck.'

A subsequent video call from Camp David went viral. A beaming President Biden, perched on a chair in between his brother Jim and his sister Valerie, congratulates the Irish rugby team on their victory over the All Blacks, the third since they banished their New Zealand hoodoo five years earlier. In the conversation with the team at the Shelbourne Hotel in Dublin, Jim Biden opens by exclaiming: 'How the hell did you do it without the Kearney brothers?' The president adds, addressing the squad:

> Our cousins. We're so damn proud of you, really and truly. By the way, when I was down in New Zealand not long ago, I was bragging

about you guys. They almost didn't let me off the island, you know what I mean? Congratulations, fellas! The three of us are gigantic fans.

His cousin, who helped facilitate the call that day, says the Irish connection is very genuine. 'I was blown away in the message to the Irish rugby team, when [Biden] was like, "I hope you guys don't forget me when I come back to visit." I'm sure he will be back in time.'

That jubilant video call is not the only time Joe Biden's public declaration of his Irish credentials trended on social media to an audience of millions.

I'm Irish . . .

As Joe Biden made his way through a crowded corridor during the 2020 election campaign, BBC's New York correspondent, Nick Bryant, shouted out: 'Mr Biden, a quick word for the BBC?' Without missing a beat, the president looked around and answered: 'The BBC – I'm Irish . . .' before flashing a cheeky grin. The video from the campaign trail went viral, simultaneously drawing approving smiles in Ireland and uncomfortable grimaces across the water in Britain. Biden's ethnicity is measured at five-eighths Irish, two parts English with one part French, but there's no doubt that Irishness is baked into his identity. It was fed into his psyche in his formative years growing up in the most Irish of American cities, Scranton, Pennsylvania – well before he ever entered the political arena.

Outside of New York and Boston, there are probably more Irish neighbourhoods per square mile in Scranton than in any other city in the United States. While Irish immigrants have scattered from their initial dyed-in-the-wool green districts over the centuries,

Scranton's Irish have tended to stay in the same streets, the same blocks, with houses handed down from one generation to the next. The president of Scranton's City Council, Bill Gaughan, says the city is full of second and third generation Irish. 'Being an Irish American was one of the big things that we knew when we were growing up. There are so many people of Irish descent. We're proud of it, we wear it as a badge of honour.'

Where Biden grew up in Scranton's Green Ridge neighbourhood, it is said that 'Irish-Catholic Democrat' was one conjoined word. The city is one of the few places where the tribal allegiance to the Democrats endures, especially when one of their own is in the running for office. The Irish heritage is evident in the names of the businesses there: Kelly's pub, Kelleher's tyres, Kildare's Irish Pub, and on and on.

Mayo is the big connection leading to Scranton, which is also twinned with the county's bustling provincial town of Ballina. Joe Biden's west-of-Ireland maternal ancestors give him an even greater affinity with the east coast American city where he spent the first ten years of his life.

'My grandmother's mother was from County Mayo and my dad's grandfather was too,' explains Bill Gaughan, whose council has issued an invitation to President Biden to come to Scranton, where they have named a street in his honour. 'We have not only a president who literally grew up five minutes away from where I live now in Scranton, but his ancestors are right up the road from where my ancestors are from in Ireland – a Hollywood producer couldn't write it,' he adds.

For RTÉ's Washington correspondent Brian O'Donovan, Biden's affection for Ireland made his job a bit easier in the press corps scrum in the US capital in the aftermath of the 2020 election. The media had camped out at Biden's HQ at his hometown in Wilmington,

Delaware, to catch soundbites from the president-elect. On 24 November, outside the Queen's Theatre, where he was holding meetings, aides informed the mostly American press pool that Joe Biden wouldn't be stopping to take questions, so they trouped back onto the media bus. The Irish station is small potatoes compared to the CNNs and NBCs of the world, but when a seasoned US correspondent recognised the RTÉ station microphone still waiting outside the theatre, she informed her colleagues and they filed off the bus and stood next to the Irish correspondent. Sure enough, when Brian shouted, 'A question from Ireland,' the president-elect walked over to the camera.

In answer to O'Donovan's question about the importance of maintaining an open border on Ireland post-Brexit, a masked Joe Biden firmly stated: 'We have worked too hard to get Ireland worked out . . . the idea of having the border north and south once again being closed, it's just not right, we have got to keep the border open.'

While President Obama famously told the British people they would be at the 'back of the queue' when it came to striking a trade deal if they voted for Brexit, President Trump U-turned this dictate during his bromance with Boris Johnson in the dying days of his term. With President Biden in office, the scales were again tipping in Ireland's favour, certainly when it came to any question of Britain reneging on any elements of the Good Friday Agreement. Irish-American Democratic congressman Richard Neal, chair of the Friends of Ireland caucus, and significantly chairman of the powerful House Ways and Means Committee which signs off on any trade deals between the UK and US, has proved to be another powerful bulwark for Ireland as he has repeatedly warned Britain against overwriting any part of the historic Northern Ireland peace deal.

Irish poetry recited in Mumbai and Beijing and Auckland

James Joyce, Seamus Heaney, William Butler Yeats . . . the list goes on. Lines from his favourite poets find their way into Joe Biden's speeches in the most surprising of places. During an address at the 2013 United States–India Partnership at the Bombay Stock Exchange in Mumbai, the then vice president evoked Yeats's 'Easter Sunday 1916' to describe the 'state of the world as we find it today'.

In December later that year, at a breakfast with the American Chamber of Commerce and the United States–China Business Council in Beijing, he quoted Yeats again before remarking: 'My colleagues always kid me about quoting Irish poets all the time. They think I do it because I'm Irish. I do it because they're the best poets,' he wisecracked to more laughter. Yeats was also quoted during his aforementioned New Zealand visit in 2016.

While he has had a lifelong love affair with Irish culture, Biden was unsure of the minutiae of his lineage until he was sworn in as vice president. When Megan Smolenyak posted a story online about his family tree around 2008, she was astonished to get a call out of the blue from the Pennsylvanian politician.

'"This is Joe Biden, Vice President Joe Biden," announced the voice down the line. He just called. He really does that,' smiled Megan. 'We talked all about his aunty Gertrude and his grandfather Finnegan.' The genealogist ended up meeting Biden in person after doing an ancestral profile on him when he was selected for the Irish America Hall of Fame. 'He shouted me out during his remarks and then he proceeded to start inviting me to his St Patrick's Day breakfast each year. I've been to it six or seven times – there were all these big names, and then people like me, and his pets' veterinarian.'

Biden's mother's side of the family is completely Irish while his father also has English ancestors. 'He's got multiple lines,' Ms Smolenyak explains:

> I was the first to say he was five-eighths Irish. He was raised in that environment. He had older single relatives who lived with him in the house at different times and he would have soaked up a lot [of Irish culture and heritage]. If you know him personally, he really does tell a lot of stories about his grandfather, Ambrose Finnegan, and shares other family memories. He's very proud of his Irish heritage; he knew of it, but he didn't know the specifics.

Given that he comes from Scranton, the Mayo connection felt a logical one, and so the genealogist tracked down Biden's Blewitt cousins before his trip to Ireland in 2016. 'His mom had visited them in the 1970s, but the two sides had completely lost track of each other. It was only after I found them that it came out that they had met decades earlier. Joe Biden had no idea; he knew his mom had been to Ireland but he didn't know who she met when over there.'

Biden has quoted his grandmother as saying: 'Remember, Joey Biden, the best drop of blood in you is Irish.' The 46th president has also spoken of his mother telling him that being Irish means that 'you never bend, never break and that resilience is critically important' – which ties in with the Scranton narrative. Before visiting Ireland in 2016, Biden stated that Northeastern Pennsylvania will be written on his heart, but Ireland will be written on his soul.

The late son who inspired the Irish visit

As vice president, Biden would draw on that resilience in the year before his state visit to Ireland when his son, Beau, an Iraq War veteran, who served as the attorney general of Delaware, passed away at the age of forty-six after battling brain cancer. When he touched down in Dublin Airport on Air Force Two on 21 June 2016, accompanied by his daughter, Ashley, his sister, Valerie, his brother, Jim, and his grandchildren, he was fulfilling a promise he'd made to his late son to make a family trip to Ireland. Beau Biden was the second of Joe Biden's children to precede their father in death – the vice president's one-year-old daughter Naomi was killed in a car accident at Christmastime 1972 along with his first wife, Neilia. Three-year-old Beau and his younger brother Hunter were injured but survived the accident. Joe Biden was sworn in as senator at the hospital bedsides of his sons a few weeks later.

The trip to Ireland was also in memory of his late mother, Catherine Eugenia 'Jean' Finnegan Biden, who had died at the age of ninety-two in 2010, having lived to see the son in whom she had instilled her own Irish heritage sworn in as vice president of the United States. The six-day trip to Ireland mixed high-level political talks with a personal pilgrimage. Rising at 5 a.m. every day, Biden would take care of diplomatic business before spending the remainder of the day reconnecting with his ancestral birthplaces.

While Megan Smolenyak tracked down the Blewitts in County Mayo, Irish genealogists Fiona Fitzsimons and Helen Moss were contacted by the White House to dig further into the Ballina line. Their research uncovered the little-known Finnegan and Kearney maternal ancestors deep in the Cooley peninsula on the east coast of Ireland. When Fiona Fitzsimons presented the findings to the vice president at the American ambassador's residence in Dublin, he explained how the original idea for the visit came from his son Beau after the death of his Finnegan grandmother.

'Beau and his dad decided they were going to bring the entire family back to Ireland,' Fiona remembers. 'Beau got sick, much sicker than anybody realised, and he died very quickly before they had a chance to do that.' Criss-crossing Ireland with the politician and his extended family as their genealogical guide, Fiona felt she was witnessing a 'leave-taking, of Beau and of Jean . . . This was a real Biden family thing; it was very personal to them.'

It is a sentiment echoed by his cousin Rob Kearney. 'When Beau was still alive it was the big family thing they wanted to do together, all of them, to reconnect with their Irish past and their ancestors and to do a trip over to Ireland. It was a way of honouring Beau, as well, that they would all go back and do this together.'

It was also deeply personal to Joe Biden because it was so important to his mother. The daughter of the late Ambrose Finnegan and Geraldine Blewitt had made her own pilgrimage to Ireland in the 1970s, when she was in her fifties. She carried out old-style genealogy in Ballina by knocking on doors until she found people with the same Blewitt surname as her mother. 'It meant a hell of a lot to her that she found someone of that name,' said Fiona Fitzsimons.

Looking back at nineteenth-century documents, the genealogist discovered that Biden's great-great-great-grandfather Edward Blewitt had married Mary Reddington in 1826. It was deduced that the family were most likely native Irish speakers as Mary Reddington's name was originally Muldearg, with '*dearg*' being the Irish word for 'red'. Working with her colleague Helen Moss, Fiona found out that Edward Blewitt and his brother James were land surveyors, who worked for the Ordnance Survey and the Valuation Office. 'They were part of the rising middle class,' she said, explaining that 'they got not only a national school education but a secondary school education.'

Between 1848 and 1850, Edward Blewitt was an overseer of public relief schemes during the famine which helped to save the lives of the poorest of the Irish poor who were employed in labour gangs to dig ditches, build walls, or repair roads. 'He probably saw some of the worst of what happened,' said Ms Fitzsimons, 'and saw an awful lot of people dying in front of him.'

In 1850, the Ballina Poor Law Union had laid off all their employees, including Biden's ancestor. In 1849, Edward's teenage son, a young seaman called Patrick, went ahead of his family to the US to scout out a home for his parents and his siblings before returning to gather up his family and shepherd them back across the Atlantic. Just a few months after being let go from his job, Edward, his wife and their eight children made the rough winter crossing to America on board the *Excelsior*, arriving in the port of New York on 28 January 1851.

The Joe show

Just over 164 years later, Patrick's great-great-grandson returned to find the streets of Ballina lined with thousands of people chanting 'Joe, Joe, Joe' as they waved stars and stripes. One enthusiastic lady in the crowd declared, 'Ain't no show like a Joe show,' appropriating the catchphrase used to describe the late great Irish country singer Joe Dolan. Flanked by the Mayo-born then Taoiseach, Enda Kenny, and his wife, Fionnuala, the smiling vice president stopped for chats, stepped in for selfies, shook outstretched hands, got down on his hunkers to engage with youngsters before later making his way into a thronged pub for a traditional music session.

'It was such a pleasure to set the seeds during the visit to Mayo in 2016 to what is now a lovely connection between the Blewitts and the Bidens,' said Laurita Blewitt, who hit it off famously with her relative during the Ballina leg of the trip. 'He talked very passionately about his mother's connection to Ireland and how he and his siblings were brought up with very strong Irish values. Since he was child, he was constantly reminded about his Irish roots and connections. His grandmother used to speak Irish to him.'

Before taking his leave of Mayo, Biden, standing alongside his sister, Valerie, and his brother, Jim, placed his hand on his heart under the VPOTUS emblem on his navy jacket as he spoke of feeling extraordinarily at home with the Ballina Blewitts. 'We met our grandmother Finnegan's side of the family, the Blewitts. It was the strangest thing, it was like we'd known each other forever,' he said, adding that during this visit his family had grown.

The following day, while touring Trinity College with his family, he reflected on being among the ranks of American political leaders who walked the corridors of Ireland's oldest college.

> President John Kennedy and his brother Ted Kennedy both spoke here while in office. Woodrow Wilson spent a day wandering around Trinity before he became president, his thoughts full of Edmund Burke. Even Benjamin Franklin was drawn to this beautiful campus when he visited Ireland in 1771 and found, in his words, 'all Ireland is strongly in favor of the American cause'.

Laurita Blewitt experienced the full razzmatazz of a US presidential election when she flew over to Las Vegas in February 2020 to join her relative on the presidential campaign trail. 'I had the chance to see the inner workings of an American candidate's campaign trail and I loved it,' she recalls, adding, 'We cannot wait to welcome him and the family back to Ireland soon as US president. He knows all about the mural in Ballina of him and is so proud of his Irish connection and his ties with Ballina.' And, since his election in 2020, that giant Biden mural with its stars-and-stripes backdrop beams down on the town's square.

From contemplation in Knights Templar cemetery to revelry in centuries old bar

The maze of narrow, sloping roads along the Cooley peninsula, a remote headland jutting out into the Irish Sea, contain the secrets to

Biden's maternal grandfather's people. In contrast to the wildness of the west, there is a stillness to the sea at the northeastern tip of Ireland around the village of Whitestown where the Finnegan family eked out a living in a tiny two-roomed thatched cottage.

The Louth parish of Cooley was the last stop on Biden's whistle-stop tour of Ireland to reacquaint himself with his centuries-old lineage. A path through the Mourne Mountains overlooking the parish is named Maeve's Gap after the Irish queen who led a huge army over the mountains to capture the greatest brown bull in Ireland.

As the line of more than two dozen black cars making up the vice president's motorcade entered Cooley, they passed a roadside sign with the stars and stripes next to the tricolour printed simply with the words 'Welcome home, Joe and Family'. The vehicles pulled in to the picturesque town of Carlingford Lough, the port where his ancestors would have departed Ireland. Today it's a place of adventure sports and its winding streets are full of lively, painted storefronts and boutique cafés.

Before he arrived, genealogist Fiona Fitzsimons briefed Biden and his family on the new information she had unearthed on his mother's father, Ambrose Finnegan, and his side of the family. 'The other side is actually the Finnegans and the Kearneys, who married into the Finnegans.' It was discovered that an entire community from the Cooley peninsula had settled in upstate New York in Seneca, with gravestones in the American county engraved with the deceased's Irish place of birth in the seaside Louth parish. Cross-referencing US records with Irish church and land records helped to unlock the identities of the American politician's ancestors.

From there, the Irish genealogists were able to pinpoint the exact spot where the family's house would have once stood in a sub-townland called Mara Na Trá. 'We traced them back to the 1770s. They became prosperous over time, as much because so many people emigrated and they took over holdings and married in and built up a land bank. But in the eighteenth and nineteenth centuries, they really are subsistence level; they're living on about ten or twelve acres of rocky land.'

The Kearney family were pinpointed to a patch of land in Mara Na Trá after the discovery of a letter from their landlord. Fiona Fitzsimons explained how the Kearney family homestead had long since melted into the landscape.

> I remember he stood there and said: 'So this is what my family would have seen when they looked out?' He wanted to know the nuts and bolts of where the house was and where people were buried.

While Mayo was a very public occasion, the genealogical guide who accompanied Biden on his tour of Ireland felt his visit to the Cooley peninsula to unearth the lesser-known Finnegan bloodline was a more spiritual journey. His walk around the ancient Cill Mhuire graveyard, which dates back to the fifth century, with just his family and local parish priest Fr Malachy Conlon was a private affair.

An old iron gate topped with a white cross leads into the graveyard in the shadow of the mottled mauve and green peak of Slieve Donard, the highest of the Mourne Mountains. The hilltop cemetery in Templetown is lined with rows of mainly nameless marking stones to denote the dead, along with a few named headstones. Adding to the medieval mystery of the site are the crumbling ruins of the Cill Mhuire Church – which translates to the Church of Mary – once run by the Knights Templar. For two hundred years, they were among the wealthiest and most powerful of the Western Christian military orders, key fighters in the crusades, but by the fourteenth century, the order, who went on to inspire Dan Brown's bestseller *The Da Vinci Code*, was disbanded. Back through the centuries, Joe Biden's

Finnegan and Kearney relatives would have been brought over the mountain on horse-drawn hearses to the graveyard where they would be laid to rest.

Standing in the cemetery, Fr Conlon finds it hard to quantify the numbers buried in the graveyard as there are no records.

One of the marked stones in the graveyard is named for a Finnegan. It's not clear if Biden is related to that particular Finnegan, but it is almost certain some of his relatives would have been laid to rest there back through the centuries, as it was the main burial ground for people from Whitestown. Fr Conlon adds:

> He had been adamant he wanted to go to the cemetery where his ancestors were buried. I greeted him formally and I read a poem and we said a prayer. There were members of his family with him, so I just gave them space to be in the place. He was very moved to be at the grave and took much longer than his security people wanted him to take. You feel it when you go to Cill Mhuire. He got quiet time in the cemetery. It was an emotional moment for him, no doubt about it, I would actually say he wasn't expecting it to be.

The mood shifted on his Cooley visit as the cavalcade moved down the road to whitewashed Lily Finnegan's pub where there was quite the carnival atmosphere created by local musicians, Ceól Heads. The visit was described by one local man as 'very homely'.

Fr Conlon was struck by the intensity and the gentleness of the future president, who zoned right in on whoever he was speaking to in any given moment.

The priest heard of the impending visit two months earlier when he got a call from the American ambassador's office. He was asked if he could meet someone at Grange Church at eleven on a Monday morning. Shortly after he arrived, twelve sleek Mercedes pulled into the car park. 'It was incredible,' recalled the priest. 'They took over the GAA complex for a week.' Other locals remember seeing US army snipers in the ditch for a whole week before the visit.

When Lily Finnegan's publican, Derek McGarrity, got a call out of the blue from the US Embassy in the spring of 2016, his first thought was it was a pal playing a prank on him, so he asked the caller for some proof of identity. Pragmatically, she suggested he simply Google the number, which resolved any doubts. The bar had to close for three days prior to the visit to allow for the Garda and the Secret Service to carry out checks. A representative from every family in Whitestown was invited.

The picture-postcard pub, with its old wooden green door, dates back to the 1700s and there are records of it being a licensed premises in the mid-1800s. With the site for the ancestral home about a hundred yards away, it is pretty likely that they patronised the hostelry. 'His ancestors one hundred per cent would have been here,' the publican claims with confidence.

As the vice president made his entry into the bar that day, flanked by around a dozen agents, he turned and declared: 'I don't wanna go home.' Inside the pub, he stretched out on a table a scroll of paper with his family tree on.

In her home on the Cooley peninsula, one of his distant relations Gemma Donnelly, whose mother was called Anne Finnegan, smiles at the memory of Joe Biden pulling up a seat next to her. 'He came in and said, "I'll sit right here," and sat down beside me and they were all clapping. I was showing him old photographs, ones of my daddy and mammy.'

Peter Savage, one of the area's longest serving politicians, surmises: 'It would be safe to say all the Finnegans were related, back a few generations.'

Another Finnegan relative, Mary Mulligan, was delighted when the vice president stopped to talk to her at the door of the pub. 'He actually kissed me,' said Mary. 'My granny was Mary Finnegan. He's very human, I felt there was a bond. When he came back on his private visit, he got pictures taken next to my grandchildren in their Cooley GAA jerseys as he had one of them at home.'

She has since discovered through contact with Joe Biden's American cousins how the tragic death of one of the Irish Finnegans helped to spark the suffragette movement in the United States. The story goes that a young girl called Roseanne Finnegan, a daughter of George Finnegan from Templetown in Louth, died of terrible injuries she sustained in a mill accident when she was seventeen. As a result, the Seneca Falls Convention took place in 1848 to highlight the bad conditions for girls working in the mills. It was attended by Elizabeth Cady Stanton, who effectively launched the suffragette movement at the New York meeting.

Before taking his leave of Cooley that day, Biden signed a book for Fr Conlon with a handwritten quote from *Ulysses*:

> As the Poet said, 'History is a nightmare from which we are trying to wake.'
>
> But we are writing a new history. Joe Biden 6-25-16.

Return of the tourist vice president in a hire car

The following year, when President Trump had taken over the White House, Derek McGarrity got a call to the landline in Lily Finnegan's pub. Out of the blue, an aide asked if he would be around if the former vice president dropped by. This time, in September 2017, there were no flag-bearing diplomatic cars, just Joe Biden pulled up at the wheel of a Jeep with a couple of companions and two aides. The publican remembered Biden telling him on the previous trip, in answer to a question from his car-mad nephew about what kind of vehicle he drove, that vice presidents and presidents in the US couldn't drive.

> There was no fanfare; they were basically retracing everything they had done the year before. His return visit to Whitestown couldn't have been any more different from the first one. He drove himself in a single vehicle accompanied by his brother, son, and two aides. It couldn't have been any more laid back. He was there in casual clothes and he had an updated version of his family tree and he spoke to few people about that and he mentioned that he'd visited the old grave-yard again. A few locals asked him if was planning on standing for election in 2020, to which he replied, 'I'm not sure, maybe I'm too old!'

Back in Dublin during that visit, his brother Jim called up Rob Kearney to invite him to meet them for dinner. The rugby international remembers:

> He was staying in the Shelbourne. The three of us went out for dinner into town and again that was pretty surreal. At the time there was no security; we just walked from the Shelbourne Hotel a few hundred metres down the road for dinner and a lot of people obviously recog-nised him, but he's just so good with his time. He's a gentleman and he's very charismatic. I was just blown away by the level of intellect of the conversation, he was an expert on every single topic we dis-cussed, be it history, war, cancer, politics, banking crisis: whatever the topic, he just knew the whole thing inside out.

Rob Kearney believes there is a genuine quality to the bond, even though the family tie is quite distant. 'Any time we speak to them, it's like *you're our cousins, you're our blood.*'

On that same trip, Biden also reunited with the Blewitts in Mayo and both communities celebrated his election to president in 2020, and eagerly await his return trip to Ireland. For Irish Americans still attached to their ancestral heritage, it can be seen as a closing of the circle, an acknowledgment of the winding journey of their forebears who never got a chance to make it back to Ireland.

Scranton politician Bill Gaughan believes those pictures of home-coming visits beamed back to the United States can still strike a deep chord with generations who listened to tales of living wakes for travellers departing in the certain knowledge they would never again see the faces of their parents and their siblings.

> I've heard the stories from our grandparents who couldn't go back, my mom had an aunt, Margaret Murphy, and she would cry just thinking of County Mayo. To see Joe Biden be able to go back as president of the United States and say, 'Thank you, I'm home.' It's a point of great pride. This is the story of our generation and our life; it's very, very emotional.

For the generations who came after millions of Irish crossed the ocean, the only evidence that often remains of their existence are tombstones with the carved placenames of Irish parishes pointing back to a small island in the north of the Atlantic. In nearly two dozen cases, the descendants of these fleeing immigrants would rise to the highest office in the New World. But their journey would take a different path down through their family trees, beginning with the one American president who'd lost every member of his immediate Irish-born family by the tender age of fourteen.

Ellis Island, New York Bay, where millions of
Irish people arrived into the New World.

CHAPTER EIGHT

THE SPECIAL RELATIONSHIP –
WHERE IT ALL BEGAN

---

*The genealogists cracked the ancestral trail with the
help of a thick brown leather bible which came over
on the boat with Thomas Fitzgerald from Bruff.*

T HE FIRST US PRESIDENT WITH AN IRISH BLOODLINE was born
to his grief-stricken mother in a simmering continent on the
brink of the American Revolution. His birth in a backwoods settlement along the border of the Carolinas on 15 March 1767 was just two
weeks after the death of his father, Andrew Jackson Snr. His parents
had crossed the Atlantic two years earlier with their two-year-old
son, Hugh, and one-year-old baby Robert, leaving behind the
familiarity of their white stone cottage in the village of Boneybefore
near Carrickfergus in Antrim in Northern Ireland to board a ship to
America at the port of Larne in Antrim. A series of tragedies during
the American War of Independence would wipe out Jackson's entire
family during his turbulent childhood, with his mother and two
brothers dying prematurely in the New World, leaving him an
orphan at the age of fourteen in 1781. At this stage, America was in
its infancy, with the Declaration of Independence, written by Thomas
Jefferson, accepted by the US Congress on 4 July 1776, an act which

had sparked the revolutionary war. Decades after the United States won independence from Britain in the 1780s, Andrew Jackson would accede to the highest office in this new country in 1829 at the age of sixty-one, but none of his Irish-born family lived to see him being inaugurated.

Andrew Jackson was the first president to emerge from the hundreds of thousands of Presbyterian immigrants exiting Northern Ireland to arrive in America through the seventeenth, eighteenth and nineteenth centuries. The arrival of Christopher Columbus to American shores at the end of the fifteenth century had led to the colonisation of the continent from 1600 onwards by the European powers of France and Britain. Birth, death, marriage and some shipping records from the American colonies show the presence of Irish-born people as early as the 1630s. But the first large swathe of Irish emigration came from 1715 onwards through much of the eighteenth century with the exodus of Presbyterians from Northern Ireland. Many of the ancestors of Irish-American presidents come from the migration of entire families, and in some cases entire communities of Protestant dissenters, across the Atlantic in the crammed holds of cargo ships in search of religious liberty. The communities known as Ulster-Scots or Scotch Irish were also fleeing the oppressive regime of high taxes imposed by the established Anglican Church in Ireland. There was also some migration of Anglican Protestants and Catholics from Ulster and Munster, but in small numbers in the eighteenth century. This pattern continued until the early part of the nineteenth century.

From 1815 to the start of the Irish Famine in 1846, between 800,000 and one million Irish sailed for North America with roughly half settling in Canada and the other half in the United States. In the eighteenth and nineteenth centuries and the first half of the twentieth, the scions of Ulster-Scots were sworn into the presidency while the descendants from southern Irish became commanders-in-chief in the twentieth and twenty-first centuries.

American frontiers

The 11th president, James Knox Polk, was born in Mecklenburg, North Carolina in 1795. His great-great-grandfather, William Polk, was thought to be born in Donegal more a century earlier, around the year 1664, and to have died in Maryland, America, in 1739 or 1740 when America was still a colony. William Polk arrived on the east coast with his Donegal parents, Robert Pollock and Magdalen Tasker, from the parish of Lyford, around the turn of the eighteenth century. His descendant was sworn into office in 1845, the second Irish American to become commander-in-chief.

The parents of James Buchanan Jnr, who was the 15th president to reside in the White House, arrived in Pennsylvania in 1788 from Donegal four years before his birth in a log cabin. His father, James Buchanan, was Irish while his mother, Elizabeth Speer, was English, but it's understood that her father was originally from Ireland. James Buchanan Jnr, a lifelong bachelor, was sworn into office in 1857, serving his term immediately prior to the American Civil War.

His successor Abraham Lincoln — one of the most iconic US presidents — was removed from his Irish relatives by many generations, but the records suggest he probably had a great-great-great-great-grandmother called Martha Lyford, who was born in Ireland before 1624, making her one of the earliest known of all presidential ancestors, although Lincoln scholars can't find documentation to confirm her birth back in Ireland. The president who issued the Emancipation Proclamation to abolish slavery was the son of a Kentucky frontiersman. A few months before he received his party's nomination for president, he wrote an account of his humble background:

I was born Feb. 12, 1809, in Hardin County, Kentucky. My parents were both born in Virginia, of undistinguished families – second families, perhaps I should say. My mother, who died in my tenth year, was of a family of the name of Hanks . . . My father . . . removed from Kentucky to . . . Indiana, in my eighth year . . . It was a wild region, with many bears and other wild animals still in the woods. There I grew up . . . Of course, when I came of age I did not know much. Still somehow, I could read, write, and cipher . . . but that was all.

The Irish connection comes through Lincoln's paternal line. The dangers of frontier living are evidenced in the death of his namesake grandfather, who was recorded as killed by 'Indians' in Jefferson County in Kentucky around 1786. He would have been a great-great-grandson of the aforementioned Martha Lyford, who had settled in Massachusetts after travelling to America from Ireland in the mid-seventeenth century. Leading presidential genealogist Gary Boyd Roberts says her father, Reverend John Lyford, who in 1597 was a graduate of Magdalen College, Oxford, went on to preach at Leverlegkish in Armagh before leaving Ireland for Salem, Massachusetts. 'This minister is basically English, has a ministry in Ireland and a daughter probably born in Ireland, and she married Samuel Lincoln, an emigrant from England, in Hingham, Massachusetts,' explained Roberts. 'They are Lincoln's emigrant ancestors.'

Andrew Johnson succeeded President Lincoln in the White House after his assassination on Good Friday, 14 April 1865, at Ford's Theatre in Washington by John Wilkes Booth, an actor, who is believed to have thought he was helping the South with his actions. Johnson led the US government's efforts to re-establish the Union following the conclusion of the Civil War. He also made history as the first US president to be impeached, though he was kept in office by the Senate.

An old gaming table in the Johnson homestead, inlaid with over 500 pieces of Irish wood, is believed to have been a political gift to celebrate his Irish ancestry, possibly from the Fenians. But the actual records are sketchy for the president who grew up in poverty in North Carolina in the early 1800s before being apprenticed to a tailor as a young boy. The Ulster Scots Agency states that his grandfather left Mounthill outside Larne in Antrim and arrived in America around 1750. Gary Boyd Roberts says his mother's maiden name of McDonough would certainly point to his Irish ancestry.

Ulysses Simpson Grant, the 18th president to be sworn into office, was a Civil War hero who had the distinction of being the first American leader to visit Ireland. His maternal great-grandfather, John Simpson, was born in Northern Ireland. Grant, who served two terms as president from 1869 to 1877, visited Ireland in January 1879, for five days as part of a world tour he undertook with his wife Julia, after leaving the White House. Less than a decade later, Chester Alan Arthur became America's 21st president in 1881, succeeding President James Garfield upon his assassination. Arthur's father, the Reverend William Arthur, was a Baptist preacher who had left his whitewashed, thatched cottage in the Draen outside the town of Ballymena in Co. Antrim for New York before the birth of his son. His emigration from Northern Ireland took place in the 1810s, almost a century before his child was sworn into office.

Arthur was succeeded in March 1885 by another Irish-American politician, Grover Cleveland, whose grandfather, Abner Neal, left Ireland towards the end of the eighteenth century. His great-great-grandmother, Ann Lamb, was from Dublin, making her the first US presidential connection outside of Ulster. In addition, their descendant had the distinction of being the only US president to serve two non-consecutive terms in office. But, sadly, Ann had a tragic start to her life in America. Around the year 1736, her father, Richard Lamb, died at sea on their way to Boston when she was between fourteen or fifteen years old.

Benjamin Harrison, America's 23rd president, who was born on a farm by the Ohio River below Cincinnati, is thought to have had a maternal great-grandfather called Archibald Irwin Jnr who left Ireland in the mid-1700s. Then, just before the turn of the twentieth century, William McKinley was sworn into office in 1897. Records show that his great-great-great-grandfather, David McKinlay, heralded from Ireland. While delivering a speech in Buffalo, New York at the end of his first term in office, in September 1901, President McKinley was assassinated by an anarchist called Leon Czolgosz in a receiving line; it was over a week before he died from complications from the bullet wounds.

His vice president, Theodore Roosevelt, who assumed the presidency, spent the next eight years in the White House. His Irish lineage was similar to his predecessor's pedigree, as it went right back to the eighteenth century. His great-great-grandfather, John Barnhill, was born in Ireland in 1729 and died in Philadelphia towards the end of the century, John Barnhill's father Robert hailed from Antrim, making Roosevelt another Ulster Irish president.

Both the US presidents in the White House during the two World Wars of the twentieth century had Irish connections. Woodrow Wilson's paternal grandfather, James Wilson, came from Ulster while his paternal grandmother, Ann Adams, was also born in Ireland. He went down in history as the president who oversaw America's entry into the First World War and later became one of the founders of the League of Nations in its aftermath. Although there has been much debate over the years as to whether his grandfather, James Wilson, came from Co. Down or Co. Tyrone, Erick Montgomery, the executive director of Historic Augusta, wrote a paper in recent years casting doubt about whether Wilson came from

Strabane. The paper, which delved into numerous records relating to the family of the 28th president, found the family had made repeated, though inconsistent, reports of their origins in Co. Down.

Most Irish of all presidents

There was a forty-year gap from when Wilson left office in 1921 until John Fitzgerald Kennedy put his hand on a Limerick bible to be sworn into office. The 35th president of the United States is generally regarded as the most Irish of all the American commanders-in-chief. He was the first Catholic president to reside in the White House when he was inaugurated in 1961. All eight of his great-grandparents were from Ireland, but in a marked departure from his presidential predecessors, Kennedy's ancestors were mainly from the counties of Limerick, Wexford, Cork and Clare in the south of Ireland with only one great-grandparent hailing from Ulster. The parents of JFK's maternal grandfather, John Francis Fitzgerald, known as 'Honey Fitz', the irrepressible Boston mayor, were Thomas Fitzgerald from the town of Bruff in Co. Limerick and Rose Anna Cox, who is thought to be from Fermanagh. The mother and father of President Kennedy's maternal grandmother, Mary Josephine Hannon, were Michael Hannon, who hailed from the lakeside beauty spot of Lough Gur, a couple of miles outside Bruff, and Mary Ann Fitzgerald, who was also born in Bruff. On JFK's paternal side, his great-grandfather, Patrick Kennedy, hailed from Dunganstown in Wexford while his wife, Bridget Murphy, came from Owenduff in Wexford. His other paternal grandfather, James Hickey, was born near Newmarket-on-Fergus in Clare, close to Dromoland Castle, while his wife, Margaret Field, was born in Rosscarbery in County Cork.

'It took us a long time to get the Irish origin of the eight great-grandparents,' said Gary Boyd Roberts, 'but we finally did.'

The genealogists cracked the ancestral trail with the help of a thick brown leather bible which came over on the boat with Thomas Fitzgerald from Bruff, and subsequently listed the marriages and births of family members across the nineteenth and twentieth centuries. This bible, which listed the birth of JFK on 29 May 1917 in 83 Beals Street, would later be requested by the president-elect to swear him into office in on 20 January 1961. It also showed his grandparents, Honey Fitz and Mary Josephine Hannon, were second cousins with records confirming they got a dispensation from the local archdiocese to get married for what was called 'consanguinity in third degree', which refers to one descendant marrying another descendant.

Gary Boyd Roberts explained how he worked on the paternal side of the family tree. 'There will be plenty of Patrick Kennedys, but there will only be one Bridget Murphy Kennedy, so you find her.' He did find a paper trail relating to JFK's great-grandfather by finding the death record for his wife Bridget Murphy Kennedy in Massachusetts in the local depository. He added that his friend and colleague Richard A Pierce did much additional research before contacting Senator Ted Kennedy, who was curious about the new information.

Mr Pierce painstakingly pieced together the details of the eight different lines over years of flying back and forth to Ireland to pore over records in churches and other Irish institutions.

JFK's Texas successor, Lyndon B. Johnson, had ancestors much further back than his predecessor in the White House with a great-great-great-great-grandmother, Hannah Taggart, who was born in Ireland in 1745. When Richard Nixon came to Ireland in 1970 during his presidency, he referred to his great-great-great-great-great-grandfather, John Milhous, in speeches during his tour of the country. His mother, Hannah, was descended from the Milhous family, Irish Quakers who came to America from Timahoe, Kildare, although John Milhous and his wife Sarah Mickle were originally from Antrim. He made a moving speech at the Quaker graveyard in Timahoe in remembrance of these maternal ancestors, but records show he had a closer relative on the Nixon side of the family in Irishman Isaac Brown, who was his great-great-great-grandfather, although his birth location is unknown. Another great-great-great-great-grandfather on the Nixon line was James Moore, who arrived from Ballymoney in Antrim in the 1700s.

Ford, who assumed the presidency following Nixon's resignation in 1974, had links that were many generations back in the distant past. His great-great-great-great-great-grandfather, John Blackburn Jnr, was born in Killmore in Co. Armagh in 1720, while his great-great-great-great-great-great-grandparents Moses Harlan and Margaret Ray were from Donnahlong in Co. Down – both were born in 1683. President Jimmy Carter, in common with President Ford, was unaware of his Irish connections while in office, but records show he had a great-great-great-great-grandfather called George Brownlee, who was born in Co. Antrim in 1757, while he had a great-great-great-great-great-great-grandfather called Joseph Scott from Ballymacran in Co. Derry.

In the 1980s, Ronald Reagan discovered a much closer connection than his predecessors with his great-grandfather, Michael Regan, hailing from Ballyporeen in Co. Tipperary while his wife, Catherine Mulcahey, was also from Ireland on his father's side of the family. His other paternal great-grandfather, Patrick Cusick, was from Ireland while his wife, Sarah A. Higgins, was either from Ireland or New York. President George H.W. Bush had a great-great-great-great-grandfather called William Holliday from Rathfriland in Co. Down, while you would add another great for his son, President George W. Bush. The 42nd president, William Jefferson Clinton, has Irish ancestry on both sides of his family, but the records are very patchy. His father, William Jefferson Blythe III, died two weeks after his son was born and Bill later took his stepfather's name of Clinton. On his paternal bloodline, he had one great-great-grandfather called Ayers and another great-great-grandfather called Hayes. His mother was called Virginia Dell Cassidy. Despite the incomplete records, genealogists are quite satisfied of his Irish heritage with names such as Cassidy, Grisham, Hayes and Ayers in his family tree. At the end of his time in the White House, he often alluded to an old mid-eighteenth-century farmhouse in Roslea, Fermanagh, which was linked to his mother's Cassidy relatives.

Into the twenty-first century, presidential ancestors were discovered principally in the south of Ireland.

President Obama's forebears came from his maternal line from a tiny village in the heart of Leinster, while President Biden's were born on opposite sides of the island, on the windswept west coast counties of Mayo and Galway and along the sheltered shores of the Cooley peninsula. In common with millions of other Irish immigrants, they crossed the Atlantic in and around the famine years. Their children had children and their children had children and, within the space of a century and a half, their offspring took the oath of office on the steps of the US Capitol.

The last photograph taken of Abraham Lincoln before he was assassinated. It's thought that he has an ancestral link to Ireland, but this has never been proven.

CHAPTER NINE

FRONTIER PRESIDENTS IN THE MAKING OF AMERICA

I have told them of the courtesy and hospitality I have experienced under your roof, and at your table, and that I always placed it to the a/c of being an Irishman.

A N INTERMINABLE TRAIN OF threadbare Irish immigrants made their way unsteadily down the gangplanks of tall ships into teeming American ports during a mass exodus which would span three centuries. Millions lured by the promise of the American dream and vast plains of land pulled up stakes, gathered their belongings and moved their families thousands of miles into an unknowable future. A tiny fraction of this vast movement of people was quite unaware their descendants would one day become the future CEOs of America. The first significant wave of Irish emigration to the colonies came in the eighteenth century, with relatives of many future Protestant presidents disembarking in ports along the east coast of America, although records show arrivals of Irish-born people as far back as the 1600s. Maryland, Delaware and the Carolinas pop up on the records of the presidential antecedents, but by far the most common destination was Pennsylvania followed by Massachusetts.

There is a neat dozen presidents with Irish bloodlines before President Kennedy – although the records are not definitive on President Andrew Johnson. They come from largely Presbyterian Northern Ireland stock who travelled to the colonies in the 1700s. Of these first twelve presidents, three had one or more Irish parents, while three could lay claim to an Irish grandparent or grandparents, another two had Irish great-grandparents, while the remaining four had links further back in their family tree. Ulster was the main breeding ground for the ancestors of the presidents who ascended to the White House in the late 1700s through the 1800s and into the start of the 1900s. Antrim was the birthplace of at least six presidential ancestors, while Donegal is recorded as the family seat for President James Polk and President James Buchanan.

By the time these Irish-American presidents were born a generation or two – or more – after the arrival of their pioneering relatives, their families were largely part of the Protestant elite in America. Many of these presidents who served in office throughout the nineteenth century and into the beginning of the twentieth century were university-educated in colleges such as Harvard, Princeton and various other East Coast universities, with the majority of them practising law before entering the White House. The exceptions were President Grant, who attended the West Point Military Academy, President Theodore Roosevelt who went to Harvard but entered public service after studying a year of law, President Lincoln, who passed the bar after educating himself with borrowed law books, and President Andrew Johnson who grew up in poverty and became a tailor before entering politics.

Quite a few were the sons of ministers or had a minister a few generations back in their family. But, by and large, by the time the future Irish-blooded presidents were born in America, their parents were part of a hard-working, land-owning class of new emigrant on the American frontier who could afford a college education for their offspring.

The three Ulster ports of Newry, Belfast and Londonderry accounted for the highest number of ships crossing the Atlantic, although there was also a trickle of immigration from the southern Irish ports of Cork, Waterford and Dublin in the 1700s. A sizeable minority of the passengers were indentured servants, poverty-stricken immigrants who signed up to seven years of free labour in exchange for their passage to the New World: some of their own free will; others, among them political prisoners, were forced into bondage.

From the 1750s onwards, most Ulster immigrants went mainly to Philadelphia, but they also poured into the neighbouring ports of Baltimore and Charleston. They were escaping religious persecution, along with a succession of poor harvests, droughts, escalating rents and crippling tithe payments, the latter a form of discriminatory tax. Penal laws brought in by the Protestant-dominated Irish parliament in the early eighteenth century were apartheid-style laws mainly against Catholics but also Presbyterians who refused to conform to the Church of England. The laws affected almost all aspects of life from the validity of marriages and succession rights to being banned from public office. It is estimated that around 200,000 Ulster Presbyterians bolted from the north of Ireland to America between 1700 and 1775 to a world full of promise and possibility, but scant records mean that the numbers could in fact have been anything from 40,000 to 400,000.

While most Ulster immigrants left the province in the nineteenth and twentieth centuries, the majority of the relatives of US presidents arrived in the 1700s. Dr Patrick Fitzgerald, head of research and development at the Mellon Centre for Migration Studies at the Ulster American Folk Park, believes religious discrimination certainly helped push Presbyterians towards the docks but that the promise of a wide-open colony was an irresistible draw.

> There is also the pull of America increasingly from the middle part of the eighteenth century, that sense of opportunity and ambition was drawing on Ulster Presbyterians to encourage them to cross the Atlantic. Relatively poor tenants could come to own a significant quantity of land. Throughout the eighteenth and early nineteenth century this is a constant dream, the Ulster Presbyterians had the desire to own their own land and to acquire quite big quantities of it.

Many Presbyterian ministers used their pulpit to persuade entire communities to uproot their lives and sail to the colonies during this century. New laws had left non-Anglican ministers stripped of their powers to legally perform marriages and funerals, while the British Empire's cancellation of the annual salary paid to Presbyterian ministers who refused to conform left many impoverished and searching for a new path for themselves and their flocks. The flow of Presbyterians is thought to have accelerated in 1718 when Massachusetts' Governor Samuel Shute offered free land in the colony for Ulster settlers.

The voyage on tall sailing ships in the 1700s could take up to six to eight weeks or more depending on the wind, but there were horror reports of passengers being stuck on boats for twelve weeks. During stormy passages they could be confined to between decks for days or even weeks at a time. On board, families crammed into wooden berths amid the stench of vomit and the odour of human bodies packed together like livestock. Fever, dysentery, rampant lice, scurvy from poor diet and unsanitary water were among the conditions that could run rampant through passengers confined to their quarters below deck for much of the journey. Along with the sickness and hunger, the immigrants and their small children often had to sail through violent Atlantic storms. 'Crowding, darkness, damp, boredom were things that were often reported in letters and journals kept by immigrants in the eighteenth century,' noted Dr Fitzgerald. 'Yes, there were horrors, yes, there were occasions when people died, yes, there were shipwrecks, and food and water could run out after fifty days or sixty days afloat, but most of the time that didn't happen.'

While some younger, single Ulster Presbyterians came across as bonded servants, most were families who paid the fare of three to six pounds sterling, disembarking in ports like Philadelphia to stock up on supplies before heading out to the American frontier and down through the backcountry of Appalachia stretching from southern New York to northern Mississippi.

This was the stagecoach era – brought to not entirely unproblematic life on the silver screen in Westerns for the captive audiences of the 1950s and 60s – and families in horse-drawn Conestoga wagons shuttled along the rutted paths carved into the vast landscapes for weeks and months at a time. All their earthly possessions were piled under the canvas cover as they made epic journeys down the length of the Great Wagon Road. The well-worn, ancient path, etched into the land over centuries by Native Americans, began in Philadelphia and ran down the east coast of the continent. Communities would form trains moving at a painstakingly slow pace of three or four miles an hour with the lead coach pointing towards the North Star at sunset before making camp for the night. As Dr Fitzgerald explains:

> They're moving down the Great Valley of Virginia down into the backcountry of the Carolinas and ultimately on through to Tennessee and Kentucky. They're also going to the backcountry of Pennsylvania. This was the area where most of the Presbyterians from Ulster had settled in the eighteenth century. They were acquiring land on the open market in America. The land in and around Philadelphia by the

end of the eighteenth century has become very densely populated so they need to move further and further to the west.

Arthur Dobbs, a Scottish-born member of the Irish parliament, acquired swathes of North Carolina while still in Ireland before leaving his home in Carrickfergus in Antrim to become the governor of the state in the 1750s. 'He acquired large holdings of land and he sought to settle it, with people who he knows will want to come out from Carrickfergus. The land, of course, has come from Native Americans. Native American land has ultimately, through the course of the seventeenth and eighteenth centuries, been eaten up by white European settlement.'

The settlers encountered extremities of weather, worlds away from the mild Irish climate, and dangerous wildlife such as bears and snakes. Although there were conflicts, the Indigenous people also helped the settlers to adapt to their new and somewhat hostile environment. As Dr Fitzgerald emphasises: 'A point to bear in mind is how much they learned from Native Americans, certainly in the early stages of first settlements.'

While the pioneers set up log cabins on farms larger than they could ever have envisaged back in Ireland, the commercially minded Presbyterians also helped to build towns, but mainly they enjoyed the freedom of their new life. 'They talk quite a bit in the letters about the capacity to establish their independence, and of course it's not unconnected to the War of Independence that America fights against Britain in the revolutionary period,' notes Dr Fitzgerald. 'One of the things they were best known for was their dissenting spirit: they buy into the idea of political freedom.'

In the New World, the Scottish-Irish populations enjoy many more advantages than the Irish who would flee the famine the following century. 'They are white, they are Protestant, they are literate, they are often part of a backcountry elite, if they've got land or they've become involved in business,' notes Dr Fitzgerald. And with that as their springboard it's perhaps not surprising their descendants went go on to occupy the White House for much of the nineteenth century.

Orphan of American Revolution, original birther letter and a controversial hanging

In a smoky log cabin in the backwoods of Waxhaws in the Carolinas, the first Irish-American president was born to his recently widowed mother on 15 March 1767. After crossing the Atlantic in 1765, Elizabeth Jackson was among the rush of early settlers who had made their way down the eastern states of America with her husband Andrew Jackson Snr and their two small sons. But by the time their third son, Andrew Jackson Jnr, was born amid the rolling hills of their new home, Elizabeth was grieving the loss of her young husband a mere two weeks earlier.

Local folklore has it that her husband's coffin was placed on a sled on a cold winter's morning in 1767 to be dragged around from house to house as was the custom of the traditional Irish wake. But when the funeral party arrived at the cemetery of Old Waxhaw Presbyterian Church two days later, they couldn't locate the coffin. But eventually the body was recovered and buried in the graveyard. Left alone to raise her three young sons in the turbulent years of the American Revolution, the young widow, described as a vibrant red-haired woman with snapping blue eyes, moved to the nearby home of her sister and brother-in-law, the slaveholding farmers, Jane and James Crawford.

When the Continental Congress approved the US Declaration of Independence, sparking the American Revolutionary War over a decade later on 4 July 1776, all three Jackson brothers enlisted to fight for their new country's freedom against British forces. The future president was just thirteen years old. His oldest brother, Hugh, died of heatstroke following the Battle of Stono Ferry in June 1779 while, two years later, Jackson and his brother Robert were captured.

During this time, the story is told that a British officer slashed Jackson with his sword after he refused to polish the officer's boots. Both boys contracted smallpox in prison and were gravely ill when their mother arranged for their release in a prisoner exchange, but Robert died two days later.

After she nursed her youngest child back to health, Jackson's Antrim-born mother travelled to Charleston to nurse injured and sick soldiers on prison ships in the harbour. While there, she contracted cholera and died, leaving Jackson a brotherless orphan at the age of fourteen. However, while he was a teenager, he did receive a modest inheritance from a grandfather still in Ireland. After his mother's death, Andrew went to live with relatives, going on to study law and become licensed as an attorney. Tall and lanky with red hair and piercing blue eyes like his mother, Jackson was known for his fearlessness, playful personality and volatile nature which got him embroiled in several duels.

During his lifetime, the president searched in vain to find where his mother had been laid to rest in the confusion of the revolution. It had been feared she may have died on the roadside, but the mystery of her final days was solved in 1918 with the discovery of a funeral notice of a fellow Antrim woman called Agnes Barton. A letter in the *Nashville Banner* from a man called John explains how he unearthed an obituary dating back to 1846 which relayed how Elizabeth Jackson was nursed in her final days by Mrs Barton. After she died, the future president's mother was dressed in Mrs Barton's clothes and laid to rest in a coffin made by her carpenter husband – although they couldn't afford a marker for her grave. Sadly, Andrew

Jackson died never knowing that his mother had had a Christian burial in the presence of Irish mourners.

Throughout his life, there are records of the Irish-American president purchasing slaves. His thousand-acre cotton plantation relied completely on the labour of enslaved African-American men, women and children. At the time of his death in 1845, Jackson owned approximately 150 people who lived and worked on the property. Another eight presidents would be sworn into office after Jackson departed Washington before the 16th president, Abraham Lincoln, finally issued the Emancipation Proclamation that declared forever free those slaves within the Confederacy in 1863.

As a military general, he became a national hero after he won the Battle of New Orleans in January 1815 against the British. Then in 1828, he was elected to the Senate before being sworn in as the 7th president of the United States. In his first term, Jackson infamously signed the Indian Removal Act into law to grant lands west of the Mississippi in exchange for Indian lands within existing state borders. The forced relocation of the Cherokees to the west by the government in the nineteenth century caused thousands of deaths. The harrowing journey would become known as the Trail of Tears.

There is evidence that Jackson was probably the first president to have his birth country questioned – in his case in a letter from a man called James Kerns. Kerns declares it 'very important that I should prove you are a Country man' and asks him '*whether or not you were born in Ireland*'. It appears Kerns had a wager going about where Jackson was born – Ireland or the American Colonies – although the letter is dated February 1815, years before Jackson's White House bid.

In 1819, his Irish heritage was marked when he was elected an honorary member of the Hibernian Society of Philadelphia for the Relief of Immigrants from Ireland. At the docks, members of the society from the Irish community would board ships and seek out fellow country folk in need. His certificate of membership now hangs in his Hermitage estate in Nashville. The gilt-framed certificate is engraved with an emigrant ship with the flag of Erin along with a harp at the feet of four floating female figures adorning the foreground. It reads:

> These are to certify that Maj. Gen. Adw. Jackson has been admitted a Member of the Hibernian Society, for the relief of Emigrants from Ireland, established in the City of Philadelphia and incorporated agreeably to Law; and he having paid the sums required by the Rules and Regulations of the said Society is entitled to Membership during his Life.

In another series of letters, Jackson references his Irish parents amid a furore over a presidential pardon he made in 1830 when he was in office. Two men, a US man named George Wilson and his Irish-born accomplice James Porter, were sentenced to execution by hanging for robbing a United States mail carrier. When President Jackson issued a formal pardon saving American-born Wilson from execution there was an outcry from the Irish community over his failure to grant a similar reprieve to Porter.

The day after Porter was hanged before a crowd of a reported 40,000, mainly his fellow Irish folk, in Philadelphia on 2 July 1830, an Irish-born Philadelphia merchant, James Gowen, writes to President Jackson to say how it was suggested among the Irish community that he pardoned Wilson and executed Porter 'merely because he was an Irishman'. He added in the letter, dated 3 July 1830, that he defended the president against accusations of bigotry:

> I pledged myself for the purity of your motives and the absence of all partiality—That had you a bias twas Irish—I have told them of the

courtesy and hospitality I have experienced under your roof, and at your table, and that I always placed it to the a/c of being an Irishman.

Gowen went on to praise the large Irish crowd for resisting the urge to save their countryman from the gallows. 'Thank God no rescue was made ... no other class of men in this community, feeling as much as the Irish did feel on the day of the Execution, would have so respected the Laws ... how easy it would have been for them, to have rescued Porter.'

In a reply a few weeks later, Andrew Jackson insisted he was not prejudiced against his own countrymen. He declared:

> The absurdity that I should have pardoned Wilson because he was an American, and permitted Porter to be hung, because he was an Irishman is too palpable to deserve one single comment from me, when it is known my parents were Irish ... I never shall regret my action in this case. I am very respectfully yr mo obdt. servt. Andrew Jackson.

But in another twist to this controversial case, Wilson rejected the pardon as he was still set to serve twenty years in prison for other charges against him. There are conflicting reports as to whether he was hanged or whether he served his time behind bars.

In personal correspondence during his presidency, Jackson was sent a family tree by his Secretary of State and future president Martin Van Buren on 10 December 1832, stating that Jackson's father, Andrew Snr, emigrated from Ireland in 1765 and had three sons, Hugh, Robert and Andrew. It was sent to Van Buren by a man called Thomas Suffern after he heard a speech by the president's secretary months earlier at Tammany Hall, the headquarters of the powerful New York political society, stating that the president hadn't a single blood relative in the world. In his letter to Jackson, Van Buren corrects his assertion saying: 'The enclosed is from a highly respectable source & may amuse you at least. At your leisure drop me a line upon the subject. My remark was, or was intended to be, that you had no blood relation in this Country.'

Jackson says in his reply to Martin Van Buren: 'I thank you for the enclosure—the statement made of the time when my father came from Ireland, and the names of his children, are correct... I shall, when I have more leisure, look at it with more attention, and scan the relation with more scrutiny.' Owing to the loss of his entire family in such traumatic circumstances at the tender age of fourteen, the president was not well versed on his Irish extended family. He left office in 1837 after serving two terms and died in 1845.

President James Polk vetoes famine aid but makes Irish sympathies clear in private diary

Jackson was still alive to see another Irish American, James Knox Polk, become the 11th president to be sworn into office in March 1845. The start of Polk's presidency coincided with the Irish Potato Famine which saw huge numbers of starving immigrants make the trip across the ocean to the US, sparking anti-Catholic, nativist backlashes. Census figures show an Irish population of 8.2 million in 1841, 6.6 million a decade later, and only 4.7 million in 1891. It is estimated that as many as 4.5 million Irish arrived in America between 1820 and 1930. To put this number into context, between 1820 and 1860, the Irish constituted over one third of all immigrants to the United States, while in the 1840s they comprised nearly half of all immigrants to the US. Although there were substantial numbers crossing the Atlantic in the 1700s from Ulster, it was only a fraction of the deluge of people who crossed the ocean the following century.

Boatloads of famine-stricken, often disease-laden immigrants arrived on boats that earned the bleak moniker of coffin ships, as so many passengers would die on their desperate journey in search of a new life. Before the humanitarian disaster of the famine, immigrants from Ireland were predominantly male, although whole communities often departed together from Northern Ireland. In the famine years and their aftermath, entire families boarded boats in the south of the country. In later years, the majority of Irish immigrants were women, with many going straight into domestic service on their arrival in America.

The descendants of those wearily moving down the gangplanks of east coast ports would in turn pour into every facet of popular American culture. In Hollywood in the mid-twentieth century, the 'Celtic Club' included director John Ford, plus actors such as Spencer Tracy, Gene Kelly and Bing Crosby. Later, Mariah Carey, George Clooney, Tom Cruise, Mark Wahlberg, Matthew McConaughey, Jennifer Connelly, Alicia Keyes and Billie Eilish are among those who could claim Irish genes. There's Katy Perry's Irish great-great-granny and two-thirds of Melissa McCarthy's family, who hail from Longford and Armagh. The list goes on . . .

Irish people are famous for their love of conversation; they are synonymous with phrase 'the gift of the gab'. So it's no surprise that legendary talk show hosts such as Stephen Colbert, Jimmy Fallon and Conan O'Brien all have strong family ties to Ireland. The news networks of the US are also populated with Irish-American voices – from Megyn Kelly to CNN's John King and Fox News's Sean Hannity. Then there are the politicians themselves, for whom the gift of the gab is almost a job requirement.

President Polk's own great-great-grandfather, William Polk, made the journey across the Atlantic with the earliest Irish immigrants to the colonies in the seventeenth century. The president's father, Samuel Polk, was the son of Ezekiel Polk, who was the son of

William Polk Jnr. His father, William Polk Snr, was born in Donegal, Ireland in 1664 and he emigrated to Somerset County in Maryland with his parents, Robert and Magdalen, in the 1680s on a British-built Dutch fluyt. Letters from during Polk's time in the White House show he was very curious about his Irish stock and wanted to establish a thorough family tree for later generations.

Polk received a letter from Templemoyle in Londonderry on 6 February 1846, from a man called John Pollock claiming to be his cousin. He told him he had heard from an American called William Ross of Philadelphia that 'you seemed somewhat desirous to know something of your genealogy from Ireland'. He added:

> This, sir, I think can be easily obtained. I as a near relative of yours can give you a little intelligence on the subject. As I understand that your grandfather was Ezekiel Polk. He and my grandfather were brothers children. They were both born in Templemoyle where I now reside.

He continued: 'I frequently heard my father speak of him as being a stout active man.' Further on he said: 'I can assure you sir that you and I are sprung from a good staunch branch of Presbiterians [sic]. Our ancestors came from Scotland about the year 1609 (and were in high estimation in their native land) and settled in and about where we now reside. And as nothing in life could give me so much pleasure as to have a personal interview with so near a relation more especily [sic] when raised to high an eminence in life.' In a later letter to a William H. Winder in 1848, the president professes a strong interest in obtaining more information on his family tree.

Through the late 1840s, he received desperate letters from Irish people looking to escape the famine by emigrating to America. One lady called Rose Savage from Dublin wrote to him on 13 May 1847, setting out her dire circumstances. She tells him:

The President will know the deplorable state of poor Ireland at this time, & that there is no such thing as earning a support in this poor Country. I am anxious to go to Boston or some of The States, where I would make a livelihood, but I have not the means of paying my way out. I have applyed [sic] to our Queen for assistance having no friends, who can give me money, but she lends a deaf ear to all such applications... If therefore The President will be good, & charitable enaugh [sic] to send me the means of going to Boston I will for ever bless, & pray for him, & The Almighty will reward him, if not here, hereafter.

Rose gives him her address and tells him how the death of her brother has left her alone and penniless. She says she could tell him 'a tale which I will venture to say, will draw tears from his eyes,' adding:

I trust The President w[ill] for The Almighty God's sake, send me the relief I sue fo[r;] otherwise, I know not what I shall do ... Our country is in a dreadful state at present, I may say, w[e] are all almost starving here, [...] every prospect, they say, of thing[s] being worse. Rose Savage [P.S.] I should be sorry to trouble The President could I do otherwise, but I am absolutely destitute of the means of support.

American officials in London and Ireland also reported on the bleak conditions of Ireland to President James Polk and his Secretary of State, James Buchanan. These horrific descriptions, however, were followed by the observation that the failed potato crop had resulted in an increased demand for American food.

In his first dispatch to the president after landing in London in November 1846, the US Minister to Great Britain, George Bancroft, details how there is a big increase in demand for American corn. In a letter a few months later from his residence in Eaton Square in London on 4 January 1847, he observes: *'The affairs of Ireland are much worse for them than you can conceive.'* But he goes on to tell Polk how this will benefit American exports to Britain. 'As to commerce you may rely that the demand for American produce will continue. This year of famine is not to end the demand. On the contrary England & Ireland will for the next year be dependent upon us.'

In another letter in 1847, Bancroft says the famine is an 'all-absorbing topic'. He adds: 'The evils of abject poverty and well-grounded discontent are heightened by famine; & the ministry, & the British public, & the opposition, & most of all, Ireland itself, knows not what to propose.'

While the president received dispatches on the growing demand for corn, on 8 February 1847, Congressman Washington Hunt of New York introduced an Irish relief measure to his legislative colleagues. The bill requested that the United States government spend $500,000 to purchase articles of subsistence for Ireland and to provide the necessary transport. The relief bill died in committee. Weeks later, the same bill was proposed in the Senate by Senator John J. Crittenden. The bill was never passed, and Polk told his cabinet he would veto the bill if it were to be passed. In an entry in his journal dated 3 March 1847 he explained:

> I informed them also that if the Bill which had passed the Senate a day or two ago appropriating half a Million of Dollars to be donated to the Government of Great Brittain for the relief of the suffering poor of Ireland and Scotland should pass the [House of Representatives] and be presented to me, I could not approve it.

In his diary he wrote his justification: 'The chief of which was the want of constitutional power to appropriate money of the public to charities either at home or abroad.' He added: 'I would be compelled to put my veto upon it. I have all the sympathy for the oppressed Irish and Scotch. A few days ago I contributed my mite [$50] for their relief but my solemn conviction is that Congress possesses no power to use public money for any such purpose.' A few days later, he reveals he agreed to place two US navy warships into civilian hands to transport provisions donated by private charities for the 'famishing poor of Ireland and Scotland'.

Repeated entries in Polk's diary the following year show just how much he sympathised with the Irish living under the rule of the British. On 29 August 1848, his Secretary of State, James Buchanan, told him of a visit from Mr Crampton, British charge d'affaires, with a despatch from his government. Polk wrote of how the British aide had been instructed to 'call on the Government of the US to perform their Treaty obligations to Great Brittain and to enforce our neutrality laws, by preventing our citizens from taking part with the people of Ireland in their present attempt to resist the authority of the Brittish Government.' These words were in reference to a failed uprising called the Young Ireland Rebellion, among the leaders of which were William Smith O'Brien and John Dillon. In the diary entry, President Polk revealed his true feelings:

> All my sympathies are with the oppressed and suffering people of Ireland, and I hope no occasion will occur to render it necessary for the Executive to act in enforcing our neutrality laws. I sincerely wish the Irish patriots success, but though this is the case, it would be my imperative duty to see our neutrality laws faithfully executed.

In the diary entry on 5 September 1848, on hearing American citizens might be under arrest for 'participating in the late disturbances in Ireland', Polk instructs George Bancroft in London:

If such was the fact, to see that they had a fair trial, and, if convicted, to procure their pardon if practicable... I had also directed him to instruct Mr. B. to interpose in a delicate way, & intimate to the Brittish Government that it would be very gratifying to the Government & people of the U. S. if that Government could, consistently with its own sense of duty, extend a general amnesty or pardon to English subjects in Ireland... We have no right to make such a demand, but simply to request it and to appeal to the magnanimity of Great Brittain not [to] execute Mr. Smith O'Bryan and other Irish Patriots who are understood to be under arrest for Treason... The whole American people with rare exceptions deeply sympathise with the oppressed and suffering people of Ireland, and if by interposing our good offices the lives of O'Bryan and other leading patriots can be saved, I am sure we will do an act of humanity and discharge a duty which will be acceptable to our own country and, indeed, to the civilized world.

Freedom-seeking President Buchanan proclaims Irish patriotism and Irish send in cavalry for President Lincoln during Civil War

Bachelor president James Buchanan Jnr was the son of a Donegal man, James Buchanan Snr, who travelled to Pennsylvania sometime in the late 1700s. The 15th president of the United States arrived into office in 1857 and served one term just prior to the American Civil War. His father appeared to have thrived in the New World; he could afford to send his son to Dickinson College, and he went on to become a lawyer.

In April 1858, just over a year into his first term, the president received a letter from a relative called Charles W. Russell telling him about his blood ties to Ireland. He begins:

In order to gratify the curiosity which you expressed to me some time ago, I have made inquires [sic]... Your grandfather was John Buchanan, a farmer, who lived near a town called Milford, about four miles from the more important town of Rathmelton in the county Donegal, Ireland ... Your father, the son of John and Jane Buchanan, was taken at an early age ... by his mother's parents to live with them. They brought him up, giving him the best education which the schools in that part of Ireland could furnish, and when he was grown, they fitted him out for America. I have heard that when he arrived in this country, and before he left the vessel, he was met by his uncle – Joshua Russel, I believe – who conducted him from Philadelphia to the interior of Pennsylvania. I have heard my aunt speak of your father from personal recollection of him in Ireland ... she well remembered his departure.

Years before he acceded to his country's highest office, the future president confirmed his pride in his Irish heritage in a letter to W.E. Robinson from his residence in Washington on 6 February 1844. 'Dear Sir,' he begins, before continuing:

In compliance with my promise & your own suggestion, I have the pleasure of informing you that my father, James Buchanan, was a native of the County Donegal, in the Kingdom of Ireland. He emigrated from that country before the date of the definitive Treaty of peace with Great Britain, having sailed from Londonderry, in the Brig *Providence* bound for Philadelphia, on the 4th July 1783. Soon after landing, he made his way to the County of Franklin in the State of Pennsylvania where he ever afterward resided until his death in the month of June 1820, in the 60th year of his age. He came to this country in humble circumstances but with a good English education; and long before his death, he had acquired a competence of the good things of this world. He was highly respected by all who knew him. I was born in the County of Franklin on the 23rd of April 1791. I am proud that Ireland is the land of my forefathers. Centuries of oppression have not destroyed the manly independence of her national character, nor been able to subdue the brave & generous spirit of her sons. May the day of her emancipation soon dawn! Yours very respectfully James Buchanan.

By the time of his departure from office, he left a fractured country on the brink of civil war. When Lincoln was sworn into office in 1861, there was a backlash against the huge influx of Irish emigrants to the States. Like the bigotry that has repeated in cycles over the centuries, with the movement of humans across borders, there was suspicion and fear that this new crop of emigrants would take jobs from the American-born population, as they would be willing to work for lower rates than settlers whose families had made the journey many years earlier. During this time a song was even coined about signs that read 'No Irish Need Apply'. And 1849 saw the founding of the American Party, which began as a secret organisation called the Know-Nothing Party, formed during a tide of anti-immigrant and anti-Catholic sentiment. It gained an initial bumper number of seats in the 1850s but by 1860 its power had dwindled.

Abraham Lincoln, the US's most iconic president, perhaps with the exception of George Washington, was not one of those nativists. As a young attorney in Kentucky, the future president and his wife, Mary, had an Irish live-in housekeeper called Catharine Gordon. Along with two of their three young sons, the eighteen-year-old is recorded in the Lincoln household in the 1850 census in the immediate aftermath of the famine. Another Irish immigrant, Mary Fagan, recalled being taken out of school and working for the Lincolns for two weeks when she was eight years old; during that time she apparently saw jelly, pig feet and celery for the first time in her life.

Lincoln famously issued the Emancipation Proclamation that

freed slaves with the stroke of his fountain pen. On his election in 1860 on an anti-slavery platform, pro-slavery states in America's south seceded from the Union, forming an unrecognised breakaway state called the Confederate States of America. These events sparked the four-year American Civil War between the North and the South, which would end in defeat for the Confederates and the outlawing of slavery. During the war, Lincoln was backed by thousands of Irish men, who fought on the side of the Union, even though most Irish backed the Democratic Party and not the president's Republican Party.

Lincoln's correspondence shows how Irish soldiers were raised by their leaders to fight in the cavalry and infantry against the southern states. One letter dated 25 May 1864, from an Irish native called James L. Kiernan, who served as a brigadier general in the war years, tells Lincoln he can 'turn twenty thousand Irish-American Copperheads in the West into good union men'. One of the most famous regiments was the Fighting 69th Brigade; formed in New York City, it served with distinction during the war.

It's likely that Lincoln was completely unaware of the possibility that one of his distant ancestors was originally from Armagh, but in truth he didn't need to play the Irish card. There is a suggestion that Lincoln's great-great-great-great-great-grandmother was a lady called Martha Lyford, who was born in Northern Ireland while her preacher father, Reverend John Lyford, was serving in an Armagh parish before he emigrated to America – but there is debate over the veracity of this claim.

In April 1865, the assassination of President Lincoln at Ford's Theatre in Washington plunged America into mourning. He was killed with a bullet to the back of the head by well-known stage actor John Wilkes Booth while watching the play *Our American Cousin*. A few days later, on 29 April, *The Dublin Evening Post* reported how a message of condolence was signed by politicians to the American people:

> *We do not think it has ever before happened that a common feeling did so completely unite governments and populations, official and unofficial bodies, hostile parties, and warring opinions, in one spontaneous and irresistible expression of sympathy with a nation, and of homage to a man . . . It is impossible, however, not to feel that every homage paid to the memory of the late President, and every message of condolence with the American people in the hour of their solemn grief sent forward to their government, more especially from Ireland, will go to swell the universal tribute of civilisation, not less to the cause than to the man.*

President Johnson and the Fenian prisoners

The emancipator president was succeeded by his vice president, Andrew Johnson, who is also believed to have Irish connections, but there is no firm paper trail of his relatives. In his annual address in 1866, he lauded a communications triumph between Ireland and the US. 'The entire success of the Atlantic telegraph between the coast of Ireland and the Province of Newfoundland is an achievement which has been justly celebrated in both hemispheres as the opening of an era in the progress of civilization.'

In the same speech, he spoke out against the treatment of Irish-born Fenian American citizens caught by the British government on a military expedition to invade Canada. In the wake of the Civil War, the discharged Fenian-leaning soldiers set their sights on taking the country from British hands, as they believed this would have a trickle-down effect of weakening the empire and freeing Ireland from its grip. When the men were charged with capital offences, Johnson appealed for leniency. 'Judgment and sentence of death have been pronounced against some, while others have been acquitted,' he said:

Fully believing in the maxim of government that severity of civil punishment for misguided persons who have engaged in revolutionary attempts which have disastrously failed is unsound and unwise, such representations have been made to the British Government in behalf of the convicted persons as, being sustained by an enlightened and humane judgment, will, it is hoped, induce in their cases an exercise of clemency and a judicious amnesty to all who were engaged in the movement.

Johnson continued that the US government had employed lawyers to defend the men, who were looking for a 'discontinuance of the prosecutions'. He went on to add:

The attempt was understood to be made in sympathy with an insurgent party in Ireland, and by striking at a British Province on this continent was designed to aid in obtaining redress for political grievances which, it was assumed, the people of Ireland had suffered at the hands of the British Government during a period of several centuries.

First US presidential visit stirs controversy in Ireland in 1879

President Ulysses Simpson Grant, the commanding army general who led the Union to victory in the American Civil War, was sworn into office in 1869 after Johnson served his single term. Grant, who worked on removing the last traces of slavery from his country, was the first Irish-American president to visit Ireland during his lifetime. He made the trip as part of a grand world tour with his wife Julia after he left office in 1877. The war hero is said to have had a maternal great-great-grandfather from Northern Ireland, who arrived in Philadelphia in the late 1700s. And so it was at the end of the following century that his descendant, a two-term US president, made the journey back across the Atlantic. He spent months in London and Paris and dined with the royal families of Spain and Portugal before crossing over to Ireland where he received a mixed reception.

Irish nationalists, who remembered how he had refused to admit a delegation representing Fenian prisoners to the White House, protested loudly at his arrival in Belfast. In December 1878, a few weeks before, the long-time US consul general in London, Adam Badeau, wrote, 'The consul at Dublin writes me that the Fenians are very hostile to him, because he refused to receive their deputation while he was President. There must be a demonstration, the Consul says, and there may be trouble.'

But in Dublin he was welcomed with open arms and given the freedom of the city, much like many of the presidents who came in his wake. In a gesture that showed his humour, he told the crowds he could now officially run for office in Ireland.

> It strikes me you did not know rightly what you were doing when you made me a freeman of your city – that you did not know the trouble you were about getting into – for I am a troublesome candidate and may trouble some of you here. I rather like Ireland . . . I have nothing more serious to say, but only to explain how I happen to make a speech of this length. I know it is because I have become an Irish citizen. I never kissed the blarney stone, and I don't think I ever shall.

During his stay, Grant toured the Royal Irish Academy, the Bank of Ireland and Trinity College. At a City Hall ceremony, the former president said:

> [I am] very proud to be made a citizen of the great city which you represent. I am by birth a citizen of a country where there are more Irishmen, either native born or the descendants of Irishmen, than you

have in all Ireland. I have had the honour and pleasure, therefore, of representing more Irishmen and their descendants when in office than the Queen of England does.

On the same day, 3 January 1879, Cork Corporation debated a letter informing the mayor that General Grant, the ex-president of the United States, was about to pay a visit to Cork within a week. One official denounced him, saying that he had 'insulted the Irish people in America. He got up a "No-Popery" cry there.' Another official added:

I can't see anything in the career of General Grant, or ex-President Grant, that calls for the sympathy of the Irish nation. I have had interviews with many persons who spent years in America, and I learned from them that he never thought of the Irish race as he thought of others, and that he actually went out of his way to insult their religion.

A week later, on 10 January, a correspondent in Washington, DC, reported General William T. Sherman's defence of President Grant.

I do not recall a single instance in which prejudice upon religious matters ever had the slightest influence in the discharge of his official duties. Many of his intimate personal friends are Catholics. His son Fred married a Catholic lady and his aunt, Mrs. Fred Dent, is a Catholic, so that I know there is no prejudice in the General's mind, such, at least, as he is accused of harboring against a class of people many of whom are his particular friends . . .

While president, Grant had given a famous speech in Des Moines, Iowa, where he stated his support for public schools and education free of sectarianism which he believes was mistakenly taken for anti-Catholicism.

Later that year, on 4 November, the president gave his views on the Cork controversy to a Chicago reporter:

> I was in Dublin at the time and had no intention of visiting Cork ...
> Their grievance, I believe, was that I was an enemy of the Catholics ...
> I cannot remember that I had ever said anything in criticism of the
> Catholic or any other church, and Catholics cannot consider me their
> enemy unless they are enemies to the sentiments I expressed at Des
> Moines.

Whether he had intention or not of visiting Cork, he headed up to the Protestant strongholds of Belfast and Londonderry, where he said, 'There are no more thrifty, self-reliant & contented people in Europe to-day than the people of north Ireland ...' At a banquet he spoke about the feeling between Ireland and America, declaring:

> There is that kindly feeling existing between my countrymen and
> yours which has been spoken of here tonight ... we all of us have
> relations on this side of the water, although some of us would, unluck-
> ily enough, have to go back five or six generations to find them. But
> we are related, and the majority of our kindred come from this side of
> the water.

Claiming to represent some 'forty-five millions of Irishmen, or descendants of Irishmen', he encouraged more to make the journey across the Atlantic: 'With industry and frugality there is a home for many more millions there yet. We hope to see more of the people of Derry and Ireland there after a while, when you become more crowded and want more room.'

But, of course, it wasn't all back-slapping speeches. At the train station on his departure the ex-president was met with a demonstration led by an Irish insurgent called John Rea. Still, shortly afterwards he left to take in the exotic world of the Orient.

Presidential sons of preacher men

The 21st president of the United States, Chester Alan Arthur, the son of an Irish Baptist preacher, took over the reins of power in 1881. His father, Reverend William Arthur, came from the Drean, near Ballymena in Co. Antrim to Quebec in the early 1800s before moving to Vermont where his son was born in 1830. He practised law in New York City before he was later made the Collector of the Port of New York. Shortly after he was sworn into office in 1881 – after succeeding assassinated President James Garfield – he found out he was suffering from a fatal kidney disease, but he kept the knowledge secret. It was seen as part of the reason he stayed above the internal politics of the Republican Party during his time in office. After his first term, he was re-nominated to run for the party but then died two years later.

The family ties to Ireland seem to have continued through the generations as Chester Alan Arthur Jnr, the president's grandson, went to Ireland on his honeymoon in the summer of 1922 in the middle of that country's civil war. Arthur appeared to support those who wanted a republic with full independence from the British Empire and he objected to the Irish Free State executing anti-treaty prisoners of war. He wrote a letter to the *New York Times* entitled 'An American Tourist's View of the So-Called Civil War'. He began by saying:

> As my wife and I spent our honeymoon in Ireland, we naturally feel the keenest interest in what is going on there … We would like to

draw the attention of our fellow citizens to the fact that there are two distinct armies there fighting a civil war, and that one of those armies has recently executed soldiers of the opposing army who surrendered themselves as prisoners of war... We happened to be in Kenmare when its Free State Garrison surrendered to an attacking force of irregulars from the hills. What would have been the fate of this Garrison had their captors adopted the policy of trying their prisoners for treason to the Republic?

Towards the end of this letter written from the Italian city of Florence on 26 November 1922, he writes: 'Those really to be pitied are the unfortunate Irish people who die between the devil and the deep sea.'

Presbyterian President Grover Cleveland, the only US president to serve two non-consecutive terms in the White House, was sworn into office before the turn of the twentieth century. His first term ran from 1885 to 1889 and he was voted back into office again in 1893. He was another son of a preacher, but in his case his father was a Presbyterian minister called Reverend Richard Falley Cleveland. However, his nearest Irish connection was his mother's father, Abner Neal, who was from Ireland. His lineage also contained a distant female relative called Ann Lamb from Dublin, which was unusual as most of the presidential relatives of the nineteenth century were from Northern Ireland. Cleveland made only a few references to Ireland in his speeches, mainly focused on the large amount of cattle imported from Britain and Ireland. In December 1896, he told Congress that the number of immigrants permitted to land during the fiscal year was 340,468. Among those he listed, he stated that just over a tenth – 37,496 – came from Ireland and of those seven per cent were illiterate. Interestingly, Ireland had one of the lowest rates of illiteracy of all the major immigrant countries that year.

The 25th president, William McKinley Jnr, who had distant links to eighteenth-century Ireland, appears to have made very little reference to his ancestral birthplace during his time in the White House. He was assassinated at the start of his second term on 14 September 1901, after leading the nation to victory in the Spanish–American War and raising protective tariffs to promote American industry. After his death, 42-year-old Theodore Roosevelt stepped into the role to become the youngest president in the nation's history.

President Roosevelt applauds Irish war heroes but urges citizens to take pride in their Americanness

It's unclear if President Roosevelt was aware he had a great-great-great-grandfather called John Barnhill, but it's apparent from his orations that he didn't care for the term Irish American. In a September 1902 speech in Tennessee, he spoke of the men who fought with him in the Spanish–American War in Cuba:

> Among my captains were men whose forefathers had been among the first white men to settle on Massachusetts Bay and on the banks of the James, and others whose parents had come from Germany, from Ireland, from England, from France. They were all Americans, and nothing else, and each man stood on his worth as a man, to be judged by it, and to succeed or fail accordingly as he did well or ill.

In Santa Fe in New Mexico in 1903, he uttered a similar sentiment, telling his audience that his regiment were 'a typical American regiment', articulating his thoughts further as follows:

> There were men in that regiment who themselves were born, or whose parents were born, in England, Ireland, Germany, or Scandinavia, but there was not a man, no matter what his creed, what

his birthplace, what his ancestry, who was not an American and nothing else.

But in remarks at the 121st Annual Dinner of the Friendly Sons of St Patrick in New York City on St Patrick's Day 1905, he also spoke of the pioneering spirit of 'these immigrants who came from Ireland to the colonies during the eighteenth century which has never been paralleled in the case of any other immigrants whatsoever', before adding:

> In all other cases, since the very first settlements, the pushing west-ward of the frontiers has been due primarily to the men of native birth. But the immigrants from Ireland in the seventeenth century pushed boldly through the settled districts and planted themselves as the advance guard of the conquering civilization on the borders of the Indian-haunted wilderness.

He namechecked Irish men who helped lead America through various battles on sea and on land. 'Among their number was Commodore John Barry, one of the three or four officers to whom our infant navy owed most.' He continued: 'On land they furnished generals like Montgomery, who fell so gloriously at Quebec, and Sullivan . . . while the Continental troops of the hardest fighter among Washington's generals, Mad Anthony Wayne.' He also namechecked 'old Andrew Jackson, the victor of New Orleans'.

He went on to say:

> In the second great crisis of our country's history – the period of the Civil War – the part played by the men of Irish birth or parentage was no less striking than it had been in the Revolution . . . The people who have come to this country from Ireland have contributed to the stock

of our common citizenship qualities which are essential to the welfare of every great nation. They are a masterful race of rugged character – a race the qualities of whose womanhood have become proverbial, while its men have the elemental, the indispensable virtues of working hard in time of peace and fighting hard in time of war. In every walk of life men of this blood have stood, and now stand, pre-eminent as statesmen and as soldiers, on the bench, at the bar, and in business. They are doing their full share toward the artistic and literary development of the country.

But he reiterated his belief in Americanism and the American spirit that had been forged by a mix of nationalities and different heritages.

Let us keep our pride in the stocks from which we have sprung; but let us show that pride not by holding aloof one from another, least of all by preserving the Old-World jealousies and bitterness, but by joining in a spirit of generous rivalry to see which can do most for our great common country.

Theodore Roosevelt, brought up in a wealthy family in the urbane environment of New York City, bookended the period of the log-cabin Irish-American presidents. In his wake the next Irish-American president, Woodrow Wilson, would be in power throughout the years of the First World War and the turbulent birth of the Irish nation.

A show of Irish power on St Patrick's Day in New York, circa 1910.

CHAPTER TEN

SHAMROCKS & SHENANIGANS & SILVER DOLLARS

America is honoured today to have back a native son who has become Ireland's liberator, Ireland's senior statesman, and Ireland's president . . . You belong to us, Mr President, just as in a very special way John F. Kennedy belonged to you.

I T WAS THE SUMMER of 1981 and the telegram from Britain's ambassador to Washington to No. 10 Downing Street had a distinctly irritable tone. Emotions were running high on both sides of the Atlantic after the young IRA leader Bobby Sands, had starved himself to death on 5 May at the age of twenty-seven after sixty-six days without food.

The subject matter of the diplomatic wire referred to the ambassador's meeting with US Congressional Friends of Ireland. The caucus had been formed a few months earlier on St Patrick's Day, by Senator Ted Kennedy, Senator Daniel Patrick Moynihan and House speaker Tip O'Neill to lobby for a peaceful settlement to end the conflict in Northern Ireland. Judging by the subtext, the diplomat's exchange with the Irish-American political titans had not been overly friendly. Dated 25 June 1981, the telegram began:

I realise the annoyance that interference by American politicians in our affairs causes in London and Belfast, where we are having to deal with the very real and serious problems raised by the hunger strike. The ignorant and partisan nature of a lot of American comment is a further aggravation and one is tempted to argue that, while we should continue to do all in our power to influence opinion here, we should not even consider allowing positions adopted in the United States to influence our policy decisions.

The dispatch marked 'Confidential' was signed 'Henderson', referring to Sir Nicholas Henderson, the British ambassador in the United States at the time. Wired to the Foreign and Commonwealth Office in London, and No. 10 the day after the Washington meeting, it gives an illuminating insight into the behind-the-scenes machinations at work in the 1980s in the uneasy triangle of diplomacy between the three countries.

The origins of the hunger strike at the notorious, now partly demolished HM Prison Maze in Belfast lay in the British government's 1976 decision to reverse a previous edict to place IRA inmates in a special category which gave them a status similar to that of prisoners of war. The category excused them from wearing prison uniforms or carrying out prison work, both of which they believed criminalised them – and they were willing to die for the principle of being classed as political prisoners fighting for a free Ireland instead of ordinary felons. The British prime minister, Margaret Thatcher, refused to budge on the seemingly trivial issues of allowing IRA prisoners to wear their own clothes, mix with their comrades along with receiving food parcels and extra visits in the prison, which lies ten miles outside Belfast.

Exactly a week after the death of Sands, his fellow Republican prisoner Francis Hughes died, followed by the deaths of prisoners

Raymond McCreesh and Patsy O'Hara, who both passed away on 21 May after sixty-one days without eating. The three men were all in their early twenties. The deaths of ten Republican prisoners by the end of August that year was a watershed moment in Northern Ireland politics, a sacrifice of young life which caused an international outcry and drew the eyes of the world to the conflict raging in Northern Ireland.

In his telegram in June, five months after the inauguration of US president Ronald Reagan for his first term in office, Sir Nicholas set out the tightrope of public opinion walked by Irish-American politicians on the subject of Republican prisoners. On the one hand, he said, they were experiencing what he described as 'heat' in their constituencies over the hunger-strike deaths. Equally they did not want to be seen as endorsing terrorism. Despite his initial testy assertion about US intrusion in their governance, the ambassador to the US cautioned Downing Street: 'We have been told by the White House that the President, with his Irish-American background, is taking an interest in the hunger strike and is regularly briefed on developments.'

Earlier that spring, a dispatch dated 23 February 1981 to Downing Street, from Britain's Permanent Under Secretary at the Northern Ireland Office, Sir Kenneth Stowe, got to the heart of this triad of diplomacy between Ireland, the US and the UK. Sir Kenneth had attended a conference on the international dimensions to the Northern Ireland situation at the Ditchley Foundation in Oxfordshire where he met representatives from the United States and Northern Ireland. The principal US guests were a powerful cross-section of the Democratic Party including Congressman Tom Foley and Senator Christopher Dodds, along with a slew of advisors to the party's heavyweights of Tip O'Neill, Senator Kennedy, New York Governor Hugh Carey and Senator Moynihan.

'The burden of their message was very simple,' explained Stowe in his memo. 'There will be a continuing interest in the United States and developments in Ireland. The US is a nation of immigrants and each national group whether it be Greek or Irish sustains a continuing interest in the affairs of its homeland.' There was the nub of the matter. America had started to actively look over the shoulder of Britain in its dealings with Ireland. The United States certainly had a celebrated special relationship with its powerful ally, with key military and economic ties to Britain, but the influential Irish lobby which reached into the presidency, the Senate and the House of Representatives was ensuring the US was adopting more of a Big Brother-style role when it came to the UK's relations with its much less powerful neighbour.

Along with direct familial links, many US presidents had Irish aides, from Woodrow Wilson's private secretary, Joseph Tumulty, to Franklin Roosevelt's advisor, Thomas Corcoran, to Kennedy's right-hand man, Dave Powers. These counsellors would have the ear of the president of the day; they were the insiders in the background of successive administrations. While the presidential term was eight years at most, career Democrats such as Cork-connected Tip O'Neill, a congressman for thirty-four years, who reigned as speaker in the House of Representatives through the late 1970s and into the 1980s, and Ted Kennedy, a senator for forty-seven years, held extraordinary sway in Washington for the best part of half a century.

Again and again, the names of O'Neill and Kennedy pop up on diplomatic documents wired between the US, England and Ireland. Kennedy was an insistent presence, eschewing violence but pushing all the time for Ireland to stay on the agenda in the White House. The mystique of America's political first family opened doors of successive administrations as the youngest Kennedy brother grew into a towering power broker on Capitol Hill.

Over the latter half of the twentieth century, O'Neill and Kennedy, along with Senator Moynihan and Governor Carey, became known as the Four Horsemen, a band of Democratic political dynamos, manoeuvring behind the scenes of successive administrations to put one of the smallest countries in Europe near the top of the political agenda. The quartet with the apocalyptic name had extraordinary access to the Senate floor, the House of Representatives, and a direct line to the White House, especially when the incumbent was a Democrat. Their names – and their imposing political presence – are all over the late-night negotiations, the shuttle diplomacy, the cross-Atlantic flights and endless phone calls which, incrementally, took Ireland to the path of peace.

The birth of the Irish political machine: ghettos, voting blocs and the Brooklyn Bridge

The persistent and wide-ranging roots of Irish power had begun centuries earlier when immigrants were channelled into organised groups, sometimes recruited by Irish societies in the dock or even before they stepped off the boat. The Irish tended to live in communities, initially in ghettos, in many cases, especially around the time of the famine, but these neighbourhoods gradually became the pillars that formed the foundation of formidable political machines. These immigrants may not have had much wealth, but after two years in America, they were entitled to naturalisation, a status which gave them citizenship and, vitally, a vote – and those votes were marshalled by neighbourhood bosses or ward leaders. In the Ireland they had left behind in the 1800s, only men who possessed a certain amount of property could vote, a category which was almost exclusively made up of the ruling Protestant class. This wouldn't be fully overhauled until the Constitution of the Irish Free State gave all citizens aged twenty-one and over the right to vote in 1922.

In this new world, Irish men and women emerging from

generations of colonial rule and voting oppression were determined to fully exercise their democratic rights. The parish-pump politics, which are still at play in parts of Ireland today, whirred along in the background, oiling the wheels of massive Irish political operations in major American cities from New York to San Francisco. These acted as an avenue for Irish Americans to secure jobs, to deal with naturalisation issues, even to obtain food or heating fuel in emergencies. Though remembered for their perceived corruption, these political machines created a community-led form of social services long before they were required by the state, while also rewarding their own through political appointments. William R. Grace became New York City's first Irish-American mayor in 1880. Four years later, Hugh O'Brien won the same position in Boston thanks to the boatloads of Irish immigrants which had poured into the city, making up a large percentage of the population. He would pave the way for JFK's grandfather, 'Honey Fitz' Fitzgerald, to become mayor of Boston at the start of the next century.

The storied American dream didn't materialise for many immigrants, but the real American dream for a people living under the hard hand of the British Empire for centuries was the opportunity for justice and freedom. A place where they could vote, where they could challenge injustice through the courts, and where they could make their homes in a continent ripe for prosperity. The Irish certainly didn't always play by the rules in engineering themselves into positions of power, with accusations of election fraud rife in the elections of the mid-nineteenth century, but as their numbers exploded, this practice later became redundant.

East coast cities such as New York and Boston saw an extraordinary flood of destitute immigrants in the late 1840s and 1850s, which caused deep alarm among the established white Anglo-Saxon Protestant elite, knowns as WASPs, who viewed political power as their birthright. In a few short years, they found themselves in danger of being outnumbered by masses of new Irish citizens, piled into tenements – like Manhattan's notorious Five Points neighbourhood, famously brought to life in the big-screen movie *Gangs of New York*. Scorsese naturally took dramatic licence in the creation of his Oscar-winning film, but historians have found records showing the depictions of prostitution, violence, bare-knuckle fighting and political corruption were all reasonably true-to-life for the city's Irish communities in the middle of the nineteenth century.

Entire families tended to live in one or two rooms at the bleakest of lodgings in sagging New York tenements. A dozen or more families often had to share one outhouse, sewage overflowed onto the streets and killer diseases like cholera spread like wildfire from the unsanitary conditions in the heaving dwellings. But the immigrants endured through this rough entry into their new life. Hundreds of thousands of artefacts retrieved from the Five Points slums in the late twentieth century revealed these communities had ornaments on their mantelpieces, pictures on their walls and decent meals at their dinner tables. From their hovel-like lodgings, they went to work in so-called respectable jobs as tailors, shoemakers, grocers, masons, liquor dealers and labourers.

Along with opportunity came discrimination from settled New Yorkers. Distrustful of the impoverished arrivals fleeing disaster, who were prepared to work for less than the city's more established population, signs of 'No Irish need apply' were regularly printed in classified employment ads in papers such as the *New York Times*. The phrase varied from 'No Irishman need apply' to 'Irishmen need not apply' to the brutally blunt 'No Irish'. And by the middle of the 1850s, a new anti-immigrant movement started to spread across the US.

'You suddenly started to see these very public displays of anti-Irish organisation in the northeast of the United States,' said Irish-American

Professor James T. Fisher, who has spent years researching the nineteenth-century Irish in Brooklyn and is the author of *On the Irish Waterfront: The Crusader, the Movie and the Soul of the Port of New York*. 'Celebrity itinerant preachers would go to cities like Brooklyn, Manhattan, Boston, and they'd stand on top of the hill in front of around 10,000 listeners saying the Irish were destroying America... they were making the country beholden to the Pope and that they had taken away their liberties and democracy.'

It wasn't all rallies and rhetoric. The hostility began to flare into violence between the settled Anglo-Saxons and the new Irish in places like Brooklyn, the third biggest city in the United States in the 1850s, and in Manhattan's Five Points.

'By the 1850s,' said Professor Fisher, 'the city of Brooklyn, which had been completely dominated by Anglo-Protestant politicians from its origins – it was only officially charted in 1834 – so, it was very Anglo and very Protestant, then very quickly in the early to mid-1850s it was completely taken over by the Irish politically, which just shocked everyone.'

The political face of the anti-immigrant sentiment was the Native American Party, more commonly known as the Know-Nothing Party, but antagonism also boiled over into pitched battles. Resentment towards Irish immigrants, which focused on their poor living conditions and their willingness to work for low wages, was often heightened by religious conflict. In 1831, Protestants burned down St Mary's Catholic Church in New York City, while in 1844, anti-Catholic nativist riots, which flared up over Bible-reading in schools in Philadelphia, left many dead and injured. 'It was serious,' states Professor Fisher:

> For a time it looked as though the Irish would be run off. It became
> very heated and violent, so in places like Brooklyn, the Irish machines

in those cities became a kind of physical protection. In the middle of all these nativist riots, churches got burned down and some Irish neighbourhoods got attacked so a lot of it began in providing a sense of security to the Irish who felt powerless at first. The political machine represented their own interests.

In the midst of open prejudice and grinding living conditions, these outsider refugees, many of them Gaelic-speaking and from rural Ireland, found salvation under the protection of the Democratic Party. Depending on the city, the Irish also sought succour from the Catholic Church, but Professor Fisher argues that the Democratic Party was the big influence in their lives, taking on the role of protector-in-chief for the masses. 'It varied by city the role the church played, but in every major north-eastern, and even some of the western and mid-western, cities, there was always an Irish political organisation by the middle of the nineteenth century. It was the dominant organisation.'

In return, their votes were expected to put the party's candidates into public office. The people were cogs in what would become one of the most powerful political machines in the United States. New York's Tammany Hall – the infamous Manhattan political society which dominated the Democratic Party in the Big Apple – grew a huge political base through the nineteenth century by helping immigrants adjust to their new life. This was replicated in other cities, as Professor Fisher states: 'Every political ward had a naturalisation committee and they would handle the paperwork. They could really make it happen pretty quickly and it was definitely a big part of how they succeeded.'

Charitable acts – such as giving a helping hand to destitute widows, finding jobs for the newly arrived and attending local fairs – were other ways in which the organisation drew loyalty. Professor Fisher said: 'Tammany had a kind of social welfare ideology; somebody like Al Smith, the first Catholic to run for president, was a product of that and he was a social reformer.'

In turn, organisations exercised political control through various Irish bosses with a blend of charity and patronage which could have been taken from the playbook of rural Irish politics. These were men like Hugh McLaughlin in Brooklyn, Blind Boss Buckley in San Francisco, and Tammany boss William Marcy Tweed in Manhattan; the latter would incidentally end up jailed for corruption in 1873 on two hundred indictment counts. The bosses would rarely run for public office, but they certainly pulled the strings behind the scenes. The cities were divided into wards, and the bosses' commands went through district captains or ward leaders. 'They worked from the ground up,' Professor Fisher added, 'and tended to control the party apparatus. They would pick the candidates for every local office.'

In the mid-nineteenth century, there were accusations of Irish immigrants voting a couple of times a day in New York's Manhattan district, stories of men going home and shaving beards and moustaches before appearing again at the ballot box. In November 1854, the *New York Times* carried a report headlined:

KNOW-NOTHING DEMONSTRATION. GRAND MASS
MEETING IN THE PARK. CHARGES OF CORRUPTION AT
THE POLLS, DENUNCIATORY RESOLUTIONS.

Another sphere of influence targeted by the Irish was the judiciary. Professor Fisher believes this focus is another legacy from their past of colonial oppression: 'They were obsessed with taking over the judiciary, the local judges, and the local courts. There was this amazing sense the Irish had that they could fight back in court and beyond that, they could even take over the court and get all these judges elected and then they'll basically do their bidding and that's exactly what happened.'

The historian says this was partly to help cover up election rigging:

It's pretty stark in Brooklyn, some of the Irish neighbourhoods relied almost on entirely on what they called ballot stuffing. They didn't want to take chances. Then the other side, the Republicans, would sue them but they ran the courts too, so the Irish political figures became almost immune from prosecution. There were reform movements where usually Anglo-Protestants would rise up and every now and then they would rebel against the political leadership, so it was this back and forth. But as the numbers grew, the elections didn't need to be fixed because they're going to win anyhow. They had this extremely narrow power base which was based on mass electoral politics and the ability to get votes.

While they never excelled in the stock markets like the Anglo-Saxons, Fisher said operations such as those at Tammany Hall operated in the same way as corporations: 'Tammany had the ability to broker contracts, like the piers and other kinds of city contracts. Most of it increasingly went through them and their candidates or local assemblymen or local councilmen would vote in favour of certain projects, and they would always get a kick-back.' The land-starved Irish and especially Irish political bosses were hell-bent on acquiring real estate.

The leadership in these democratic political organisations was very intent on acquiring property. When they built the Brooklyn Bridge in the 1870s, who are the people that knew the neighbourhoods where the Brooklyn Bridge was going land on both sides of the river? It was the Irish politicians – they bought all the land knowing how incredibly valuable it was going to become.

While there was certainly corruption, historians argue that the organisations had an important social function along with an irreverence for the Establishment after years of suffering under the rule of free-market capitalism in Britain. By the twentieth century, Tammany's influence had faded. In the 1900s, not only did the Irish start voting their own into Congress, mayoral offices and the presidency, they also moved up through the power structures of the country's police forces and firehouses. The sons of Irish immigrant families joined precincts in New York and Boston, first on the beat and later rising all the way up through the ranks. Right up to the twenty-first century, a long line of Irish Americans have occupied top jobs in the New York Police Department; most recently, the son of two Irish immigrant parents, Dermot Shea, was appointed police commissioner in 2019. Shea took over the role from James O'Neill, whose grandparents came from Ireland. He in turn was preceded by Irish-American William Bratton, while one of the longest-serving commissioners was Raymond Kelly, who ran the department from 2002 to 2013.

Immigrant communities were also card-carrying members of GAA organisations and other Irish-affiliated societies with nostalgic prefixes like 'Emerald' or 'Hibernian'. Another forgotten factor is just how much the Irish reached into popular culture in the late nineteenth century and into the twentieth century. They possessed the drive to reach the highest echelons of sport, film and literature.

As early as the 1870s, the prize-fighter John Morrissey became a household name, but his countrymen also reached into all the most all-American of sports. 'There's a tremendous number of Irish athletes among early baseball players,' observed Professor Fisher. The Irish rose really quickly, too, in other areas of public spectacle in the realms of professional sports, boxing, popular culture, music and theatre.

> The Irish thrived in these areas that didn't require a formal accreditation from fancy colleges or generations of wealth behind them or social status. The whole idea of the Democratic Party is the party of the people – and what is it that makes the Irish synonymous in America with the people? It's one of the great coups. The Irish people just brought joy to all these public activities. It was really attractive.

1916, Woodrow Wilson, the Irish Question and the firebrand congressman

By the time it looked like Ireland was finally breaking free of the British Empire, when Irish Republicans revolted in the 1916 Easter Rising, President Woodrow Wilson was in the third year of his first term. In Congress, there was a flurry of motions tabled by fired-up Irish Americans in support of the rebellion which was front-page news across America. Missouri representative Leonidas Dyer tabled a resolution looking for Congress to support the Easter Rising, one which denounced the British response and praised the patriotism of those in Ireland willing to follow 'the inspiration of the American Revolution'.

In 1917, after initially following a policy of neutrality, President Woodrow Wilson led America into the First World War with a landmark speech to the US Congress, urging them to declare war on Germany to 'make the world safe for democracy'. The Democratic president emphasised that the United States must undertake a principled intervention in the war to protect the right of self-determination for small nations.

Jumping on this assertion, one week later Representative Thomas Gallagher of Illinois tabled a resolution calling for the United States to make the independence of Ireland a condition of any agreement to end the First World War. On 28 April, Representative William Cary of Wisconsin proposed a similar resolution. Speaker of the House Champ Clark of Missouri along with 136 members signed a telegram cabled to British prime minister David Lloyd George, which reiterated Wilson's position on the rights of small nations and emphasised the importance of Irish independence to the American people.

This was followed by a 14 May resolution to 'declare the liberation of Ireland one of the purposes of the present war'. This audacious motion, proposed by Illinois representative William E. Mason, outlined explicit terms for the 'separation' of the island from the United Kingdom, demanded that Ireland play a part in the post-war peace process, and authorised the US Secretary of the Treasury to purchase up to $100 million in bonds from the newly constituted Irish government. But these zealous resolutions were never passed by the US branches of government.

Throughout 1917, Irish societies ramped up the pressure on President Wilson, urging him to intercede with England to free Ireland from colonial rule. Letters and petitions flooded into the White House, often through his right-hand man, Joseph Tumulty. The network of associations and clubs demanded Ireland's immediate liberation in exchange for America entering the war on the side of Britain against Hitler. At one stage, firebrand Republicans remind Wilson's administration that nearly half of the American army have Irish blood.

The *New York Times* carried a dispatch from London on 22 January 1918, reporting: 'The *Daily News* says there is reason for stating that President Wilson quite recently made urgent representations to the British Cabinet on the desirability of an Irish settlement.' Two days later, the paper led with the headline '*Absolute Denial For Wilson*'. An official in a position to speak for the president said there was no truth in the reports that the president had sought to influence the British government in regard to the Irish question.

In 1919, New York-born Irish revolutionary leader Éamon de Valera placed the Irish Republic at the heart of American affairs during an eighteen-month tour of his birth city where he was welcomed with open arms. During one event hosted by the Friends of Irish Freedom at a sold-out Madison Square Garden, de Valera's arrival onstage was reportedly met with a ten-minute standing ovation. Styled in New York as the president of the Irish Republic, de Valera was treated as a statesman by the Irish diaspora. His incredible popularity bolstered petitions by political leaders in organisations like the Friends of Irish Freedom and the Sons of St Patrick who were making appeals in Washington to back Ireland's bid for independence.

Despite his paternal grandparents hailing from Down in Ireland, Wilson would fall out of favour with Irish Americans in the aftermath of the Great War over his failure to bring up the Irish question at the Paris Peace Conference. The international summit of world leaders was convened on 18 January 1919 by the victorious Allied powers of France, Italy, United Kingdom and the United States, and its work was to lay the foundations for a permanent peace in Europe.

Wilson conceived the peace conference as a forerunner to a new world order based on an idealistic fourteen-point speech made to Congress in 1918. One of the fourteen points referred to an impartial adjustment of colonial claims, which precipitated heavy lobbying by Irish Americans on Wilson to plead the case for Ireland's independence in the French capital. At the Paris Peace Conference, the Treaty of Versailles was signed, ending the war, and Wilson did succeed in establishing the League of Nations, an international organisation, headquartered in Geneva, Switzerland, to provide a forum for resolving international disputes.

A *New York Times* article on 18 September 1919 reported that

President Wilson had for the first time finally set out publicly how he saw his League of Nations covenant affecting Ireland. In reply to a series of questions sent to him by the San Francisco Labor Council, he said:

> The case of Ireland was not heard at the Peace Conference because the Peace Conference had no jurisdiction over any question of that sort, which did not affect territories which belong to the defeated empires. My position on the self-determination for Ireland is expressed in Article XI of the covenant, in which I may say I was particularly interested, because it seemed to me necessary for the peace and freedom of the world that a forum should be created to which all people could bring any matter which was likely to affect the peace and freedom of the world.

Wilson's pronouncement did not impress Éamon de Valera, who issued his own statement to the *New York Times* from his headquarters at the Waldorf Hotel in the American city:

> I need only say that the narrowing down and limitation of the Peace Conference to only such matters as affected territories belonging to the defeated empires was altogether out of accord with the war aims of America as enunciated by the president and the professions of the Entente statesmen during the war.

Wilson would face accusations from Irish Americans that he championed Poland's independence at Paris while staying quiet on Ireland, but it is argued that he could only apply informal pressure on his ally and fellow superpower, Britain. In the end, the Irish lobby felt, rightly or wrongly, that Wilson didn't push for Irish self-determination with the British in Paris. This has frequently been given as a reason as to why a large part of the Irish-American vote left its traditional home in the Democratic Party, leading to the election of Ohio Republican Warren Harding as the 29th president of America at the end of the Democratic president Woodrow Wilson's eight-year term in 1921.

Sleepy start to Ireland's diplomatic relationship with America

The United States officially recognised the Irish Free State as a state in 1924 under President Calvin Coolidge, who was in power following President Harding's death from a heart attack in August 1923. Diplomatic relations began when Timothy A. Smiddy presented his credentials as Minister Plenipotentiary of the Irish Free State in Washington when the American Embassy in Dublin was established on 27 July 1927, and when Frederick A. Sterling presented his credentials as American Envoy Extraordinary and Minister Plenipotentiary.

In 1948, a young diplomat called William Howard Taft III – a grandson of US President William Taft – was posted to Ireland to work in the US Embassy. Five years later, he was made US ambassador to Ireland. His time in Dublin in the 1950s was calm and informal with none of the terrorist activities which turned Ireland into a highly volatile posting in the 1970s and 80s. In an oral history interview, he would tell US Foreign Affairs:

> It was a place where Barbara, my wife, and I could live in a very nice embassy with the children and have no problems. It was generally peaceful. We did have negotiating matters concerning, for example, whether or not Pan American or TWA would have the right to come to Dublin Airport rather than Shannon.

The US ambassador also noted that the Irish in Congress were expert lobbyists who successfully pushed to have funds channelled into building a good relationship between Catholic and Protestant communities in Northern Ireland in the 1980s:

> The Irish moved through Capitol Hill and made friends, as indeed now they have done in recent years, where you have a scheme to pay money to the Northern Irish to generate better approaches to Irish people living together, the Catholics and Protestants, and by making any new US loans to industry up in the North contingent on fair employment for all people. So it's not the White House really which generated this activity except that they think – and I think – it's a good thing. It really comes from the Congress, and, of course, their large Irish constituency here among the Congressional districts. Anything favourable like that to improve the political climate in the North and feelings between the North and the South is a good thing. But I'm not sure that if these matters were put to the American people generally, they would subscribe to lavish assistance.

St Patrick's Day – the ultimate diplomatic date

In 1952, Irish ambassador to the US John Hearne sent a small bowl of shamrocks to President Truman to mark St Patrick's Day. Truman was out of town at the time, but later sent the ambassador a message, in which he said that he hoped 'relations between the two countries will continue to be on a good and effective level for generations'. By any account, it was an unremarkable way to commence what would become an extraordinary diplomatic coup. The first recorded celebration of St Patrick's Day in the American colonies had been in Boston in 1737, and the first St Patrick's Day celebration in New York City was held at the Crown and Thistle Tavern in 1756. But this hugely significant day in the Irish calendar didn't turn into a standing diplomatic date between Ireland and the most powerful country in the world until halfway through the twentieth century.

Hearne could not have foreseen that those shamrocks would sow the seeds of decades of an open-door policy to the White House, which peaked during the Clinton administration. Four years after that first bowl was delivered, Irish Prime Minster John Costello was received in the White House for St Patrick's Day and three years later Seán T. O'Kelly was the first Irish president to arrive at the invitation of President Dwight Eisenhower. At Washington Airport on 17 March 1959, the Irish president made a shrewd symbolic gesture of pinning a shamrock on Eisenhower's collar, an image beamed into millions of homes all over America.

He was accompanied by Ambassador Taft, who was under instructions by Eisenhower's Republican administration to keep the Irish leader out of the clutches of Tammany Hall Democrats who would be looking to monopolise his time to play to their Irish-American base:

> I was assigned a political role: to keep Mr Costello next to me the whole time, because in his going up to New York to the parade and so forth, the Republican Party seemed to feel that there was a danger he might be kidnaped by the Democrats. What would have happened I have no idea, but that was a concern, and I did my best to stay with him. When there was a motorcade, I leaped into his car rather than being shunted behind anywhere.

He remembers almost losing the Taoiseach to a swarm of Tammany Hall politicians when they went to a crowded party at Averell Harriman's house – the official who had been head of the Marshall Plan. He recalled:

> He had elevators in his house and there was a vast crowd getting into his party and before I knew it, Mr Costello was pushed into the

elevator in a crush and the doors shut. I thought, Heavens I'm not going to see him again for several hours, but luckily I was able to get into the next elevator and I found him without difficulty. I was young enough to feel this was a very important political assignment and I didn't want to botch the job.

When Taft got the opportunity to stay on for a second term in the role, he declined President Eisenhower's offer as he felt that being a diplomat in 1950s Ireland was on the uneventful side. 'There was not all that much to do, and I thought it would be a bad thing for my continuing moral fibre; I enjoyed my golfing afternoons too much . . . one had a lot of pleasant, leisure time.'

The St Patrick's Day tradition at the White House continued when JFK was elected with Ambassador Tommy Kiernan arriving with the now obligatory bowl of shamrocks and a scroll with the Kennedy family crest and his family tree. The seasoned diplomat was determined to leave no doubt about the power of the Irish blood tie to the glamorous young leader.

Former Irish ambassador to the US, Seán Donlon, who had joined the Foreign Service shortly before Kennedy's visit, remembers JFK's advisors blocking any suggestion that the president would signal US interest in the Northern Ireland situation.

'The Irish ambassador in Washington, Tom Kiernan, had tried in advance of the visit to get Kennedy to say something about partition and reunification but that had been knocked on the head by the advisors to Kennedy,' he explained. 'It was eventually felt there was no point in adding a disruptive factor to what was a very successful, emotional visit.'

In the run-up to the president's European tour, which also took in Italy, Germany and the UK, a call to the US Department of State by the Spanish ambassador Don Antonio Garrigues on 25 April 1963, requesting that Spain be included in President Kennedy's tour of Europe, illuminates the status of Ireland in the White House. A memo of the conversation reveals that the Spanish ambassador was looking for 'some gesture of friendship from the US'. It continued:

> In this connection Ambassador Garrigues mentioned that the president was not planning to visit Spain ... the impression had been created that this Administration was less friendly to Spain than the last ... As to a presidential visit ... the fact was that the president had visited only two countries in Europe and was now adding only two more (Ireland was a special ancestral case). A visit now was simply not possible.

In a sweep of international press after the visit, the White House gauged the reaction to the young Democratic president's European tour in a memo sent to JFK on 9 July by the acting director of the United States Information Agency, Donald Wilson:

> In Europe generally, your visit to Ireland was seen as a 'sentimental journey' and a 'homecoming' without political implications. Within Ireland, no event in modern times has received such detailed press, photographic and TV coverage. There is still no consensus about the political significance of the visit, but there has been speculation about Ireland's role in world events and relationships with NATO.

In the same memo, the president was told that Peking viewed the tour as a 'cunning diplomatic move with evil designs'. Wilson added: 'A Red Chinese labour official asked: "How can this Satan incarnate be viewed as an envoy of the people?"'

In the wake of JFK's four-day visit to Ireland in June 1963,

Taoiseach Seán Lemass visited the young president in the White House in October 1963, at his invitation. One month later, President Éamon de Valera returned to the US Capitol for the funeral of the much-loved leader.

The following May, an almost blind 81-year-old de Valera returned to address the US Congress. As the elder statesman moved with dignified posture up the aisle, he was applauded by a standing audience. In his speech, the leader gave thanks to Congress, that he felt were forty-five years overdue, for the United States' support for his country's struggle for independence. He had never forgotten congressional support for the Irish cause in 1919 and 1920, referencing 'its votes of sympathy for the aspiration of the Irish people for a government of their own choice'.

He set out how the solidarity from the US Congress to the Irish cause mirrored the attitude of the 'American people as a whole'. He continued:

It's not necessary for me to tell you how heartened our people were by these expressions of sympathy and friendship. We were in a very difficult struggle facing very great odds and it was a comfort, and an earnest of ultimate success, that this great freedom-loving nation of America and its people were behind out efforts.

The Irish people . . . what was their gratitude? It was clearly evident to anyone who saw the reception that was given to your late president, President Kennedy. He was welcomed not merely because he was of Irish blood, not merely because of his personal charm and his great qualities of heart and mind, not even because of the great leadership which he was giving to the world in critical moments.

But he was honoured because he was regarded by our people as the symbol of this great nation because he was the elected president of this great people . . . [words which were met by a spontaneous burst of applause] ... and in honouring him they felt that they were in some small measure expressing their gratitude to the people of the United States for the aid that had been given to them.

The previous day, the interlinked complexity of the family ties between the two countries were referenced on the White House lawn by President Lyndon B. Johnson when he spoke of de Valera's birth in America.

America is honoured today to have back a native son who has become Ireland's liberator, Ireland's senior statesman, and Ireland's president. To no other Irish leader do we owe a greater debt than you for the contributions which Ireland has made – and is making – to the building of a world community under the rule of law. This is the country of your birth, Mr President. This will always be your home. You belong to us, Mr President, just as in a very special way John F. Kennedy belonged to you.

On the question of his own blood ties, President Lyndon B. Johnson appears to have known there was a record suggesting he had a great-great-great-great-grandmother called Hannah Taggart, as he alluded to his Celtic genes in a speech in Honolulu in 1966: 'My forebears came from Britain, Ireland, and Germany.' It is suggested that he continued to receive the gift of shamrocks for St Patrick's Day as homage to President Kennedy. In Post Office Square in Boston in 1964, Johnson spoke movingly of the city's loss of their young Irish-American leader:

No memory is more fresh and none is so bright, and none so mingles pain and gratitude as the memory of John Fitzgerald Kennedy of Massachusetts. He led an entire nation, and he found his way to the secret hopes of man. But he was Irish, he was Massachusetts born, and he was Boston bred.

During the 1970s, there were five visits to Washington by Irish leaders with two falling on St Patrick's Day. In the Nixon years, the president used the shamrock ceremony to herald political appointments or to make announcements such as his state visit to Ireland in 1970, in which he visited the graves of his Quaker relatives. The same year, Taoiseach John Lynch attended the White House dinner held to mark the twenty-fifth anniversary of the United Nations in 1970.

US career diplomat Roger Sorenson, Deputy Chief of Mission at the US Embassy in Dublin from 1969 to 1974, observed that Irish Americans in the US did not always act at the behest of the Irish government, especially when it came to the operations of the Irish Republican Army, who were carrying out a guerrilla war in the north of the country in protest over English rule in Ulster.

In a Foreign Affairs oral history interview in 1990, Sorenson noted:

> The support that the IRA receives in the United States has been a source of considerable and genuine embarrassment to the Irish government. Unfortunately, much of the money that keeps the IRA going comes from Irish Americans who still think romantically of the old IRA and its role in the Irish Rising. I remember attending a meeting in Seattle where the Irish Consul from San Francisco argued all evening with IRA supporters from the Irish-American community, imploring them to discontinue supporting the IRA, noting that the continuing terrorism and killing in Ireland and the UK is largely financed by the Irish-American community.

Sorenson continued:

The Consul's pleas fell largely on deaf ears. There was a great deal of violence during my tour of duty in Ireland, and inevitably members of Congress would arrive demanding to go wherever they thought there might be a photo opportunity, usually to a funeral, a demonstration, or sometimes even to the border to be photographed looking at British outposts. On occasion, their activities were directly contrary to the wishes of the Irish government, which made its views known to us while turning a blind eye to the offending activities of the congressional member.

It was the way the game was played, but it was certainly a demonstration of the power of the Irish-American vote in the United States as perceived not only by members of Congress but by the Irish government as well. In short, the Irish government could mobilise this constituency for its own purposes in certain areas. In other areas, however, they contravened its interests.

He remembers Senator Ted Kennedy visiting Ireland during his time in Dublin.

The Irish adored the Kennedys. Several presidents have been of Irish extraction, but Kennedy was the first who was also Catholic, which carries with it a tribal identification in Ireland. This was the reason that John Kennedy ignited such a flame there. If you travelled in the country you'd find in humble cottages a picture of the Pope, one of the Sacred Heart of Jesus, and a third of President Kennedy.

President Ford, who was sworn into office from 1974 following President Nixon's resignation amid the Watergate scandal, was vaguely aware he had four Irish great-great-great-great-great-great-grandparents, two from Down and two from Armagh, in his family tree. Receiving Irish Taoiseach Liam Cosgrave with full military honours on the south lawn of the White House on 17 March 1976, he spoke warmly of blood ties:

> I welcome you not only as Prime Minister of Ireland but as a kinsman, very distant in genealogy but very close in affinity. My mother proudly told me one time that I am partially Irish in heritage, and I can assure you that I am fully Irish in spirit.
>
> Throughout our history – beginning with the many Irish Americans who fought for freedom in 1776 and the eleven who signed the Declaration of Independence – men and women from your country have brought Irish courage, Irish energy, Irish strength, Irish devotion, and Irish genius to the United States of America. Ireland, which became a free nation only in this century, is part of the new as well as the old.

While President Ford didn't officially visit Ireland during his short presidency, he did stay overnight in Kilfrush Stud in Limerick, the Georgian property owned by the Mulcahy family which had hosted Nixon during his state visit, after his presidency:

'There was just a handful of security people with him,' said Kevin Mulcahy, the son of Irish-born hotelier, John A. Mulcahy. 'We had an absolutely lovely evening; he was a charming man. We talked about American football and golf as his home was only a few hundred yards from my dad's home in California. They were very close friends and golfing buddies.'

US intervention in Irish affairs begins with 'Outside President'

President Jimmy Carter had a great-great-great-great-grandfather called George Brownlee from Antrim, but Irish diplomats believe he was oblivious to the link during his time as CEO of the United States from 1977 to 1981. It was Carter, not Kennedy or even Nixon, who is credited with becoming the first US president to set out America's interest in resolving the turmoil in Northern Ireland. Before the peanut farmer from Georgia was elected to the White House, American presidents, even those as wholeheartedly Irish as Kennedy, viewed Northern Ireland as an internal issue.

But when civil rights tensions started to rise in Northern Ireland in the late 1960s, the Irish Northern Aid Committee, or Noraid, was founded in America to raise funds for the cause of a united Ireland. Biscuit tins passed around in bars in Irish strongholds such as the Bronx and South Boston brought in a flood of dollars to the Republican movement. Second, third or even fourth generation Irish Americans, some forty million of them in the 1970s and 80s, often tended to have a more romanticised view of the political struggle in Ireland, with the expanse of the Atlantic Ocean between them and the hard, brutal reality of the Troubles. The British authorities insisted that the truth was the funds went to buy arms for the IRA, but Noraid would counter that the money went directly to the families of Irish political prisoners.

Heavily influenced by John Hume's view that Americans should not send money for IRA guns, the Four Horsemen broke with the political status quo to issue a joint St Patrick's Day message in 1977, strongly urging Irish Americans to be on the side of moderation, dialogue and an end to the violence. The quartet, who were determined to push for a non-violent path to peace, also began to pressure Carter to launch an unprecedented presidential initiative encouraging England to moderate its support of the Protestant government in Belfast, which existed at the expense of the Irish Catholics.

Former Irish ambassador to the US, Seán Donlon, remembers having 'good contact' with the president, who became best known in later years around the world as a champion of human rights. Coming to Washington straight from his role as governor of

Georgia, he was an outsider in Capitol Hill, which worked in Ireland's favour:

> He had never been elected to anything in Washington before he became president. So he was a little bit lost when he arrived and, luckily for Ireland, the Speaker of the House, who was just elected at the time was Tip O'Neill. Jimmy Carter had to lean very heavily on Tip O'Neill – because they were both Democrats and because the president had no background in how to navigate the complexities of Washington politics. And that gave us an opening through Tip O'Neill to Jimmy Carter.
>
> Through that connection, Jimmy Carter became the first American president to offer to be of assistance in relation to the problems of Northern Ireland. It was a remarkable success for people like my colleagues and John Hume, in particular, because President Carter was approaching international affairs from a human rights point of view. He was very interested in the civil rights background to what was happening in Northern Ireland. But we wanted the focus to be a little bit more on the division of Ireland, the difficulties in the Anglo-Irish relations and how he might be recruited to help.

In August 1977, President Carter made a sharp departure from centuries of previous US policy when he issued a historic statement promising aid to all parties in Northern Ireland to support a peacefully negotiated democratic settlement. 'He issued a statement basically saying the United States is interested in helping both parties,' Seán Donlon recalled. 'And furthermore, if we succeed in getting some sort of an arrangement between the parties in Northern Ireland, the British and Irish governments, the US would financially back it. It is important to recognise in a practical, political sense that Jimmy Carter became the first American president to do something for Ireland.'

In August 1979, in the wake of the IRA murder of the English queen's cousin, Lord Louis Mountbatten – in his fishing boat, *Shadow V*, in the waters off the pretty village of Mullaghmore, his much-loved Sligo bolthole – the US Embassy and the Irish government joined the British in the condemnation of the terrorists. In a telegram to Downing Street around that time labelled 'US Attitudes to Northern Ireland', British ambassador to the US, Sir Nicholas Henderson, sets out his concerns on the extremist element of Irish-American Republicanism:

> The murders have produced a wave of revulsion against the IRA. Although there is no significant unionist voice in the United States, commentators have been forced to pay serious attention to the Protestant dimension. But the mood will not last and extremist pro-Republican Americans have been unaffected. The heart of the problem here lies in the fact that these extremists, led by the Irish National Caucus and the Northern Ireland Aid and supported in the House of Representatives by 130 members of the Ad Hoc Committee on Irish Affairs led by Biaggi, have harnessed and distorted for their own purposes the sentiments of the thirteen million Irish Americans in favour of Irish unity.

He continued that the rationale behind various American congressmen denouncing alleged human rights violation in Northern Ireland was to keep a firm grip on the Irish-American, Catholic vote.

Thanks to heavy lobbying from Tip O'Neill and Ted Kennedy, President Carter ran with the ball and passed it on to successive administrations which were now pressurised to keep the Irish question on the table throughout the administrations of Reagan and both Bushes, until President Clinton delivered a home run.

President Reagan was another first, in that he was the first

Republican president to broach the subject of Ireland with the British – even though he enjoyed a famously close friendship with Margaret Thatcher. During his two terms, it also became clear that the Irish vote was no longer locked up by the Democratic Party. Former ambassador Seán Donlon remembers:

> President Reagan was the first Republican president to break into what I would call the Irish vote in America which was typically in the Democratic side. By the time Reagan was running for the presidency, a lot of Irish democrats had moved up the social scale in the world. It was not unusual for the father who was a fireman or a policeman, for the son or the daughter to become a lawyer or a doctor or an accountant. So, the Republicans under Reagan realised this was happening, and they were trying to break into the Irish-American vote.

Today, contemporary Irish Americans are not seen as a distinct ethnic group whose vote can be counted on to be cast in a certain way. Like many other groups, successive generations have dispersed widely, intermarried and diversified the scope of their lives, all of which has gradually diluted the more fixed, tribal element to their vote through the generations.

By the Reagan era, the movie-star president began the St Patrick's tradition in earnest with Irish Taoiseach Charles Haughey and Garret FitzGerald both paying two visits each to the White House. From the 1990s onwards, it was firmly established that the Irish Taoiseach would fly in for a full schedule of St Patrick's Day events. In the twenty-first century, irrespective of a presidential blood tie to Ireland, a full day of his diary is almost completely given over every year to a round of engagements around the saint's holiday with only the Covid pandemic getting in the way of the annual appointment in 2021.

In total, Irish leaders have paid fifty-three visits to the White House, with fourteen in the 1990s and another fourteen taking place in the 2000s at the height of the Northern Ireland peace negotiations. This is in stark contrast to countries such as Angola with just four visits and Bangladesh with six audiences in the White House. Even America's close neighbour Argentina has had twenty-six visits, Poland thirty-two, Greece twenty-three. Italy has had seventy-eight visits, France fifty-seven and Britain, as a major power, has had far more trips to the Oval Office. But as a small country with inconsequential military or trade resources, Ireland's presence in Washington far outweighs any strategic importance its relationship might possess to the most powerful country on earth.

In Capitol Hill, the names have changed over the past fifty years but there has always been a roster of Irish Americans in key positions: 'The first time I was over there with Brian Linehan Snr and John Hume was in 1983,' recalled Mr Ahern. 'We went into Tip O'Neill and it was the Four Horsemen. Then afterwards, Ted [Kennedy] and Chris Dodd were the two big guys on Ireland.' Today in Washington, the Israeli lobby is probably the only country to have a more influential special interest group. 'In Capitol Hill, the British never had politicians as powerful as John F. [Kennedy] or Teddy [Kennedy] and Chris Dodd, even if you look at it now, Nancy Pelosi has Bray connections that she's very proud of. This is a regular thing and it's known and noted.'

What is not in doubt is that Ireland's ability to punch above its weight in Washington is thanks to Republican and Democratic power brokers, both behind the scenes or behind the desk in the Oval Office. The influence of these deeply embedded Irish groups was brought home to Bertie Ahern over a few bowls of green porridge when he spent one memorable St Patrick's Day in Savannah, Georgia, which has one of the biggest parades in the world:

I remember being down at this Paddy's Day breakfast and meeting an old priest there, who was ninety, who was inviting me to the Fenian Society and reminding me that the Fenian Society was about twenty years older than Dáil Éireann. Then I went off down to the Daughters of Éireann, which was probably also about a hundred and ten years old, where about six hundred people were eating green porridge.

The former Irish leader is of the opinion that the sheer scale of the Irish lobby across America has long been underestimated.

Over the years, meeting a lot of senators, a lot of governors and congressmen, when you ask them about [it], they say, 'Oh, you know, some of our great campaign workers, some of our great canvassers, some of the great characters, are Irish...' Whether they're Republicans or Democrats, they kind of meet it at that grassroots level and that's right across the whole of Capitol Hill, right across governorships.

Sometimes it's missed out. When you go to their constituencies you realise how their constituency politics are so like ours. It's not the same in size, we're talking about thousands and they're talking about millions, but it has the same structures. They do door-to-door canvassing, even in the last election in 2020. The Irish were taskmasters at that, particularly on the Democratic side.

When the former Taoiseach was Minister for Labour between 1989 and 1991, he acquired first-hand experience of the Irish lobby in the US.

So many of the key guys in the craft unions and in the big, blue-collar unions were of Irish descent. There was a time you would not get a job if you weren't Irish. If you were a politician in those constituencies, you were going to be dealing with the Irish in the sports organisations, in the community organisations, in the trade union organisations. The Irish were incredibly powerful, not to mind in the churches, which were so strong in the old days as well.

And it continues right up to the present day: 'In the various state legislators, there are literally hundreds of people with Irish connections all around the country.'

Ahern believes politics is in 'our DNA': 'It probably comes from eight hundred years of fighting the neighbours.' This Taoiseach, who has spent more time in the White House than any other Irish leader, believes the Irish influence over American presidents begins long before they ever set foot on Capitol Hill.

They all get it back at their own bases. This is where presidents such as Obama and Clinton would have first come across the Irish political machine, even before genealogists went searching into their ancestral past. The first thing with all of them is they pick up a lot of that interest in Irish affairs – even when their direct bloodline mightn't be that close – from their own areas where they are growing up, meeting Irish people, Irish lobby groups, St Patrick's Day committees, GAA clubs ... It's the history of it. In terms of economic power or military power we are not in the game, that's the hard reality. But it is from that connection power and the influence of the Irish caucuses, the old family connections – that's really where that comes from.

And St Patrick's Day? Amid all the green pints and twirling batons, it's a show of power, according to Bertie Ahern, who got an up-close look at the Irish involvement in the US when he was Minister for Labour in the 1980s. 'Back then at least forty per cent of the unions were led by Irish Americans, we're talking about unions with millions of members and a lot of these unions have huge resources and investment funds and have these very strong Irish connections. That's where the Paddy's Day parade in New York comes from.' Ahern concludes: 'This is their day to show their strength and, by God, do they show it.'

I'm Irish ... win friends and influence people

Aside from all the lyrical declarations, what do these old family links to the United States mean to Ireland in terms of economic and political capital? A clip of Joe Biden cheekily telling the BBC 'I'm Irish...' had the simultaneous effect of delighting Ireland while causing consternation across the Irish Sea with their British neighbours. Since the inception of the independent state, the relationship with the US has significantly bolstered Ireland's fortunes at different times over the past century.

Before William Howard Taft III became ambassador to Ireland in 1953, he was posted to Ireland as a young diplomat in 1948 to help roll out the Marshall Plan, the famous US programme set up to provide aid to Western Europe following the devastation of the Second World War. Ireland's inclusion raised eyebrows as de Valera had kept Ireland steadfastly neutral during the war, much to the annoyance of both the British and the Americans. In an oral history interview for the Library of Congress, the diplomat, who would later be appointed US ambassador to Ireland in 1953, said the Irish programme was a small one:

> I have always wondered, except for the political process, why the Irish deserved even a small programme? After all, they had been neutral during the war.

The Marshall Plan in Ireland was political; there is no harm in saying that the Irish seemed to have conceived over all the years that they have a closer connection with the United States than almost any other country. Like the Israelis, and unlike other countries, up till lately anyway, they have spent their time as a diplomatic unit, I think, more on Capitol Hill than they have in an orthodox way in their connections with the State Department, which is supposed to be the avenue of diplomacy.

Roger Sorenson, who was economic counsellor to the US Embassy in Dublin in 1969, at around the time Ireland was in the process of joining the European Economic Community, also noted in his oral history testimony that Ireland benefitted from the plan even though as a country it had suffered no real war damage. 'When it came time to rebuild Europe following the war, Congress guaranteed that the Irish would be among the beneficiaries of American largesse, notwithstanding their lack of involvement in the war.'

Sorenson was also involved in the cross-Atlantic negotiations on airline landing rights for national carriers between Ireland and US – although the real horse-trading appears to have gone on in the corridors of Capitol Hill. 'In the aftermath of the Second World War, the Irish had negotiated a treaty with the United States that was extraordinarily favourable to Ireland, allowing Irish airlines to land in Boston, Chicago, and New York while restricting American airlines to Shannon, which of course is not where the Irish population is,' he explained. 'The result was that the bulk of the traffic was with the Irish carrier. We were determined to change this, that is, to renegotiate the agreement to get landing rights for our airlines in Dublin as well as Shannon.'

He was amazed to find out why the US had tolerated this lopsided flight arrangement for decades.

Our government had been trying without success to renegotiate the treaty for several years. And the reason our negotiators had failed was that the Irish were especially skilled in mobilising the Irish-American lobby in the United States where there are a good many people who are still proud of their Irish descent. They had played the State Department off for years by the simple tactic of agreeing to discuss the treaty a year later, the year agreed to always coinciding with congressional elections at which time congressional candidates from districts with large numbers of Irish Americans would unfailingly signal to the State Department that it was an inopportune moment to try to change the treaty. It took us five years, but we finally broke their pattern of manoeuvring to negotiate only on election years and succeeded in getting the treaty rewritten. I was on the inaugural flight of the first TWA plane to land on a scheduled flight to Dublin.

But, of course, the most significant chunk of American funds has gone directly into the cause of securing peace in Ireland. 'When the Anglo-Irish Agreement was signed in 1985, President Reagan announced not only his support for the agreement politically, but that America would back the agreement with financial capital,' recalled former US ambassador Seán Donlon. 'That was a realisation of the commitment made by Jimmy Carter back in '77. The financial capital came in the form of the creation of a special fund for Northern Ireland and for border regions, and that fund is still active.'

The United States has poured $544 million to the International Fund for Ireland, which was established in 1986 to finance projects to promote the peace process and cross-community engagement and enhance economic opportunity in Northern Ireland and the border counties of Ireland.

Today, many tech giants – among them Google, Facebook and

Twitter – base their European operations in Ireland. On the trade balance sheet, the United States is a major goods exporter to Ireland, ranking second only to the United Kingdom, while about twenty-seven per cent of all Irish goods exports are shipped to the US, making it Ireland's top export destination.

The late Irish-American entrepreneur Donald Keough is widely credited with bringing Coca-Cola to Ireland. Sean Reidy, former CEO of the JFK Trust, believes the Irish heritage of the former Coca-Cola president and chief operating officer influenced the location of the soft drink giant's new plant in 2011. 'I had gotten to know him well,' said Mr Reidy.

> He made a speech the day of the official opening, saying the fact that his great-grandfather was from Wexford and the fact they were opening the factory in Wexford was totally coincidental. But that was his humour . . . because it was a lot to do with it. Portugal and other countries had been mentioned for that plant. That's one tangible example where his Irish heritage influenced the investment of Coca-Cola in Ireland. How many times has that happened?

Ireland's membership of the EU attracts US companies who are keen to use Ireland as a base to sell into Europe and other markets. There are approximately seven hundred American-owned firms operating in Ireland, employing about 155,000 people across high-tech electronics, computer products, medical supplies and pharmaceuticals, not to mention retailing, banking, finance and other services. Likewise, Irish firms are significant investors in the United States across a wide range of sectors. More than five hundred Irish companies operate in the US, having invested more than $225 billion and employing some 110,000 workers as of 2019. In 2020, the US spent $66,016 million on imports from Ireland – thirty-seven times more than the $1755 million spent in 1990 which, even taking inflation into account, paints a clear picture of the burgeoning trade relationship between the two countries.

It's an undeniable fact that the open door to the White House on St Patrick's Day is immeasurably beneficial to the Irish government. In diplomatic circles, it's known as soft power. 'We would line up the issues we would want to discuss,' noted Bertie Ahern on the subject of those March meetings:

> There were the obvious ones like the north and European issues, but we were always watching things that the IDA would be worried about such as tax loopholes being closed that might affect us. When I moved our corporation taxes, which used to be thirty-eight per cent, and then we had this narrow manufacturing tax of ten per cent and then we moved everything to 12.5 per cent, we had to delicately get them on page with us. We never would have been able to get that through if it wasn't for our connection with America.

Ireland's sacrosanct corporation tax rate of 12.5 per cent – which was brought in during the era of the Celtic Tiger in 2003 when President George W. Bush was in the White House – was a key feature in attracting foreign investment during the first two decades of the twenty-first century. The Taoiseach said the EU was opposed to the change, but the Irish government had its access to the top echelons of the US administration to set out their case for the tax change. 'We used those meetings to explain our position. Like in every country, if the president and the secretary of state express interest or support, it goes through the system. And,' Bertie Ahern admits, 'we used that to great effect for the last thirty or forty years.' However, after a long negotiation, the Republic of Ireland agreed to support a deal to set a global minimum corporation tax rate of fifteen per cent for large firms with a turnover of more than €750 million at the tail-end of 2021.

The effect of this hike on the multinational unicorn companies based in the country remains to be seen. While the Irish connection may open doors, former ambassador Seán O'Huiginn observes that sentimentality doesn't wash when it comes to business dealings. 'No matter how fanatically loyal a businessperson might be to Ireland they owe a duty to the shareholders, so no serious person can frivolously throw billions of their company's money at an enterprise unless they know that it's soundly based.'

By any measure, there is an economic, diplomatic and even spiritual connection between the two nations, shaped by millions upon millions of hopeful Atlantic crossings. When future US president Joe Biden stood at Dublin Castle in 2016, he mused over the remarkable similarities of the immigration paths of his Louth ancestor and President Obama's Kildare ancestor, both shoemakers, who boarded ships bound for America within five weeks of each other in the summer of 1844.

It's doubtful they ever knew each other. But one thing we do know – they left everything behind for an uncertain future. And in all of their dreams, could they ever have dreamt that 160 years later, two great-great-grandsons of shoemakers from Ireland would be sworn in as president and vice president of the United States of America?

ACKNOWLEDGEMENTS

T HIS AUTHOR'S THANKS and best wishes to:
John B. Murphy in the US Embassy, who sent me on my way
with a list of invaluable sources, fact files and a file of photographs
documenting various presidential homecomings.

Archivists and librarians in the presidential libraries from the JFK
Library to the William J. Clinton Presidential Library and Museum
to the Ronald Reagan Presidential Library and Museum, the George
W. Bush Presidential Library, the Nixon Presidential Library and the
Barack Obama Presidential Library were vital in sourcing documents
and material relating to Ireland.

The Library of Congress, across the manuscripts, history and
genealogy divisions, and other departments, never failed to answer a
question or return a call or email. The papers of the US presidents at
the Library of Congress, containing letters and diaries, gave an
illuminating real-time look into their thoughts while in the Oval
Office.

The presidential libraries into the earlier Irish-American presi-
dents were also hugely helpful, starting with Marsha Mullins at the
Andrew Jackson Foundation in the Hermitage in Tennessee,
President James K. Polk's Home and Museum in Tennessee and the
Andrew Johnson National Historic Site.

The University of Tennessee was very beneficial in the

exploration of President James Polk's correspondence. The Lancaster County Historic Government records gave a window into President James Buchanan's life and times, while the *Collected Works of Abraham Lincoln*, along with the Abraham Lincoln Presidential Library and Museum, gave an insight into his dealing with Irish soldiers. *The Papers of Ulysses S. Grant* at Mississippi State University were immensely helpful in researching his trip to Ireland.

The American Presidency Project was a fantastic source of presidential speeches. Papers, telegrams and dispatches from the Margaret Thatcher Foundation and declassified documents from the National Archives of the UK (TNA) gave a fascinating glimpse into behind-the-scenes manoeuvrings in the three-way relationship between the United States, Britain and Ireland. Oral histories gathered for the *Frontline Diplomacy: The Foreign Affairs Oral History Collection of the Association for Diplomatic Studies and Training* at the Library of Congress gave a window into the lives of diplomats in Ireland from the first years and throughout the twentieth century. The Office of the Historian at the US Department of State was a key source of information on Ireland's relations with the US.

The examination of Irish links to the White House is wide in breadth and scope, much more extensive than I envisaged, spanning dozens of administrations. Irish-American presidents were serving in the White House during slavery and the displacement of Native Americans from their lands. As this book focuses on the history between American and Irish immigrants, I did not delve into this difficult, tragic part of the history of the United States, as a surface examination would not do their plight justice.

Researching the family trees of the American presidents with links to Ireland simply wouldn't have been possible without the help of some of the world's best-known genealogists on both sides of the Atlantic. Leading New England genealogist Gary Boyd Roberts very kindly gave me hours of his time during a marathon conversation, while his book, *Ancestors of American Presidents*, was my bible when it came to the backgrounds of dozens of presidents.

Megan Smolenyak, who has worked on the TV series *Who Do You Think You Are?*, was equally as generous with cross-Atlantic phone calls as she patiently went through the intricacies of the family trees of Barack Obama and Joe Biden. She turned bloodlines, DNA and old records into clear-cut lineages linking immigrants to the White House. Solving history mysteries, as she would put it herself.

In America, genealogist R. Andrew Pierce, who is an absolute authority on the Kennedy family, was an invaluable source of information on all their bloodlines in Ireland and helped enormously in evaluating the authenticity of lesser-known lines to JFK, along with details on the nuts-and-bolts of everyday life for the various great-grandparents. David Dearborn guided me through the records to Bill Clinton's Irish background in the South. Erick Montgomery, executive director of Historic Augusta, Inc, furnished me with his detailed research on the Irish origins of President Woodrow Wilson.

In Ireland, genealogist Fiona Fitzsimons from Enclann went through her painstaking process in finding some of Joe Biden's relatives, her observations about his poignant motives in finding his family, and her research into Barack Obama's family, which she presented to Michelle Obama in Trinity. Historian Celestine Murphy was a vital source of information on the branches of the Kennedy family in Wexford – particularly in relation to his great-grandmother Bridget Murphy – and went above and beyond in furnishing me with the smallest of details. Down in Cork, historian Tim Crowley gave an intriguing look into the Michael Collins connection to JFK. In Kildare, local historian Seamus Cullen gave a lively account of Nixon's high-octane arrival, while in Limerick, Michael O'Sullivan relayed his vivid memories of the Republican president descending on his town.

Thomas A. Fitzgerald Jnr, JFK's first cousin, was very generous with his time and access to his own charming book, *Grandpa's Stories*. In Limerick, distant cousins Pat Moloney and Michael Fitzgerald helped paint a picture of the family's origins. Sean Reidy, the former CEO of the JFK Trust in New Ross, was a fount of knowledge of all things related to the Kennedy family and their visits to Ireland. In Wexford, Patrick Grennan brought history alive with a poignant three-hour tour of the Kennedy homestead, his home. He's passionate and highly informative about the connection.

In Kildare, Marian Moore was very generous with her time in explaining how she ended up on the White House tapes after her own personal audience with Nixon and Kissinger in the Oval Office as a teenager. Rob Goodbody gave a moving account of his grandmother Olive's bravery in staying true to her Quaker beliefs in front of the world's media during the Nixon visit to Timahoe.

In Ballyporeen, former landlady Mary O'Farrell gave an insight into her time as a media darling, the intense preparations for a presidential pint and her affectionate connection with the president long after he left the town, while I loved Neil Donovan's dry observations on the preparations for the biggest day in his town's lifetime. The former manager of Ashford Castle, Rory Murphy, evoked the fun of a presidential visit with his gems of stories about the Secret Service's bumper catch of salmon and his own skittish encounter with the officer guarding the nuclear codes during the Reagan visit.

Kevin Mulcahy, son of John A. Mulcahy, and the host of no fewer than three presidents, was full of humour and insight about the trips of Nixon, Reagan and Ford to his father's homes and hotels.

The legendary Frank Quilter and Jackie Donovan keep me entertained with one colourful Ballybunion story after another. Former golf captain, Brian McCarthy, regaled me with behind-the-scenes stories of the putting greens with Clinton.

Henry Healy, the famous 'Henry the Eighth' cousin of Barack Obama, and Ollie Hayes spent a few hours describing their meetings with the Obamas and the wonderful rapport built up with America's first family during the 2010s. Reverend Stephen Neill was very helpful in talking me through the Obama ancestors.

In Louth, Peter Savage was a fantastic tour guide all over the Cooley peninsula during the summer, taking me on the full gamut of Irish life from the local pub to the graveyard. I went back in time with Fr Malachy Conlon on our walk about the graveyard and church run by the Knight Templar, where Biden's relatives would have been laid to rest.

Publican Derek McGarrity was very interesting on Biden's visit as vice president and his equally interesting low-ley arrival behind the wheel of his own car a few months after to the quaint pub in the east coast beauty spot. His cousin, Mary Mulligan, explained the link of Biden's Irish relatives to the suffragette movement and his homely charm when they met up. The president of Scranton's City Council, Bill Gaughan, captured the incredibly strong links between his American city and Mayo. While in Galway, Liam Hanniffy was a great host who brought me on a tour of the farm on the edge of Galway Bay, where Biden's paternal ancestors lived.

Painting the picture of Irish immigration across the American frontier spanning four centuries took much research. Several eminent academics gave me a steer across this very dense subject. Dr Patrick Fitzgerald, head of research and development at the Mellon Centre for Migration Studies at the Ulster American Folk Park, gave a detailed look into Ulster migration from the first settlers in the 1600s right up to the twentieth century. Professor James Fisher, the author of *On the Irish Waterfront: The Crusader, the Movie and the Soul of the Port of New York*, brought Tammany Hall in New York to life, along with insights into how the Irish political machine began with the masses of penniless immigrants and went all the way to the office of the president. US presidential authority Professor Russell Riley was enlightening on the Kennedy mystique, President Clinton's affinity for Ireland and the Irish political machine. Dr Michael Kennedy at the Royal Irish Academy offered a broad expanse of US relations with Ireland since the birth of the Republic.

RTÉ's Washington correspondent Brian O'Donovan took time out from his schedule to give me a very current perspective on Irish-American relations from his ringside seat in the American capital.

Former US ambassadors, Seán O'Huiginn and Seán Donlon gave compelling insight into Washington's corridors of power and their relationships with various twentieth-century politicians. After spending time in their company, it's easy to see why they were chosen for a career in the diplomatic corps. I have to reserve a special word of thanks to former ambassador Donlon for taking the time to compose the brilliantly written foreword. Bertie Ahern and Dick Spring were also very generous and offered a real insight into the political and human sides of various presidents in the White House, and that soft power they used so effectively.

To my husband, Anthony, for all his support and mucking in while I was missing in action, my children, Katie, Cali and Luke (three 'star bars' to borrow a phrase). My biggest thank you on the book front has to go to my brother, Michael, right-hand man and constructive critic. To my dad, Tom, who sparked my curiosity about the world; my mother, Sheila, an amazing lady, for constant support and delicious dinners; my sister, Helen, for daily doses of coffee and advice, plus pandemic office space; my brother, Neal, for helping back at the ranch.

Thanks to the photographers and publications who helped source and supply this book's photographic material. Finally, to all at Black & White, in particular Emma Hargrave, for her valuable input and long hours in putting this book together over the best part of a year.

BIBLIOGRAPHY & SOURCES

Prologue – Cracking History Mysteries

Megan Smolenyak, genealogist, author, Who Do You Think You Are? consultant and former chief family historian at ancestry.com, interview with author.

Renegades: Born in the USA, conversational series between President Barack Obama and Bruce Springsteen (spotify.com/show/42xagXCUDsFO6aolcHoTlv).

National Archives of Ireland, Dublin (nationalarchives.ie).

Irish Emigration History, University College, Cork (ucc.ie/en/emigre/history).

Chapter One – JFK

Sean Reidy, former CEO of the JFK Trust in New Ross, Ireland, interview with author.

Patrick Grennan, custodian of the Kennedy Homestead in Dunganstown, Wexford, interview with author.

Celestine Murphy, historian, interview with author.

Letter from Patrick Kennedy to his cousin Jim Roche in Wexford, 24 December 1907: courtesy of the John F. Kennedy Library Foundation.

Letter from JFK to Professor Jim Burns, 25 August 1959, courtesy of Patrick Grennan of the Kennedy Homestead.

Letter from PJ Kennedy to John F. Fitzgerald: courtesy of the John F. Kennedy Library Foundation.

Report of the Committee of Internal Health on the Asiatic Cholera in Boston in 1849: Boston College, Massachusetts (globalboston.bc.edu/index.php/cholera-report).

Fitzgerald, Thomas A. Jnr, *Grandpa Stories*, courtesy of Thomas Fitzgerald Jnr.

For story of Honey Fitz's return to Limerick in 1938: *Limerick Leader*, 28 June 1963.

R. Andrew Pierce, genealogist specialising in Irish-American connections, who has written on Kennedy and Reagan connections to Ireland, interview with author and access to articles on JFK's Irish ancestry.

Reminisces of Rose Kennedy: courtesy of the John F. Kennedy Library Foundation.

Declan Hehir, historian, interview with author on newly unearthed JFK homestead.

Pat Moloney, distant JFK cousin (on Fitzgerald side), who produced *Life* magazine article and detailed family tree, interview with author.

Tim Crowley, historian, the Michael Collins Interpretative Centre and Museum, interview with author.

Letter from Jacqueline Kennedy to Mrs Ryan: courtesy of Patrick Grennan.

Chapter Two – President Richard Nixon

For log of President Nixon's conversations: Richard Nixon Presidential Library (nixonlibrary.gov/sites/default/files/forresearchers/find/tapes/finding_aids/tapesubjectlogs/oval783.pdf).

National Archives and Records Administration, the White House Tapes (archives. gov).

Richard Nixon Presidential Library and Museum, the White House Tapes (nixonlibrary.gov/white-house-tapes/783/conversation-783-007).

Marian Scully Moore, interview with author.

Bell, Raymond Martin, *The Ancestry of Richard Milhous Nixon*: courtesy of the Richard Nixon Foundation.

Seamus Cullen, historian, interview with author.

Michael O'Sullivan, historian, interview with author.

Kevin Mulcahy, son of industrialist and hotelier John A. Mulcahy, interview with author.

For the 1966 census detailing 571 people in Hospital: cso.ie/en/media/csoie/census/census1971results/volume1/C_1971_V1_T8.pdf

Chapter Three – President Ronald Reagan

Mary O'Farrell, landlady of O'Farrell's aka The Ronald Reagan, interview with author.

Neil Donovan, son of local county councillor and shop owner, the late Con Donovan, interview with author.

Seán Donlon, former Irish ambassador to the US, interview with author.

Letter of introduction to de Valera from Ronald Reagan: National Archives of Ireland (nationalarchives.ie/topics/PRES/image_pages/25.htm).

For information on Barbara Riggs: United States Secret Service (secretservice.gov /press/releases/2004/09/barbara-riggs-appointed-deputy-director-united -states-secret-service-30-year).

Kevin Mulcahy, son of industrialist and hotelier John A. Mulcahy, interview with author.

Rory Murphy, hotel manager of Ashford Castle, interview with author.

Ronald Reagan's White House Diaries: courtesy of the Ronald Reagan Presidential Foundation & Institute.

Margaret Thatcher on Garret FitzGerald: margaretthatcher.org/document/ 109185

For Margaret Thatcher's briefing cards, October 1985: margaretthatcher.org/docu- ment/150700, via the Reagan Library: NSC Exec Secretariat files, Peter Sommer RAC Box 4

Chapter Four – President Bill Clinton

Dick Spring, former Tánaiste and minister for foreign affairs, interview with author.

Frank Quilter, Ballybunion lobbyist and hotelier, interview with author.

Brian McCarthy, former captain of Ballybunion Golf Club, interview with author.

For information on civil rights: The CAIN Archive (cain.ulster.ac.uk/events/ derry/chron.htm).

Public Papers of the Presidents of the United States: William J. Clinton (1996, Book I): govinfo.gov/content/pkg/PPP-1996-book1/html/PPP-1996-book1- doc-pg425.htm

Roberts, Gary Boyd, *Ancestors of American Presidents* (New England Genealogical Society, 2009).

Democratic Candidates Forum 1992: c-span.org/video/?25402-1/democratic- candidates-forum&playEvent

Bertie Ahern, former Taoiseach, interview with author.

Gerry Adams, oral history interview: courtesy of the Miller Center, University of Virginia (millercenter.org/the-presidency/presidential-oral-histories/ gerry-adams-oral-history).

Professor Russell Riley, US presidential authority and co-chair of the Miller Center's Presidential Oral History Program, interview with author.

Séan O'Huiginn, former Irish ambassador to the US, interview with author.

Cable on Unionist Concerns: courtesy of Clinton Presidential Library, Little Rock (clinton.presidentiallibraries.us/exhibits/show/northern-ireland/item/57319).

Children's letters to Clinton: The Clinton Presidential Library (clinton.presidentiallibraries.us/files/original/405cd5948c1ce1a024eee6c7819e1599.jpg).

The American Presidency Project: presidency.ucsb.edu

Declassified documents on Clinton's telephone conversations, page 196 – 2013-0472-M (presidentiallibraries.us).

Public Papers of the Presidents of the United States: William J. Clinton (1998, Book II): govinfo.gov/content/pkg/PPP-1998-book2/html/PPP-1998-book2-doc-pg1526.htm

For Bill Clinton on golf: irishcentral.com/sports/bill-clinton-names-his-favorite -golf-course-ballybunion-in-county-kerry-53047277-237654631

Chapter Five – The Bush Presidents

Letter to Bono dated 1 June 2007: the National Archives Catalog, Records of the White House Office of Records Management (George W. Bush Administration), (catalog.archives.gov/id/30910053 - Collection GWB-WHORM).

Correspondence between Bono and President George W. Bush on the President's Emergency Plan for AIDS Relief (PEPFAR), July 2007: the National Archives Catalog, Records of the White House Office of Records Management (George W. Bush Administration), (catalog.archives.gov/id/31490774 - Collection GWB-WHORM).

The George W. Bush Library, Dallas: georgewbushlibrary.gov/bush-family/george-w-bush

The George W. Bush Presidential Center: bushcenter.org (Forum on Leadership a conversation with President Bush and Bono, see: youtube.com/watch?v=6FHuzGaOfuM).

The American Presidency Project: presidency.ucsb.edu

On Northern Ireland's political process, political parties and elections: The CAIN Archive (cain.ulster.ac.uk/issues/politics/government.htm).

Chapter Six – President Barack Obama

Ollie Hayes, publican and uncle of Henry Healy, interview with author.

Henry Healy, Barack Obama's distant cousin from Moneygall, interview with author.

The American Presidency Project: presidency.ucsb.edu

Obama, Barack, *Dreams From My Father: A story of race and inheritance* (Canongate Books, 2007).

On the Obama presidency: obamawhitehouse.archives.gov

Chapter Seven – President Joe Biden

Liam Hanniffy, President Biden's distant paternal cousin, interview with author.

Megan Smolenyak, genealogist, author, *Who Do You Think You Are?* consultant and former chief family historian for ancestry.com, interview with author.

Fiona Fitzsimons, genealogist, family historian, writer, researcher, director of Eneclann, interview with author.

Brian O'Donovan, Washington correspondent for RTÉ News and author of *Four Years in the Cauldron: Telling the extraordinary story of America in crisis*, interview with author.

On Biden's trip to Ireland as vice president: ie.usembassy.gov/vice-president-bidens-trip-ireland; obamawhitehouse.archives.gov/the-press-office/2015/05/30/statement-vice-president; obamawhitehouse.archives.gov/blog/2016/06/21/bideninireland-follow-along-vice-presidents-trip; obamawhitehouse.archives.gov/vp; obamawhitehouse.archives.gov/the-press-office/statement-vice-president-joe-biden-0; obamawhitehouse.archives.gov/the-press-office/2016/06/24/remarks-vice-president-irish-people

Laurita Blewitt, broadcaster, podcaster and President Biden's distant maternal cousin from Ballina, Co. Mayo, interview with author.

Peter Savage, former county councillor in the Cooley peninsula in Co. Louth, interview with author.

Mary Mulligan, President Biden's distant maternal cousin (Finnegan line) of Whitestown, Co. Louth, interview with author.

Derek McGarrity, publican at Lily Finnegan's in Whitestown, Carlingford, Co. Louth, interview with author.

Fr Malachy Conlon, pastor of Cooley Parish in Co. Louth, interview with author.

Rob Kearney, Irish international rugby player and cousin of Joe Biden, interview with author.

Chapter Eight – The Special Relationship – Where It All Began

National Archives of Ireland, Dublin (nationalarchives.ie).

Andrew Jackson's Hermitage, Nashville Tennessee (thehermitage.com).

Roberts, Gary Boyd, Ancestors of American Presidents (New England Genealogical Society, 2009).

Shannon, Dr Catherine B., Irish Immigration to America, 1630 to 1921 (reprinted courtesy of the New Bedford Whaling Museum).

Library of Congress, Washington, DC (loc.gov).

National Library of Ireland, Dublin (nli.ie).

Irish Emigration History, University College, Cork (ucc.ie/en/emigre/history).

The White House (whitehouse.gov).

Ulster-Scots Agency, Belfast (ulsterscotsagency.com).

Chapter Nine – Frontier Presidents in the Making of America

On important ports and Ulster-Scots settlement: Dr Patrick Fitzgerald, head of research and development at the Mellon Centre for Migration Studies, Ulster American Folk Park, Omagh, interview with author.

On immigration numbers and Presbyterian ministers: Shannon, Dr Catherine B., *Irish Immigration to America, 1630 to 1921* (reprinted courtesy of the New Bedford Whaling Museum); (nantucketatheneum.org/wp-content/uploads /Irish-Immigration-to-America.pdf).

On voyages: eyewitnesstohistory.com/passage.htm; nifhs.org/wp-content/uploads /2021/04/Cheapest-and-Shortest-Sea-Passage.pdf; cmich.edu/library/clarke /ResearchResources/Michigan_Material_Local/Beaver_Island_Helen_ Collar_Papers/Subject_Cards/EmigrationandImmigrantLife/Pages/ Transatlantic-Crossing.aspx

Andrew Jackson's Hermitage, Nashville Tennessee (thehermitage.com).

The White House website (whitehouse.gov).

Gaines, J.W., *General Andrew Jackson's mother did not die on the roadside, Nashville Banner* (Nashville, 18 August 1918). Library of Congress (loc.gov/item/ rbpe.1750430a).

On slavery and slaves: thehermitage.com/learn/mansion-grounds/slavery; whitehouse.gov/about-the-white-house/presidents/andrew-jackson

On the Trail of Tears: guides.loc.gov/indian-removal-act

For Jackson's Hibernian Certificate: loc.gov/resource/maj.06162_0316_0319

For letter from Kerns to Jackson: Jackson, A. & Kerns, J. *James Kerns to Andrew Jackson* (1815). Library of Congress (loc.gov/item/majo24076).

For letter from Gowen to Jackson: Jackson, A. & Gowen, J. *James Gowen to Andrew Jackson, July 3.* (3 July 1830). Library of Congress (loc.gov/item/majo11995).

For letter to Gowen on Wilson and hanging: University of Tennessee, Knoxville (trace.tennessee.edu/cgi/viewcontent.cgi?article=1006&context=utk_jackson (pp 439–440)).

William [Bavet?] to Martin Van Buren, December 5, 1832, Library of Congress (loc.gov).

US Reports: *United States v. Wilson,* 32 US (7 Pet.) 150 (1833). (loc.gov).

For the letter from Van Buren to Jackson: University of Tennessee, Knoxville (trace.tennessee.edu/cgi/viewcontent.cgi?article=1008&context=utk_jackson).

On Irish emigration figures: Library of Congress (loc.gov/classroom-materials/immigration/irish/irish-catholic-immigration-to-america).

For letter from Rose Savage to President Polk: University of Tennessee, Knoxville (trace.tennessee.edu/cgi/viewcontent.cgi?referer=&httpsredir=1&article=1002&context=utk_polk).

For letters to President Polk: University of Tennessee, Knoxville (trace.tennessee.edu/cgi/viewcontent.cgi?referer=&httpsredir=1&article=1001&context=utk_polk).

For letters relating to President Polk: University of Tennessee, Knoxville (polk.lib.utk.edu/exist/apps/polk-papers/resources/pdfs/polk.pdf).

For letters from the James Buchanan Family Papers: courtesy of Lancaster History (collections.lancasterhistory.org).

On hired help in the Lincoln family: Abraham Lincoln Home National Historic Site, Illinois (nps.gov/liho/learn/historyculture/hired-girls.htm).

For Abraham Lincoln letters: Library of Congress (loc.gov).

Abraham Lincoln and the Dublin Evening News: Office of the Historian of the US Department of State (history.state.gov/historicaldocuments/frus1865p4/d663).

President Andrew Johnson Second Annual Message, 3 December 1866: The American Presidency Project (presidency.ucsb.edu/documents/second-annual-message-10).

The Papers of Ulysses S. Grant: Mississippi State University (https://msstate.contentdm.oclc.org/digital/collection/USG_volume/id/26272/rec/30).

Chester Alan Arthur Jnr in the *New York Times* on 13 December 1922 (timesmachine.nytimes.com/timesmachine/1922/12/13/107086992. html?pageNumber=20).

For Megan Smolenyak on Bruce Springsteen, Katy Perry, Melissa McCarthy and Stephen Colbert: Irish America magazine (issuu.com/irishamerica/docs/ia_ october_november_2015; plus February/March 2015; August/September 2016; and August/September 2017).

Chapter Ten – Shamrocks & Shenanigans & Silver Dollars

From the National Archives, Kew:

First telegram dated 25 June 1981 sent by Sir Nicholas Henderson, British ambassador to the US (1979–82), from the British Embassy in Washington to the Foreign and Commonwealth Office in London and No. 10 (https:// c59574e9047e61130f13-3f71d0fe2b653c4f00f32175760e96e7.ssl.cf1.rackcdn. com/130AEF149B6A4DD9984651B788C061B6.pdf).

Second telegram dated 25 June 1981 – *Prime Minister's Visit to the United States – Northern Ireland* – Northern Ireland Office, declassified letter from Sir Kenneth Stowe to No. 10 (https://c59574e9047e61130f13-3f71d0fe2b653c4f-00f32175760e96e7.ssl.cf1.rackcdn.com/810223%20NIO%20to%20 No.10%20%28600-217%29.pdf).

On hunger strikes: National Archives of Ireland, Dublin: Irish government papers (nationalarchives.ie/wp-content/uploads/2021/01/2020_23_3.pdf); The CAIN Archive (cain.ulster.ac.uk/events/hstrike/chronology.htm).

On the inauguration of Ronald Reagan: Library of Congress (loc.gov/rr/program /bib/inaugurations/reagan/index.html).

On immigration and assimilation: Library of Congress (loc.gov/classroom-materials/immigration/irish/adaptation-and-assimilation).

On naturalisation: VCU Libraries Social Welfare History Project (socialwelfare. library.vcu.edu/federal/naturalization-process-in-u-s-early-history).

Professor James T. Fisher, researcher into nineteenth-century Irish in Brooklyn, interview with author.

New York Times on Know Nothing Demonstrations: (nytimes.com/1854/11/10/ archives/knownothing-demonstration-grand-mass-meeting-in-the-park-charges-of.html).

On police chiefs: irishamerica.com/2019/03/hall-of-fame-nypd-commissioner-james-oneill

Library of Congress, papers on Woodrow Wilson (loc.gov).

For information on the Easter Rising: history.house.gov/Blog/2016/June/6-30-EasterRising; history.house.gov/HouseRecord/Detail/15032448838; history.house.gov/Blog/Detail/15032434694;history.house.gov/Blog/Detail/15032434694

New York Times, 22 January 1918: 'Reports Wilson Urged Settlement of Irish Issue' (nytimes.com/1918/01/22/archives/reports-wilson-urged-settlement-of-irish-issue.html).

New York Times, 23 January 1918: 'Rebukes Effort to Involve Wilson' (nytimes.com/1918/01/24/archives/rebukes-effort-to-involve-wilson-prompt-denial-of-london-times.html).

New York Times, 18 September 1919: 'Wilson Defines Stand on Ireland' (nytimes.com/1919/09/18/archives/wilson-defines-stand-on-ireland-says-the-league-sets-up-a-forum-for.html).

Oral histories taken from: *Frontline Diplomacy: The Foreign Affairs Oral History Collection of the Association for Diplomatic Studies and Training* (loc.gov/resource/mfdip.2004taf02).

Kennedy, C. S. & Sorenson, R. A. (1990) *Interview with Roger A. Sorenson.* Library of Congress (loc.gov/item/mfdipbib001101).

For Spanish ambassador's memo about JFK's trip: Office of the Historian at the US Department of State (history.state.gov/historicaldocuments/frus1961-63v13/d371).

Seán Donlon, former Irish ambassador to the US, interview with author.

For telegram on US attitudes to Northern Ireland and the murder of Lord Mountbatten: Northern Ireland: UKE Washington telegram 2515 to FCO (2350Z) ('U.S. Attitudes to Northern Ireland') (Warrenpoint ambush and murder of Lord Mountbatten: influencing US opinion), declassified 2009, Margaret Thatcher Foundation.

US Department of State on bilateral relations: state.gov/u-s-relations-with-ireland

US Embassy on relationship with Ireland: ie.usembassy.gov/our-relationship/policy-history/?_ga=2.212605844.1275382824.1634137953-1910764367.1634137953

United Census Bureau on foreign trade with Ireland: census.gov/foreign-trade/balance/c4190.html#2019